Splitting the Baby

ERUPTIONS
New Thinking across the Disciplines

Erica McWilliam
General Editor

Vol. 20

PETER LANG
New York • Washington, D.C./Baltimore • Bern
Frankfurt am Main • Berlin • Brussels • Vienna • Oxford

Linda Myrsiades

Splitting the Baby

The Culture of Abortion
in Literature and Law,
Rhetoric and Cartoons

PETER LANG
New York • Washington, D.C./Baltimore • Bern
Frankfurt am Main • Berlin • Brussels • Vienna • Oxford

Library of Congress Cataloging-in-Publication Data

Myrsiades, Linda S.
Splitting the baby: the culture of abortion
in literature and law, rhetoric and cartoons / Linda Myrsiades.
p. cm. — (Eruptions; v. 20)
Includes bibliographical references (p.) and index.
1. Abortion. 2. Abortion in literature. 3. Abortion—Law and
legislation. 4. Abortion—Caricatures and cartoons. I. Title. II. Series.
HQ767 .M97   363.46—dc21   2001050666
ISBN 0-8204-5816-3
ISSN 1091-8590

Die Deutsche Bibliothek-CIP-Einheitsaufnahme

Myrsiades, Linda:
Splitting the baby: the culture of abortion
in literature and law, rhetoric and cartoons / Linda Myrsiades.
–New York; Washington, D.C./Baltimore; Bern;
Frankfurt am Main; Berlin; Brussels; Vienna; Oxford: Lang.
(Eruptions; Vol. 20)
ISBN 0-8204-5816-3

Cover design by Joni Holst

The paper in this book meets the guidelines for permanence and durability
of the Committee on Production Guidelines for Book Longevity
of the Council of Library Resources.

© 2002 Peter Lang Publishing, Inc., New York

Printed in the United States of America

Contents

Preface

T he purpose of this work is to provide what has yet to be provided in abortion studies—an opportunity for readers to explore the rich cultural landscape of abortion literature, cartoons, and rhetoric to access a deeper, more humane way of addressing an issue that has provoked a pressing and painful social split in the American psyche. This work explores the wisdom, and sometimes the lack of it, of Supreme Court opinions, the lessons of history, the visual, literary, and rhetorical expressions of abortion culture with special focus on the last quarter of the twentieth century. The material reviewed here may provide an opportunity to step back from the fray and remind ourselves that the dilemma that abortion poses is a human dilemma and a cultural dilemma that is survivable only in shared human and cultural terms. Approaching the culture of abortion not through one way of seeing or one form of knowledge but through several interrelated ways of knowing the work capitalizes on the potential richness such an approach entails without the limitations of a singular political or disciplinary perspective.

Where abortion will largely be treated in this work in an American venue, it has—front and back of the work—found some of its grounding in European origins. The tale of King Solomon has allowed some fine-tuning of its views on the human character of judgment, and cultural anthropology and English common law have provided some sense of its rootedness in precursory bodies of experience that helped form or contextualize the American experience. But essentially, and without excuse, this book is about abortion in twentieth-century America. The work explores a law that is not transcendent but human and that, being human, is best understood through the experience of human culture. The more it is couched in culture, the work contends, the better the law will be understood and the better it will resonate with that which it presumes to rule.

There is nothing neat about abortion. Its exercise, and resistance to that exercise, involves many different ways of seeing, feeling, and codifying it as an experience. The variety of voices that are heard put us in touch with the deep well of care and concern behind the legal and political problems that arise in addressing an experience so fundamental to the human condition. Abortion, after all, is an issue that touches both life and death, the cradle and the grave. It will not go away, nor is it likely to be fully resolved.

Chapter One introduces the work with the early history of abortion law in America. It provides a cross-cultural view of abortion and background to the association of abortion, witchcraft, and midwifery. English common law, colonial American law, and slavery are presented in a discussion that takes us through the first systematic assault on abortion rights with the nineteenth-century physicians' campaign. Chapter One speaks to a woman's agentive ability, her culpability, and her vulnerability, both at her own hands and those of the state, religion, law, and medicine. It speaks, as well, to society's interest in the basic social compact, to its desire for individual autonomy in private acts, to a sense of fairness in its dealings with women, to its protective feelings for the unprotected, and to its responsibility for providing safely for life and the living. Included in this picture is the public's desire for safe medical care and qualified, expert medical authority. Moreover, it is clear that society has an interest in preserving social order so that scandals are prosecuted and crime is punished with certainty. As part of that order, law is expected to produce clarity if it is to achieve legitimacy, even if it must do so within a complex of powerful cultural forces and diverse legal venues that result in an incoherent rather than a resolved body of law. It must do so even across centuries that express a chain of discontinuity rather than continuity in the history and traditions related to abortion.

Chapter Two frames the rhetorics used to give body to the abortion debate. This chapter examines the profiles of the abortion and antiabortion movements and explores the evolution of legal and political abortion rhetorics: the themes and images they develop, the constructions they give to the main players, and the language they use. The chapter then analyzes selected advertising campaigns and considers emerging images of the fetus—personal and public—and the effect of ultrasound technology on the "transparent" mother. Constructing "choice" as a lesser Apocalypse leading to the larger Apocalypse of social suicide, antiabortion forces propose a mythic Holy War around the fetus, a figure construed in its political and technological guises as a self-generated entity. Organic motherhood having been relegated to the past in this construction, proabortion rhetoric itself disavows the bodily uniqueness of woman; it sees the body as a construction and not a given. But the rhetoric of abortion yields clues to future ways of seeing for the abortion debate, including the not-altogether-salutary prospect of disappearing women as well as the more appealing notion of a network of social relations that includes men on potentially equal terms. Perhaps the most constructive contribution to the on-going conversation, however, is the prospect rhetoric offers for a greater overlapping of ideas shared by proabortion and antiabortion forces, a broader range of common ground, and a greater flexibility that marginalizes vilification and oppositionality.

The next three chapters study abortion culture from 1973 to 2000, incorporating the visual arts through a survey based on over 200 cartoons and the language arts through a survey based on 60 works of poetry and 150 works of short and some selected long fiction. Drama and film have been excluded from consideration because of the length of the work, with the hope that someone else will take up that piece of the cultural puzzle. The handful of works of long fiction treated here were included to give fuller representation to race-d experiences of abortion and to treatment of the fetus in abortion literature. Judith Wilt (1991) has already given us a good start on examining novels of abortion.

Chapter Three takes up abortion cartoons and looks at them in relation to contemporary historical events and legal issues. The chapter reflects three decades of cartoons from 1973 to 2001, covering the work of forty-three master cartoonists such as Tony Auth, Paul Conrad, Don Wright, Jimmy Margulies, Herblock, Chuck Haynies, Nicole Hollander, and Signe Wilkinson. It creates a national snapshot of commentary on abortion politics from such widely ranging newspapers as the *Philadelphia Inquirer*, the *St. Petersburg Times*, the *Atlanta Constitution*, the *Los Angeles Times*, the *Des Moines Register*, the *Spokane Chronicle*, the *Oregonian*, and the *New York Daily News*. Centering on several key metaphors—the hanger, the scales of justice, the pregnant male, the earthquake fault line, and the maze, among them—this chapter considers the differences that arise among members of the Supreme Court in delivering a decision, being delivered from it, and "delivering" *Roe v. Wade*, either by reaffirming or by disconfirming it. Cartoon art provides a visual history that ranges from clinic protests to bombings and assassinations, from the prohibition of Medicaid payments for abortions for the poor and the obstacles posed by undue burdens on abortion access to consideration of death row inmates juxtaposed to death "*Roe*" fetuses. As a history, cartoons offer more than a time-line or a testimony; more importantly, they offer the possibility of unpacking oppositional rhetoric, exchanging messages, and diminishing tension between opposed positions by means of humor and irony. The visual metaphors provided by cartoons act to open the possibility of conversation and to invite the participation of the reader. They constitute an open forum that enables us to see through a different set of assumptions, question our own assumptions, and thereby interrupt our hold on singular ideas to produce new possibilities. The dislodging of fixed notions offered by cartoons provokes the prospect of more fully engaging the abortion conversation, making it more difficult to discount the argument Justice Scalia puts forward. Scalia challenges *the Planned Parenthood of Southeastern Pennsylvania v. Casey* plurality holding that "calls the contending sides of a national controversy to end their national division by accepting a common mandate rooted in the Constitution" (in Friedman 1993, 362). It may, indeed, be more realistic for the nation to face its differences directly and forcefully without expecting that can be done speedily or be finally settled. Certainly in cartoon culture, abortion is given a full and wrenching hearing.

Chapter Four initiates the discussion of literature with a consideration of how abortion is treated in poetry. Here, as well as in Chapter Five, the range of experiences appears almost infinite as abortion poetry deals with such broad issues as relationships, conflicts, structural conditions, and agentive actions. The chapter looks at the actual occasion of abortion, then its effects, followed by questions of a woman's identity and the male perspective. The poetry explored includes, among others, that of Anne Sexton, Adrienne Rich, Marge Piercy, Lucille Clifton, Alice Walker, and Gwendolyn Brooks, as well as W.D. Snodgrass, Frank O'Hara, Robert Lowell, and William Carlos Williams. Like the cartoons and the short fiction, the poetry sample largely covers the period from *Roe v. Wade* (1973) to the aftermath of *Planned Parenthood v. Casey* (1992) in *Stenberg v. Carhart* (2000), but it expands outside that frame in places to access works of special importance like Ben Jonson's "To Fine Lady-Would Bee." The situations and motives treated in poetry extend from coerced sex, sexual confusion, and suicidal impulses to duress, self-assertion, and animal instinct in pursuing an abortion. Abortions occur in both middle-class and poor families, urban and rural settings, in small as well as large families, with married as well as unmarried women, and in pregnancies that are unexpected, desired, or unwelcome, constituting a pattern that reflects the complexity of real world abortion experiences. Abortion as treated in poetry can be a merciful experience or one ridden with guilt and regret; it can express itself as a desire by a mother for her own obliteration as often as a celebration of liberating her body. A discussion of gender perspective finds, in addition, that oppositional distinctions between male and female poetry do not hold up well over an extended sample of poems. Rather, some themes may receive more attention by men (the male desire for progeny) or by women (the threat to a woman's independence) but not at the expense of shared concerns (the anxiety experienced at the loss of progeny), so that there is more ambiguity than clarity in the difference of gendered perspectives.

In the short fiction treated in Chapter Five, we find a richness and range of experience comparable to that of poetry, demonstrating again the prospect for a shared group of themes that goes well beyond the rank oppositionality of the political battles over abortion to remind us of the common ground that exists at the local level of human concerns. Short fiction offers a base of work significantly broader than poetry, though less broad than cartoons, to provide such work as Toni Cade Bambara's "A Girl's Story," Warren Adler's "An Unexpected Visit," Marshall Klimasewiski's "Jun-Hee," and Alice Walker's "The Abortion," as well as work by Patty Lou Floyd, Bobbie Ann Mason, Sara Paretsky, Andre Dubus, Gish Jen, Joseph Epstein, and Barbara Summers, among others. Study of some longer fiction offers the opportunity to consider the contribution to abortion studies made by Gayl Jones' *Corregidora*, Gloria Naylor's *The Women of Brewster Place*, Toni Morrison's *Beloved*, and Maryse Conde's *I, Tituba, Black Witch of Salem*. We find in short fiction an expression of the depth of feeling that abortion arouses, both among those most immediately involved and within the communities of which they are a part. Generational expectations and race-d experiences contribute to the ways in which abortion is embraced or resisted. So does gender stereotyping, which finds men trapped outside and women locked within the world of abortion decisions. Class considerations, religious and ideological values, together with ethnic, family, and community traditions all play a role that is explored in short fiction.

Finally, in the Conclusion, the work returns us to the legal culture, in which the abortion wars have been most purposefully played out. Here, a root metaphor is used for the abortion wars—the tale of the wisdom of King Solomon. Solomon has been referenced in at least two Supreme Court opinions—*Planned Parenthood v. Casey* and *Madsen v. Women's Health Center* (1994)—and has preoccupied cartoonists Jim Borgman and Ed Fischer, who are fascinated by a judgment splitting the abortion "baby." It is discussed, in addition, through Bertolt Brecht's *The Caucasian Chalk Circle* to explore judicial decision-making and through Mark Twain's *Huckleberry Finn* to consider giving voice to the silenced in law. The tale of Solomon provides a legal metaphor that allows us to tie together the variety of ways of seeing embraced by this work, from history and rhetoric to the content of literature and the visual metaphors of cartooning. It allows us to access feminist perspectives as well as theories of power and politics to explore forms of knowledge ranging from the deeply experiential to the highly abstract. The tale of Solomon embodies for us the irreducible dilemma of a collision of courses and offers the choice of rendering a judgment or escaping from it. Consent and coercion, representation for the voiceless, and the legitimacy of the Court are each considered through the Solomon tale. In sum, Solomon raises the irresoluble issue of preserving halves without splitting the whole and of the power of the sword to render moot the most critical issues of personal rights.

The cultural expressions of abortion in both the visual and language arts thus provide an ameliorating experience that blunts the harshness of polarizing forces on the abortion issue and opens a discussion on finding common ground. This work represents an effort to examine how what we feel and express in cultural products presents a more human side to the abortion wars, a side that is more honest and even accurate than the ideological posturing to which we have become inured. Abortion is not treated here as merely a literary matter or mere fodder for the visual art of cartooning. Rather, both the literary and cartoon venues offer an entrée into the world of abortion that roots it more appropriately in the culture of which it is a part. Culture gives us distance from the hysteria of abortion politics, exchanging for it something that is at once both less intense and more deeply felt. At the same time, cultural expressions of abortion are products of the cultural context of which they are a part, so that they therefore necessarily inform even as they reflect their culture.

Acknowledgments

I thank here, at the end of a personally rewarding trip through women's history and sorrow, those who gave me sustenance on the way. Three women have mattered greatly in my life—my grandmother, my mother, and my daughter—two of whom almost died because they lacked access to a humane, medically safe abortion, and one who had the right to one and, mercifully, never had to make the choice. The irony of such a difference should not be lost to us. Lacking a choice, women can die; with a choice, they may never have to make one. I thank as well a good friend, Barbara Norton, Professor of History at Widener University, who has found her good fortune and helped me find mine by acting as a true and faithful reader for a manuscript that clearly needed one.

I extend once again my deep appreciation to West Chester University and the Pennsylvania State System of Higher Education. They supported this work through a Faculty Development Award and a state system grant that made it possible for me to work with some talented student researchers—in particular, Amy McDermott, who served well beyond the call of duty to provide exceptional assistance to the project—and to spend a year at Temple Law School working with two colleagues for whose support I am indebted—Peter Liacouras Professor Jane Baron and Professor Finbarr McCarthy. Finally, the welcome support of a NEH summer institute grant at Columbia Medical School is happily acknowledged; the NEH is undeniably the bread and staff of good research in the humanities, for which many of us are most grateful.

CHAPTER ONE

The History and Tradition of Abortion Law

The Anthropology of Abortion

The anthropology of abortion frames this work in terms of the motivation, techniques, and consequences of abortion as well as attitudes towards it and social actions taken in response to it. A survey of a variety of abortion practices worldwide suggests how varied different societies' responses to abortion are and how frequently societies disagree over its legitimacy internally. Because the integrity of the communal fabric is affected by abortion, the practice often does not go unremarked and is most often constrained by certain social requirements (Devereux 1955, 66). In spite of the famous line in the physician's Hippocratic oath that appears to prohibit assisting in an abortion ("Similarly [will I not give] to a woman an improper pessary," quoted in Riddle 1992, 9),[1] the ancient Greeks believed that fetuses have no souls. They "notoriously practice[d] abortion" as well as exposed infants (Devereux 54). Some cultures assume that society may demand abortion against one's will, either without one's knowledge or consent or by coercion. The rationale for such a practice might simply be to preserve a woman's or family's reputation or to protect a community's ideological or religious belief about male-female relations and roles or about nature and the cosmos. In some cases, abortion is itself the penalty for those who refuse to abort, just as beatings, divorce, shame, exile, or a fine are penalties.

The motivation for abortion among those who engage in it is thus complex and can be related to cultural, moral, religious, or even political purposes. The more obvious rationale is that abortion is used as a form of birth control or to conceal a sinful or illegal relationship and thereby avoid punishment (Devereux 1955, 7–24). It may be considered a coping strategy for women afraid of childbirth or an economic measure for those too poor to bear the cost of a child. Some pregnancies may indeed be aborted for vanity's sake, for the effect a pregnancy will have on a woman's looks or desirability. A woman may be motivated because she is too young, too old, or too ill to safely bear a child. Indeed, in one tribal society, the fetus is put on trial when its mother is ill; if found guilty, it is aborted to cure her (8). Similarly, if a father is old or sick or if there is reason to believe a pregnancy is "bewitched" and a mother is likely to bear a "monster," social codes may dictate an abortion.

In many cultures, reproduction is tied to the power of rich or powerful factions, so that a ruler may choose to ensure his line by aborting his sister's children or those of his concubine(s). In the sultan's harem, for example, one wife is designated the "bloody midwife" to perform just this function (Devereux 1955, 10). Equally, a society may choose to abort the pregnancies of its enemies; enslaved itself, it may choose abortion to resist the conquest and slavery of its offspring. Mass abortions are sometimes ordered to serve the same purpose (10). A conquered people whose native institutions have been undermined will experience a surge in abortion and population decline, a sign that it has lost the capacity for self-preservation. Dominant groups are likely to establish anti-miscegenation laws and taboos or exploit prejudices to prevent the emergence of a socially disruptive class of half-breeds (11). To protect property and ensure the inheritance of legitimate heirs in some cultures, fetuses are sometimes aborted upon the death of the father (14). Ritual abortions related to power and property as well as cannibalism of fetuses during periods of starvation are also characteristic of some cultures (16). Dreams or omens may require an abortion either because of familial superstition or a religious requirement (20).

More personal reasons for abortion include a woman's desire to retain a husband whose attention is likely to drift during a pregnancy. A woman aborts from despair while mourning a lost child; she aborts to revenge herself on her husband or to end a pregnancy resulting from coercion, incest, or rape. On the father or husband's side, men are likely to batter or otherwise assault women carrying illegitimate or undesired children, in one culture retrieving and boiling the male child's testicles to render an adulterous lover impotent (Devereux 1955, 17–18). Witchcraft, as well, can be implicated in abortion (23), sometimes by a jealous co-wife or a male sexual partner anxious to conceal his part in a pregnancy. A woman's part in a pregnancy or abortion is, by contrast, easily discernible. Her general agitation, bleeding, milk-filled breasts, and vaginal wounds are all considered signs, even where a swollen belly has been artfully concealed. A child born deformed or a woman who cannot bear children is often accepted as a sign of abortion (61).

Outside of adoption, once the decision not to give birth or to retain the child is made, virtually the only alternatives are infanticide or suicide (Devereux 1955, 24–25). The risks of abortion are themselves clear and serious: injury, death, sterility. Nevertheless, abortion techniques remain as numerous and varied as the numbers of cultures in which abortions occur. Some more common techniques create trauma to the fetus or stimulate labor. One might do so by lifting heavy loads, jumping from a height, smashing oneself against a boulder or a tree, jumping on or kicking the belly, or constriction of the belly using belts or by squeezing, massaging, and manipulating the genitals, uterus, or abdomen. Pregnant women in different cultures have been bled and starved to provoke a miscarriage, and heat has been applied to scald the belly, using hot water, ashes, or stones. In some cultures, biting ants are applied over the body, are ingested, or are inserted vaginally. Irritants are applied to the belly or inserted as pessaries (vaginal suppositories), including turpentine, tobacco, soaked sponges or cotton, animal feces, and seawater. Wires, sticks, and bottles are inserted to perforate the womb. Clysters are used in the form of bulb enema syringes, and emetics and purgatives are administered (36–38). Substances are ingested, including the hairs of an animal in bearfat, such toxic drugs as tansy and savin, and such animal secretions as camel foam or goat dung. Alternative procedures include magical rituals, baths, and psychogenic drugs.

With all the variations in the practice of abortion, there is little lore on the treatment of the aborted fetus (Devereux 1955, 44–45). Informally buried on the spot, for the most part, it is likely to be tossed as rubbish or sunk in water, sometimes stored in a pot. In times of famine, it is sometimes consumed; in ritual uses, its blood is sprinkled over the land or its parts cooked and scattered. Whereas fetuses are sometimes given names and addressed in prayer, in one tribal culture the fetus is used in ghost hauntings to prevent women from seeking subsequent or multiple abortions (46).

Midwives, Witchcraft, and Abortion

Narrowing our focus to Western medicine, it is clear that people of the pre-modern period were well informed about birth control, that abortion has always been available, and that contraception, abortion, and infanticide have been a continuing historical practice across all cultures (Riddle 1992, viii, 2–7). During antiquity, almost anything was considered permissible. Works attributed to Hippocrates or to followers of the Hippocratic school reveal extensive recipes for abortion, constituting a compendium of all then-available knowledge of abortifacients (76–81). In spite of the controversy surrounding what many regard as a misreading of the Hippocratic oath to prohibit abortion (4, 7–10, 144–153), the oath was apparently intended to proscribe only a pessary, leaving a physician free to use contraceptives, oral abortifacients, and surgical and manipulative procedures. The Middle Ages marked an important change from antiquity during which "almost nothing went unchecked" (3), and "the church and to some extent secular law now sought to control sexual behaviors and antibirth control" (109). Prohibitions included a list of practices that interfered with fertility and thereby challenged God's control over creation, signaling an alliance with the devil or denial of male authority (109–112). Prohibitions covered "sodomy, adultery, abortion, contraception, mutilation (notably castration), nudity, sexual relations during menstruation and after birth until weaning, and infanticide" (3).

Nevertheless, more than two hundred herbal methods and instruments of abortion were in common use in the Middle Ages (Kellough 1996, 24–25). Midwives controlled or were among the most effective practitioners of medical knowledge related to such practices until the development of obstetrics as a medical specialty in the nineteenth century (Leavitt 1986). They were in demand in spite of a climate in which accusations of religious heresy and attacks on suspected witches were common. Indeed witchcraft was defined in the 1486 witch-hunter's handbook, the *Malleus Malificarum* or hammer of witches, as "practicing any means of limiting the size of one's family" (quoted in Kellough 48). Common crimes for which witches were charged included contraception, abortion, and relieving the pain of childbirth (Ehrenreich and English 1978, 35; Barstow 1994, 133–134). Birth control, infanticide, and abortion, all of which implicated midwives in some way, were, thereby, connected to witchcraft. Witches were typically associated in the fifteenth and sixteenth centuries in Europe with killing unborn and newly born children, preferably unbaptized so they could be dedicated to the devil (Dresden-Coenders 1987). Mothers mainly had the largest opportunity to accommodate such deeds and were linked to midwives, whom many regarded as having special powers over the unborn and newly born (60). Women, as a result, were considered prominent among witches because of their proximity to reproductive events. Indeed, their presumed interference with reproduction was taken to risk the very destruction of the human species. In times of social disruption and economic difficulty, which put pressure on the stability of families and on the availability of medical assistance, opportunities to accuse women of witchcraft were rife. Midwives, in particular, were held to operate at the center of suspect women's networks. These networks were believed to exclude or control men by way of marriage brokers or brothels or through women's covert sharing of information and gossip. Networks appeared suspect because of women's power over bearing and rearing children (63, 67). Travelling from one household to another and overseeing reproductive events, midwives, more than other women, appeared to represent a threat as mediators among women within women's networks. Exerting control over fertility, conception, and birth necessarily put midwives at risk of the wrath of the church, which held that the power over the creation of life was the province of God alone. Indeed, in mid-seventeenth-century French-speaking lands, a treatise by Judge Boquet called *An Examen of Witches* was used to hunt witches under the theory that "Satan spoke through a female's 'shameful parts' and . . . all witches were abortionists" (Barstow 66).

The perpetual need to balance sexual urges and family size meant that, irrespective of legal or religious pressures, birth control, abortion, and infanticide would be continuing social problems (Riddle 1992, 2). The Christian church, fearful of family limitation practices, demanded control over issues related to fertility (Harley 1990, 2). Roman and Germanic legal traditions protected the right of a head of a family to the children he had fathered (Riddle 10, 140). Protections were only extended to reproductive women when there was harm to their lives as a result of medical mal-practice. Women were, on the other hand, generally preferred in law over the fetus. Both ancient and medieval codes held practitioners who used enchantments or poi-sons liable if they threatened women's lives but not if they threatened the fetus (140, 174 n47). A woman was not, however, protected against offenses related to fertility control, fornication, post-quickening abortion, or magical practices (111–112). Witch-hunters' manuals focused on those areas in their search for violators of the sacraments, participants in heresies, and magical healers or sorcerers (Harley 8,12). Midwives were suspected of relieving a woman's pain at childbirth and dis-placing it as a magical power onto someone else (14–15). Female midwives in Prot-estant countries were suspected of superstitious contamination of the young, of using Papist charms, and of conducting emergency baptisms. In Catholic countries, they were suspected of having failed to baptize the newly born. Midwives were ima-gined, as well, to have access to materials considered necessary to witches. The fat of children was thought to be used as a flying ointment for attending the "Sabbat," infant flesh for food at the Sabbat (a form of cannibalism enhanced if the flesh was unbaptized), and the bodies of infants—particularly the afterbirth—for magical purposes (3). Because eating and healing were often implicated in the practice of witchcraft by witch-hunters' manuals, folk healers and innkeepers were, like mid-wives, often caught up in the web of suspicions raised by witch-hunting hysteria and accused of medical malpractice and food poisoning.

In spite of the widespread attention given to practices associated with midwives in the witch-hunters' manuals, as well as the rather sinister regard in which the "sage femme" who specialized in obstetrics and gynecology was held (Harley 1990, 7), midwives were, nevertheless, rarely prosecuted as witches. Actual cases are few and isolated, reflecting to some extent the relatively high standing of midwives in their communities. Many among them were town notables, and they were often li-censed or elected in their communities (2). Whereas midwives were often consid-ered in the same vulnerable group as spinsters and widows (5), that they were poor or illiterate is a myth (2). Moreover, they appear to have generally been warmly em-braced by their patients, many of whom testified on their behalf (11). As David Harley attests, the only significant risks to midwives occurred when an inquisitorial system of justice prevailed and torture was permitted so that long chains of accusa-tions were created.

The association of midwives with witches was thus not of consequence in the English common law tradition that was to inform American colonial law. Among the four commonly cited cases of midwife-witches in colonial America (Anne Hutchinson, Jane Hawkins, Margaret Jones, and Elizabeth Morse), for example, none was tried for witchcraft, and only one was suspected, erroneously (Harley 1990, 17–18, 24). Nor does an association of midwives with abortion and witches appear in court cases examined by studies on abortion (like Cornelia Hughes

Dayton's on women and law in Connecticut, 1639–1789 [1995]) or by studies on midwifery (like Laurel Ulrich's on midwifery in Maine, 1785–1812 [1990]). Midwives had been condemned as witches in western tradition, and in the American colonies the most famous midwife, Anne Hutchinson, was condemned for her "authority," banished, and made a religious martyr (Ulrich 46). Such outcasting was possible because birthing was the site of both abortions and infanticide as well as a site where midwives were present and unsupervised by male authority, making the midwife a strong candidate for association with witchcraft. Studies on witchcraft in New England (Demos 1982; Karlsen 1987), by contrast, "have found suggestive references to healing activities by suspected witches, though with no strong correlations between witchcraft and midwifery per se. . . ." Midwives, apparently, were like all women in their "susceptibil[ity] to the witchcraft slander" (Ulrich 374 n12).

The period of the 1690s was one in which economic and social distress led to a rise in premarital pregnancy and out-of-wedlock births, prime conditions for abortions and infanticide from 1693–1699 (Cohen 1993, 59; Dayton 1995, 188). They also served as contributing factors to the association of midwives with abortions and witchcraft. As an ordinance enacted in New York City in 1716 suggests, the suspicions under which midwives operated were such that they were required to swear: "not [to] Give any Counsil or Administer any Herb Medicine or Potion, or any other thing to any Woman being with Child whereby She Should Destroy or Miscarry of that she goeth withall before her time" (quoted in Olasky 1992, 37).

The English jurist Edwin Hale's mid-nineteenth-century (1867) opinion of abortionists indicates that midwifery was still a tainted profession a century and a half later. He saw midwives as creatures who operated under the guise of such "apparently harmless avocations" as midwives and fortune-tellers to "ply their murdering trade" (quoted in Siegel 1992, 301).[2] In an interesting piece of cultural history, the *National Police Gazette* in 1847 published a drawing in which "a well-dressed young woman [appears] whose lower body has been transmuted into a devil, wings spread, head emerging from her pelvis, and feeding on the throat of a newborn held in her claws. The caption reads, 'The Female Abortionist'" (in Stormer 2000, 110).

Colonial History and Common Law

American abortion law from the colonial period until the early nineteenth century was based on English common law. The earliest statement about abortion as a crime in common law comes from Henry de Bracton, a justice of the Court of King's Branch in the thirteenth century (c. 1250). De Bracton established the principle that one who "strikes a pregnant woman or gives her a poison in order to procure an abortion, if the foetus is already formed or quickened, especially if it is quickened" (quoted in Keown 1988, 172 n9) is guilty of the crime of homicide. The crime was extended by de Bracton's commentator Fleta (c. 1290) to pre-quickening (quickening being "the first maternal perception of fetal movement," 3), as well as to contraception, the intent to abort, and the conduct of the woman herself. He attaches guilt to whoever "has given or accepted poison with the intention of preventing procreation or conception. A woman also commits homicide if, by potion or the like, she destroys a quickened child in her womb" (quoted in Keown 172 n10). A distinction is made here between the intent to abort, for which the abortionist is to be punished, and the actual destruction of the fetus, the only act for which the woman is to be punished.

In the fourteenth century, problems of proof were raised regarding abortions, in one case because the fetus was given no baptismal name and in a second because of the difficulty of judging whether or not the abortion itself was what killed the fetus (Means 1971, 337–342, 344; Keown 1988, 4–5). As a result, in neither case was a misdemeanor or a felony upheld (1327 and 1348, in William Staunford's *Pleas of the Crown*, 1557). By the sixteenth century, a distinction was made between killing a child "newly borne, this is Felonie of the death of a man, though the childe have no name, nor be baptized" and a child "destroyed in the mother's belly [which] is no manslayer nor Felone" (quoted in Means 342; Keown 4–5). Building on this distinction in a case in 1601, the law held that the charge is murder should a child be born, live, and then die with wounds on its body as proof of a previous beating, but if it is born dead, the charge is not murder (Means 343; Keown 9). We find an evolved expression of this law codified by Sir Edward Coke in 1641 where he distinguishes born alive from death in the womb: "If a woman be quicke with childe, and by a Potion or otherwise killeth it in her wombe; or if a man beat her, whereby the childe dieth in her body, and she is delivered of a dead childe, this is a great misprision, and no murder: but if the childe be born alive, and dieth of the Potion, battery, or other cause, this is murder: for in law it is accounted a reasonable creature, in *rerum natura*, when it is born alive" (Coke's *Third Institute*, quoted in Means 345). Finally, William Blackstone confirms this line of reasoning for the eighteenth century, making abortion of a fetus in the womb a misdemeanor (a misprision): "To kill a child in its mother's womb is now no murder, but a great misprision" (quoted in Means 349).[3]

Thus, the harshest crime ascribed in common law was homicide for the abortionist, and it incorporated contraception, a pre-quickening abortion, and the intent to abort (such as we find in Fleta in 1290). But these distinctions were not to go unchallenged. Rather, conditions requiring post-quickening, an abortion that is actually effectuated, and the demonstration that the death of a fetus resulted from the event of an abortion developed into a base line for abortion law. Moreover, if the crime were to qualify as murder, the birth of a dead fetus alone would be insufficient. The fetus must be born alive and then have died as a result of a previous act of abortion to qualify as a murder; where the fetus is born dead, the crime is a misdemeanor.

Although common law did not regard an infant as a victim of homicide unless born (Keown 1988, 4), there was some appreciation for the fetus. In *R. v. Webb* in 1602, a woman who acts as an agent to abort is considered to have done injury to the infant as well as to have offended the Crown: "not having the fear of God before her eyes, but moved and seduced by the instigation of the devil, once ate the poison called 'rattesbane' with the intention of spoiling and destroying the infant in the womb of Margaret herself . . . [and having done so] as a pernicious example to all the malefactors offending in like manner, against the peace of our Lady the Queen, her crown and dignity" (quoted in Keown 7). Further, in a trial in 1732 in which Eleanor Beare received three years imprisonment for abortion, the prosecutor was reported to have accused the defendant before the jury in the following terms: "to destroy the fruit of the womb carries something in it so contrary to the natural tenderness of the female sex, that I am amazed how ever any woman should arrive at such a degree of impiety and cruelty" (quoted in Keown 9).

An abortion case in 1742 (a case that would not be prosecuted, despite the death of both mother and fetus, until 1745 and would not conclude until 1747) was more typical. In this case, the physician-accomplice and the father of the fetus were indicted "for the 'highhanded misdemeanor' of endeavoring to destroy Sarah's health 'and the fruit of her womb'" (Keown 1988, 46). The charge was neither a felony nor a capital crime and therefore not murder. Moreover, the indictment was returned only against the doctor, the agent considered most directly involved in administering the substance, as if to say the case was limited to medical malfeasance: "By recklessly endangering Sarah's life he had abused the trust that heads of the household placed in him as a physician" (47). The sentence of public shaming and whipping, or corporal punishment, was appealed as inappropriate to a misdemeanor case. Concern for the status of the fetus was apparently one of the unsettled questions in early American law; it was "strikingly absent from these eighteenth-century documents . . . [as was] either outrage over the destruction of a fetus or denunciation of those who would arrest 'nature's proper course'" (Dayton 1991, 23).

The death of the woman in an abortion was generally handled with greater clarity than was the death of the fetus. In the late seventeenth century, Matthew Hale held that her death in an attempt at abortion would be murder, for the substance administered was intended to destroy the child, not to cure her of a disease (*Treatise of the History of the Pleas of the Crown*, 1670). The Margaret Tinckler case in 1781 (reported by Edward Hyde East in 1793) found that the deceased woman, whether or not she had consented to an abortion, could not be held to be an accessory to her own death, which must be treated like any murder. Chief Justice Lemuel Shaw of the Supreme Court of Massachusetts applied this common law to an American case in 1845 and held that the use of violence, drugs, or instruments upon a woman to procure an abortion without her consent is an indictable assault under common law. Moreover, where "the death of the mother ensues, the party making such an attempt, with or without the consent of the woman, is guilty of murder of the mother, on the ground that it is an act done without lawful purpose, dangerous to life, and that the consent of the woman cannot take away the imputation of malice" (quoted in Means 1971, 372). Whereas the pregnant woman's death was not intended, and even though she may have consented, this interpretation acknowledged the malicious nature of such an act on its pregnant victim as well as the great danger of abortion to her person.

In colonial America, a number of abortion cases dealt with the pregnant woman being coerced to take an abortifacient that did her as well as the child harm. If the woman survived, as she did in a case in Maryland in 1652, she was treated less as a victim herself than as a sinner and had to pay the penalty for fornication, in this case a whipping. As for the father, the connection between the stillborn child and the abortifacient being difficult to prove, a fine and a posted bond for future good behavior had to suffice for a charge of "adultery, fornication, and murtherous intent" (quoted in Olasky 1992, 22). As a case of rape and abortion in Maryland in 1663 demonstrates, marrying the mother, the only true witness, allowed many fathers to disqualify the principal testimony against them and thereby to escape punishment (23).[4]

In spite of shifting lines in the law, aborted pregnancies before quickening and those attempted after quickening were regarded differently. Reproach was particularly reserved for the latter when it involved a child born alive, whereas an almost benign forgiveness accompanied the former, particularly when it involved a married woman. The act of fornication, however, was without exception taken very seriously. In Connecticut, as throughout New England, "fornication was by far the largest category of criminal cases on the county court docket from about 1690 until 1770" (Dayton 1995, 160). It accounted for more than one-third of the criminal actions brought in Massachusetts between 1760–1774. In all but one of these cases (a black man cohabiting with a white woman), it was the woman who was prosecuted (Ulrich 1990, 148). In Woolrich, Maine, "half of all women but only ten percent of men accused at the local level ever appeared in county court records" in fornication or paternity suits (154). In contrast to the seventeenth century when both men and women were held equally liable, by mid-eighteenth century "fornication had become a woman's crime" (148). Nevertheless, it appears that for the most part, women who bore children out of wedlock were neither ruined nor abandoned in their communities, as both the policing of sexual mores and caretaking were controlled more effectively by informal mechanisms than by the courts (149). The midwife Martha Ballard in the late eighteenth century noted four times as many incomplete as completed legal actions for paternity, suggesting that local informal arrangements were frequently made to satisfy both parties (154). The unwed mother was questioned during labor to name the father of the child for purposes of child support. Such testimony, generally taken by midwives, was accepted in itself as sufficient to warrant child support unless there existed overwhelming evidence to the contrary. By contrast, prosecution of the responsible male for fornication required either confession or witnesses (149, 151). In any case, premarital pregnancy was common throughout New England; in Martha Ballard's experience along the Kennebec river in Maine, forty of the one hundred six babies she delivered over twelve years (1785–1797) were conceived out of wedlock (155–156).

In the early American legal story of abortion, the evidence put forward to determine the existence of fetal life was quickening. The existence of a fetus was subsequently used as legal evidence of the act of fornication, a crime where "problems of procedure and proof" had led to failed charges (Keown 1988, 5). Pregnancy was regarded as the punishment for fornication. The man in this colonial story was the seducer who bore the onus for the crime. The woman was his victim, but a victim condemned by nature to suffer a punishment dictated by her own body. Termination of the pregnancy was thereby regarded as a means of concealing the evidence of a crime and a further threat to both the life of the man's victim, the pregnant woman, and the "fruit of her womb," the fetus. Harm may attach to the fetus, recalling common law, but the true victim, whether the abortion is successful or not, is the woman, having been coerced or assaulted. Nevertheless, under common law if the woman acted as an agent to destroy a quickened fetus born alive and succeeded in doing so, she was culpable of a homicide.[5]

Prior to 1750, infanticide rather than abortion was the population limitation method that received the most attention (Riddle 1992, 10–11),[6] partly because of the life-threatening dangers of many abortive remedies. The dosages for ingested poisons and suppository insertions varied widely, so that the need for certainty in inducing an abortion often dictated a potency that was murderous to both mother and fetus. Like perforating instruments, which posed the danger of life-threatening infections for the pregnant woman, they often proved suicidal, last-ditch measures. Since daughters of well-established families more frequently married before delivery (Dayton 1995, 212), unwanted children of the poor were most at risk of infanticide.

The earliest infanticide law in the colonies, a 1710 Virginia law, covers a bastard child delivered and killed by the mother and whose death is concealed. The act was, indicatively, titled "An Act to prevent the destroying and murdering of Bastard children" (Olasky 1992, 86). In 1797, a Delaware law assigned a charge of accessory to murder to any who advise a "woman to kill the child she goes with, and after she is delivered, of such a child, she kills it" (quoted in Olasky 85); the Georgia Penal Code of 1811 followed the same route, charging as an accessory to murder whoever gives advice to "another to kill a child before its birth, and the child be killed after its birth, in pursuance of such advice" (quoted in Olasky 85). There thus grew up a spate of anti-concealment laws that expressed the state's interest in the preservation of a child's life. Extending well into the nineteenth century and across the frontier as it moved West, infanticide generally carried a term of imprisonment and sometimes a fine. Kentucky's version of such a law in 1801, for example, dictated a term of from two to seven years (89).

In Connecticut, an upsurge of infanticide prosecutions occurred after 1740, largely involving "a single woman who had allegedly concealed her pregnancy and murdered her 'bastard' child" (Dayton 1995, 211). Nearly all those charged were women of marginal status, which included African or Indian servants or slaves and white servants or household help. The sudden increase in infanticide was accompanied by social changes that saw the development of "what was evidently a growing population of unmarried women for whom domestic service threatened to become a permanent rather than a temporary way of life" (210). Families of moderate income concealed pregnancies and absorbed the dishonor of raising out-of-wedlock children or arranging subsequent marriages. Such protection of one class of women meant that "the range of women prosecuted narrowed in large part to marginal figures—poor women, domestic servants, women in interracial relationships, women who repeatedly bore children without marrying" (161). As a result, the greatest incidence of abortion, concealment, and infanticide that was prosecuted occurred among socially marginal women.

One factor that loomed large in considering prosecution for abortion or infanticide in the colonial and postcolonial periods was race. Although whites, after 1688, were rarely whipped in New England for fornication, it was common punishment for colonial blacks (Dayton 1995, 184–185), a means of explicitly distancing them from the privileges of white law. Cases throughout the eighteenth century that implicated blacks or Indians were consistently treated differently. The penalty of execution for infanticide, though rarely given, was assigned in 1701 to a household worker, Esther Rodgers, who had intercourse, concealed a birth, and killed a child on two occasions, each involving a black male partner (Cohen 1993, 59ff). A second figure, Patience Boston, sent to the gallows in 1734 was not only an Indian servant but married to a Negro servant.

During a period when the legislature was on the brink of accepting the growing unpopularity of capital punishment by reducing by half the number of crimes to which it applied, a black servant in 1768 Massachusetts was tried and sentenced to death for rape. During this same period, rape accusations for white males were routinely dismissed or reduced to attempted rape. In a charge of attempted rape in 1723 in Massachusetts, an Indian was found guilty in spite of testimony that shed considerable suspicion on the woman who accused him; he received a penalty that "was the most severe handed down to those found guilty of attempted rape in the first half of the century" (Lindemann 1984, 66). In a 1774 trial, during a period when white men were infrequently charged or convicted for adultery and where "a white woman, despite a tainted reputation, maneuvered to evade an adultery conviction

. . . a free black man had no resources to ward off a speedy trial and the pain of branding, whipping, and wearing a halter" (Dayton 1995, 171 n27). In sum, crimes were more likely to be punished when the accused were servants or transients, particularly when they were African or Indian (Lindemann 76, 80).

From 1710 to the end of the century, women were also more likely to be singled out before the bar (Dayton 1995, 168). This stigmatizing practice reversed the Puritan tradition of holding both partners responsible before the law. Fornication in the colonial period had been understood to differ little from "coerced sex" for women; by the 1740s and 1750s, however, it had become, in effect, a female crime, as men were either not charged or not convicted (178, 193–194). Indeed, beginning even as early as 1690, women had stopped accusing men of being responsible for their pregnancies; two thirds of those women in New Haven who were before the court had either to be summoned or arrested to appear. The very fact of her pregnant body was sufficient evidence of a woman's fornication. A man's guilt, by contrast, had to be proven by confession, eyewitness testimony, or otherwise overwhelming evidence.

Tracing the kind of evidence considered valid in the crimes of fornication and abortion provides in itself a trail of changes in the legal treatment of reproductive crimes. Fornication was the cornerstone of reproductive crimes not only because it was prerequisite to subsequent acts but, more importantly, because of the role it was perceived to play in the stability of social order. Marriage was understood as the keystone of the family and, therefore, of social order. Illicit sexual acts thereby threatened both institutions, not only by questioning the foundational role of motherhood but by impacting male authority and the legitimacy of inheritance. When citizens no longer reproduced in an orderly way that protected their offspring and did not burden the state (Dayton 1995, 224; Siegel 1992, 314), the welfare of the state was, indeed, implicated. In the same way, if lower-class and marginal women came more and more in the eighteenth century to be associated with fornication, abortion, and infanticide, their punishment and repentance would stand as a warning for middle-class women.

The legal picture of the colonial period had been one in which informal rules and ad hoc remedies prevailed, including "truth telling in childbirth, the midwife's testimony, community corroboration of who was keeping company with whom" (Dayton 1995, 225). A 1672 Connecticut statute reflects the early legal scene where "a woman's 'constant accusation' of one man was legally sufficient to convict him of fornication and make him liable as a parent" (158). Whereas confession was considered a lynch-pin of the early system, by 1701 young men ceased confessing to their crime, no longer considering it in their best interest. Together with the decreased value placed on a woman's oath, this meant that between 1690 and 1740, "given a man's denial of the charges, he should be criminally punished only if damning evidence existed beyond the woman's accusation" (196). This was the beginning of more rigorous standards of proof and a more formal, less communal legal system (225). As one nostalgic jurist, Zephaniah Smith, commented in 1795, "admitting the oath of the woman to prove the father of a bastard child, introduces a new mode of proof, which is repugnant to the general rule respecting evidence" (quoted in Dayton 196).

As the colonies moved out from under Puritan influence to a system based on English criminal trials (Dayton 1995, 225), eighteenth-century American courts began to concern themselves less with questions of truth and more with evidence (Lindemann 1984, 72). Simplified legal rules and a ban on lawyers had allowed residents more direct legal access to the court system. But now confessions and hearsay could no longer be freely admitted; the prosecution would have to produce witnesses to be cross-examined; the victim's testimony could no longer be believed at face value; the accused would have to answer incriminating questions in his testimony, and for capital crimes two witnesses would have to be strictly required. Lacking court stenographers for oral testimony, court records had been incomplete and unevenly kept, some cases maintaining voluminous written depositions from witnesses at a distance and others neglecting to record the actual nature of the issues before the court itself. Instructions to the jury and the judge's comments from the bench had gone unrecorded and the "practice of issuing judicial opinions to explain rulings and verdicts began, spottily, only in the 1780s" (Dayton 6). Indeed, gallows sermons, criminal conversion narratives, and polemical tracts had become important sources for the trial record of a case, to be replaced by more official trial reports in New England only after 1800 (Cohen 1993, 26ff). Courts changed greatly from the seventeenth to the end of the eighteenth century, moving from diminishing influence of the religious community on the conduct of legal affairs to, first, adoption of English common law practices, and, then, gradual accretion of American statutory law (Dayton 8).

American law was to become less variable from state to state, less "ragged and disjointed" (Hall 1989, 17). The influence of transplanted English common law was radically altered by the prodigious growth in the post-Civil War years of statutory law-making, moving the country beyond common law judicial activism to statutory interpretation (226–227). National law, lacking as an integrating force since the framing of the Constitution, began to assert its own sovereign authority to supplement that which the states had significantly retained and exercised (5). The volume of court business expanded markedly as did professionalization and specialization in the law until it came to hold a very powerful and central role in social ordering and nation building in the nineteenth century (Dayton 1995, 9). Just as licensing of professional attorneys and strict rules for evidence contributed to these developments, growing urbanization and the growth of the bourgeoisie and its ethic of commerce, individualism, and privacy changed earlier communal values (12–13).

As part of this larger pattern of legal changes, the passage of the first statutory law on abortion in England, Lord Ellenborough's Act, in 1803, was intended to clarify what until that time the common law had "not clearly delineated" (Keown 1988, 12): "the prohibition of abortion was perceived to be vague and inadequate" (13).[7] The statute in its very first clause declared a charge of felony, a capital crime with a penalty of death and denied benefit of clergy, should "any person or persons . . . wilfully, maliciously, and unlawfully administer to, or cause to be administered to or taken by any of His Majesty's subjects, any deadly poison, or other noxious and destructive substance or thing, with intent such His Majesty's subjects thereby to murder, or thereby to cause and procure the miscarriage of any woman, then being quick with child" (quoted in Keown 15). The intent to abort rather than the actual abortion of the fetus would be sufficient to incur the penalty. The state thereby relieved itself of the burden of proving that the act itself had caused fetal death, a connection that had stymied prosecution under common law. In its final form, the bill added two clauses, one that penalized a pre-quickening abortion as a misdemeanor punishable by fine, imprisonment, the pillory, or whipping and another that penalized the administration of drugs and instruments (18). It did not, however, include the woman herself among those who could be charged.

Influenced by Lord Ellenborough's Act, the General Assembly of Connecticut in 1821 passed the first statute against abortion in the colonies as part of its general crimes and punishment:

> Every person who shall, wilfully and maliciously, administer to, or cause to be administered to, or taken by, any person or persons, any deadly poison, or other noxious and destructive substance, with an intention him, her, or them, thereby to murder, or thereby to cause or procure the miscarriage of any woman, then being quick with child, and shall be thereof duly convicted, shall suffer imprisonment, in newgate prison, during his natural life, or for such other term as the court having cognizance of the offence shall determine. (quoted in Mohr 1978, 21)

The Connecticut statute addressed for the first time in American colonial law the intent to murder or affect the miscarriage of a woman whose pregnancy has reached the point of quickening. It covered a party other than the woman herself (the woman, not the fetus, was considered the victim of the crime), and it considered only the use of a poisonous substance, not instruments or mechanisms. The passage of this law was a response to a scandal-ridden trial in Connecticut seven months earlier in which an Episcopalian minister, Ammi Rogers, was convicted of charges involving "seduction and child-murder; and poisons and violence" in the concealment of an abortion (reported in the Norwich, Connecticut *Courier*, October 11, 1820, p. 3, and quoted in Olasky 1992, 93). Under the common law, Rogers' sentence for a pre-quickening "miscarriage" was two years in the Norwich jail (92).

Slavery, Reproduction, and Abortion

In the slaveholding South, sexual control was a question of total procreational control ranging from sexual relations through marriage to childbearing itself. The objective was to eliminate the possibility of generating a new racially mixed class of white servants and blacks, both free and slave, that might challenge slaveholder supremacy. As a result, racial codes were enacted from the seventeenth century that not only banned sexual relations outside of marriage and interracial marriage but punished white women who bore mulatto children (Getman 1984, 124–126). Just as mulatto children were condemned to be slaves until thirty-one years of age (Higginbotham 1978, 44–45), so were free white women required to serve the master of their black husbands until thirty years of age; equally, free blacks who married white women were to be enslaved (Getman 127; Higginbotham 44–45).

The interracial sexual activities of a black woman were not covered in the law, for a slave had no rights except the right to exist.[8] It was not a crime for a black woman to have a bastard child with a white man nor a crime for them to have sexual relations. Neither was it a crime for a white male to have raped a black female slave (Higginbotham 1978, 45).[9] Indeed, the offspring of rape became the property of the master. As a general rule, the only sexual crime against a black slave was, as a result, a crime against her master's property rather than a crime against her person (Getman 1984, 146). Whereas the master did have recourse to laws dealing with trespass on his property, he was just as liable to extend the sexual services of his slaves as an act of hospitality to his guests. The black slave woman was thereby surrounded on all sides by the appetites of both the slave and the master classes. Her only choices were to resist providing her services, abort her progeny, or flee, all carrying a whipping penalty, or take her own life.

By one argument (White 1985, 39), the black female slave was comparable to northern white prostitutes, with the exception that her offspring represented an acquisition for her owner, producing for him new property. Slavery kept her in a condition of enforced prostitution. She had become, in effect, a means of reproducing the slavery of her people by having become the chief means of maintaining the institution following the 1807 outlawing of the overseas slave trade (68). Free black women had some protection but only against black male slaves (as was apparent in six cases in Virginia between 1790 and 1833 [Kennedy 1997, 36]). Because blacks were precluded from testifying against whites,[10] free black women were, as a practical matter, unable to protect themselves against whites, no known case law demonstrating otherwise.

White southerners had successfully constructed the black female's sexuality in a way that focused on what they asserted was her natural proclivity to satisfy the male appetite. This was a view intended to justify white masters' use of their female slaves' bodies and to excuse in the law this use of her body to produce new property that would reinforce slavery as an institution.[11] Slavery allowed the slavemaster to assume "both the role of the state and the role of the family" (Davis 1997, 247), so that a black slave had not the right to be a husband or wife, father or mother (117). The denial of a legal form of marriage meant the denial of legal parentage, guaranteeing that from birth the slave's condition "would be defined as a commodity rather than as the child of a family, community, and nation" (91). To have allowed marriage would, from the perspective of slave society, have granted familial rights to spouses and parents that would have made human property a poor holding for the slavemaster. It would have challenged the very meaning of ownership should slavemasters wish to punish their slaves, split up families, or sell off children. With the slave woman a breeder and slave children a profit, slavery had to trump marriage and family if property rights were to be meaningful; parentage, marriage, and family were, as a result, unavailable in a meaningful way to slaves.

Given the almost total control of their lives, female slaves had no choice but to face the physical risks of conceiving and bearing children as well as the physical and personal risks of failing to do so. Narratives, diaries, and testimonies demonstrate that female slaves lost more time from work for problems related to menstruation than from any other causes, the former including such complaints as blocked menstrual flow, abnormal bleeding related to tumors, discharges resulting from gonorrhea, and prolapsed uterus (Savitt 1978, 115). Although census figures suggest slightly lower dangers for slaves than for whites, childbirth was itself a dangerous procedure. Poor general hygiene and ignorance of antisepsis meant that infections were sometimes carried from the sickbed to the birthing bed, affecting the health of both mother and child (119). Problems related to birthing itself included convulsions, ectopic pregnancies, uterine rigidity, breech births, puerperal fever, infections, and retained placentas, with bleeding and laxatives the preferred treatments (117). Cesareans, it is worth noting, were not only performed in some difficult births, but black women in Virginia were known to have played an important, if coerced, role in the development of such a procedure (118). The most common risks to the child were neonatal tetanus and infected umbilical stumps (Savitt 1978, 120). Slave children had a "notoriously high mortality rate" (33), attributable not only to the possibility of infanticide and to what some referred to as "overlaying" or "smothering" deaths (in later days considered SIDS or "crib deaths") (122), but more significantly to sickle cell anemia, which predisposed slave children to severe pneumococcal infections (33).

If any group was reduced to resisting tyranny by denying or resisting an oppressor's presumed rights over its reproductivity, it was thus slaves in the southern American states. American culture could predictably expect its enslaved population commonly to engage in abortion and infanticide, whether intended, imposed, or as a function of the conditions of life under which slaves were forced to live. The inability of male slaves to protect their wives and children and of slaves to exert parental custody and control meant they faced the prospect of begetting children who would only become chattel. As a result, slaves often resisted bearing or raising children. Testimonies like that in 1859 of J. W. Loguen tell of men who did not marry because "slavery must 'never own a wife or child of mine'"; in 1850, Henry Bibb "vowed that the daughter he left in slavery was 'the last slave that ever I will father, for chains and slavery on this earth'" (quoted in Davis 1997, 190). Women abstained, committed abortions, or resorted to infanticide. Motives varied, from the despair of one mother facing the sale of her children who "took an axe and chopped off their heads, and then ended her own life with the same instrument" (quoted in Davis 191) to Margaret Garner's refusal, immortalized by Toni Morrison in her novel *Beloved*, to allow another of her children to be re-enslaved once they had fled to freedom. One former slave, Jane Blake, considered whether "all bond women had been of the same mind, how soon the institution could have vanished from the earth" (quoted in Davis 191). If enslavement meant "the abrogation of natal ties" (247), the only taste of freedom a slave had was the choice to deny to the master what he had already stolen from her—her children.

Less dramatic and visible acts than infanticide made an even greater, if surreptitious, statement. Statistics suggest, for example, that slave women bore children two and a half years apart and that they did not, on average, begin bearing until between seventeen and twenty years of age (possibly two years earlier than white women) (White 1985, 97–98, 185, n31; see also Gutman 1976, 50, 75, 171). The delay between children and between menarche and a first pregnancy as well as significant testimony of the resistance of young slaves to forced sex suggest the motivation to use abortifacients as well as the substantial practice of abortion or infanticide (Gutman 80–85).

Although hardly of epidemic proportions, sources cite more frequent abortion and miscarriage among slaves than among free white women (Savitt 1978, 119; Genovese 1976, 498; Gutman 1976, 80). As one Georgia physician, E. M. Pendleton, acknowledged in 1849, many slaveowners believed "blacks are possessed of a secret by which they destroy the fetus at an early stage of gestation." Pendleton expressed the slaveowner's belief that there was "an unnatural tendency in the African female to destroy her offspring"; indeed, "whole families of women . . . fail to have any children" (quoted in Gutman 80). One physician had reported the use of "a roll of rags about two or three inches long and as hard as a stick" stuffed into the vagina. Another physician, John T. Morgan of Tennessee, however, reported in some detail in 1860 at the Rutherford County Medical Society that slave women rarely resorted to mechanical means "to effect an abortion or derange menstruation" (quoted in Gutman 81). Rather, according to Morgan, their remedies tended to be herbal and included roots and seeds of the cotton plant, pennyroyal, and tansy to effect miscarriage and camphor both for abortion and for contraception. The more ingenious techniques reported by ex-slaves included the ingestion of bird-shot, gunpowder, or turpentine, the latter for each of nine consecutive days (n82). The purchase of new slaves reportedly saw every new conception "aborted by the fourth month" (quoted in Gutman 81). Among the physicians who heard Morgan deliver his report, one spoke of a slavemaster who kept between four and six slave women over a twenty-five year period to see only two children born. As White indicates, cases of self-imposed sterility may have occurred in much larger numbers than have been reported (1985, 85).

Whereas the conditions that gave rise to abortions, miscarriages, and infanticides were not difficult to ascertain, the acts themselves were difficult to prove. It did not help that physicians were generally infrequent and expensive visitors to the slave quarters. Nor did it help that slavemasters had to rely on slaves themselves and slave midwives for evidence of such acts if they were to control abuses. Masters took deceptions perpetuated by slaves around issues of breeding as an assault on the dignity of white patriarchy in the deepest possible way. Abortions, miscarriages, and infanticides were thus significant sites of contest on the plantation, even if, as Eugene Genovese (1976) reports, "birth and reproduction rates remained high. Slave abortions, much less infanticide, did not become a major problem for the slave holders or an ordinary form of 'resistance' for the slaves" (497).

Administering aborting remedies would have been easily accomplished on the plantation, for midwives provided most of the medical care slave women would get. Midwives were almost exclusively elderly or middle-aged black women, more often than not slaves themselves (White 1985, 124). Without bringing a formal case before the law, slavemasters would have had difficulty proving that an abortion had occurred. Moreover, the silencing that prevailed within the slave quarters would have kept such matters within the slave community. Accepting abortion as miscarriage and infanticide as stillbirth was, as a result, common, in spite of the suggestive testimony of one midwife who, upon accepting Christianity, admitted that she felt as if she had been "carried to the gates of hell [as my] life as a midwive was shown to me and I have certainly felt sorry for all the things I did" (quoted in White 126).

On the other hand, there was significant motivation to bring a pregnancy to term.[12] In spite of exposed working conditions, inadequate nutrition, barrenness resulting from sexual diseases, and largely absent or inadequate gynecological care, the general attitude about breeding on the plantation encouraged pregnancy. As one source puts it, Virginians "regarded pregnancy as almost holy" (Savitt 1978, 116). Slaves were less liable to whippings, had their claims of illness taken more seriously, and were often able to get time off from work. Self-interest alone suggests why slave masters might have provided relief for pregnant slaves (Fox-Genovese 1988, 322; Gutman 1976, 79). They placed a high premium on breeding, which may have accounted for 5%–6% of their profit (White 1985, 98).[13] Using an economic argument, it was in the slavemasters' interest to create an environment for their slaves aimed at "maximizing the number of children born" (98). Prime inducements were often offered to maintain slave relationships, like marriages. Those inducements re-warded prolific breeders with privileges and goods, offsetting the prospect of later splitting up the family if offspring were sold. As Herbert Gutman concludes, "Mon-etary rewards based on family labor (such as the slave garden plot) and incentive payments for 'extra' work balanced the threat of the sale of relatives and especially of grown children. A husband and father might work harder to get extra rations for his children, to earn cash to purchase a luxury item for his wife, or to prevent his children from being sold" (79). Negative inducements played a role as well (White 101), for un-reproductive women were likely to be sold off and tolerated slave mar-riages broken off if parties failed to breed. Motherhood, in any case, gave both women and slave families some status within the slave quarters themselves and al-lowed communal traditions of child care and family life to be maintained. As a re-sult, there was motivation to counter abortions and infanticide, for a woman's status would be transformed from a positive to a negative state if she failed to have off-spring, depriving her of privileges, leaving her vulnerable to beatings and sale, and affecting the fate of other members of her family.

Pattern Shifts in Abortion Law

Under the timetable for abortion law history in the nineteenth century, nine states and one federal territory[14] had followed Connecticut's lead to make abortion a stat-utory offense between 1821 and 1841 (Mohr 1978, 20).[15] Sixteen of twenty-six states had not yet passed an abortion law, thereby remaining within the frame of the common law interpretation of abortion (43). Between 1840 and 1860, thirteen of thirty-three states had no abortion statutes,[16] suggesting that decisive movement on the antiabortion front still awaited public reaction to abortion and a major cam-paign on the part of what James Mohr asserts would be "a politically conscious or-ganization with a vested interest" in abortion law (146). During the Civil War, most antiabortion activity ceased, although five territories included abortion restrictions in their territorial codes (202).[17]

Resistance to abortion legislation had been encouraged by the open medical practice of such irregular practitioners as midwives, herbalists, and Indian and folk doctors as well as Thomsonians, osteopaths, and homeopaths (Starr 1982, 79–144). With such resistance, early laws reflect a lack of focus and interest in abortion regu-lation on the part of legislators. Certainly, the insertion of the term "intent" into bills that penalized administrators of abortive remedies meant that a loophole had been created, demanding a kind of proof that would make convictions less likely. Moreover, regulations that were passed were generally part of omnibus crime bills from 1821 until the Massachusetts statute of 1845, rather than separate abortion statutes.

At the same time, allopathic forces largely endorsed abortion legislation as a tool in their effort to gain control over the range of types of medicine practiced, medical malpractice, and quackery. Because of the strong motive to institute poison control policies in early common law prosecutions and general criminal codes, abortion laws appear to have been directed against apothecaries and physicians partly as medical malpractice indictments (Mohr 1978, 43–44). Indeed, the 1821 Connecticut Crimes and Punishment law "was primarily concerned with attempted murder by poisoning"; section 14, which dealt with "miscarriages," "might best be characterized as a poison control measure" (21). Poison control legislation in the eighteenth and nineteenth centuries was generally recognized as a necessity, because of both wide familiarity with poisons and the widespread use of poisons as purgatives. Along with bleeding and clystering (enemas), poisons were the primary means of medical management until the development of modern medicine. Given a demonstrated "intent to kill," poisons were thus of concern well beyond the practice of abortion, so that the latter fell within the purview of poison control as a crime of intention to kill. The writing of antiabortion laws became a question of inserting abortion into a poison control clause to make it a crime,[18] a practice that is reflected in the shared language of abortion and poison control bills. Thus a poison control act passed in Mississippi in 1822 and addressed to slaves provided that "if any slave, free negro, or mulatto shall prepare, exhibit, or administer to any person or persons in this State any medicine whatsoever, with intent to kill such person or persons, he or she so offending shall be judged guilty to a felony and shall suffer death" (quoted in Tushnet 1981, 79). The 1821 Connecticut abortion statute, by comparison, required that "Every person who shall, wilfully and maliciously, administer . . . any deadly poison, or other noxious and destructive substance, with an intention him, her, or them, thereby to murder, or thereby to cause the miscarriage of any woman . . . shall be thereof duly convicted, shall suffer imprisonment" (quoted in Mohr 21). In both, it is the administering of a medicine with the intent to kill that takes the primary focus.

New York abortion law provides a capsule history for abortion legislation of the nineteenth century as abortion-specific legislation became more common (Mohr 1978, 26ff, 123–124, 216–219, 227–228; Means 1968). Over the period of time from 1828 to 1881, we find, first (in 1828), the prohibition of both abortion substances and instruments, together with their administration. Liability was restricted to the practitioner, to the post-quickening period, and to a penalty of no more than a year imprisonment and/or a fine of no more than five hundred dollars. If necessary to save the life of a woman, a post-quickening exception was allowed for the first time but required the advice of two physicians. The second change (in 1845) was to charge the post-quickening death of the woman or the fetus as second-degree manslaughter. Here, liability was extended to whoever advised or procured an abortive remedy at any stage of the pregnancy. Women were, significantly, made liable for seeking, submitting to, or performing upon themselves an abortion. The penalty stayed essentially the same as the earlier law. The third step (in 1868) was the prohibition of advertisements for abortion and the elimination of the distinction between pre- and post-quickening (the distinction was to be re-introduced in 1881). Parties to a successful or an unsuccessful abortion were both given immunity and allowed as competent witnesses against other parties. Finally (between 1872 and 1875), a woman's death was made a felony (with a maximum penalty of twenty years imprisonment), as was consent to an abortion and self-abortion. A woman's dying declaration became admissible evidence. New York law over the period of half a century thus extended the number of parties liable for the crime of abortion, made the pregnant woman a party to the crime, enhanced the penalty from a misdemeanor to a felony, and reformed legal procedures to facilitate prosecution.

Between the Civil War and 1880, the most important burst of antiabortion legislation in the nation's history occurred (Mohr 1978, 200), so that by 1880 unambiguous abortion laws had been passed "in most of the states that had not already acted during the previous twenty years" (226). Finally, between 1880 and 1900, the United States completed its statutory transition "to a nation where abortion was legally and officially proscribed" (226) and where the nation's courts also ended "their historic tolerance toward those accused of performing abortions" (226). The statutes of the boom period were essentially to remain in place "unchanged in substance until the 1960s" (224), acting in tandem with the changes in trial law and evidence that had transformed the courts of the nineteenth century to make possible more effective enactment of those laws (224).

Storer's Egg, or the Physicians' Campaign

The increasing prevalence of abortion in the period between 1840 and 1860 had led to the first significant pattern shift in abortion legislation as abortion laws began to proliferate in mid-nineteenth century (Mohr 1978, 119). Indeed, falling birthrates in general would lead to a change in the perception that unmarried young girls were the primary "victims" of abortion (128), as they had been perceived before 1840 (43–44), leading to a move to revoke women's immunity under abortion laws. This move was initiated by New York's abortion legislation in 1845 and became more common with similar legislation in several other states.[19] Sensational and unsuccessfully prosecuted abortion cases constituted the second significant pressure during the same period. One particularly critical case came before Chief Justice Lemuel Shaw of Massachusetts Supreme Court in 1845; in this case the abortionist's acts were found "not punishable at common law" (quoted in Mohr 120). In the Maria Aldrich case in the same year and state, the unmarried and pregnant Miss Aldrich died; a critical witness fled the jurisdiction, and the parties accused had to be acquitted. Such cases incensed the public sense of justice and exercised its frustration at failed prosecutions (131). The third pressure for change in mid-century arose from expanded advertisement of abortion remedies, leading to the widespread commercialization of the practice of abortion through wide availability of information, distribution of substances and instruments, and access to the provision of abortion services (141–142).

To these pressures was added the significant factor that, for many, put the entire nineteenth-century body of abortion law into perspective: the physicians' campaign to license medical practitioners, control malpractice, and essentially empower allopathic doctors by eliminating their competition. In its focus on abortion, the physicians' campaign attacked irregular practitioners who treated female complaints, including pregnancy and abortion as well as the prevalent menstrual disorders surreptitiously related to abortion. Because abortion began to supersede infanticide both in practice and in cases brought before the bar in the 1840s and 1850s, physicians became increasingly involved. They formed the American Medical Association in 1847 and began an antiabortion physicians' campaign that changed the picture of abortion legislation. In New York alone, laws were "enacted, amended, and reenacted" (Olasky 1992, 96) ten times over the fifty-three year period from 1828–1881.

Reinforced by the imminence of the Civil War and the general inactivity in the legal arena on matters related to abortion control, the physicians' campaign was able to capitalize on the newly emerging organizational framework of the AMA to generate an organization-endorsed position and then to lobby state legislatures through its state chapters. Led by Horatio Storer of Boston, the committee that would draft the AMA report on abortion for its 1859 convention was populated by antiabortion physicians. Presenting themselves as speaking on behalf of the profession, Storer and his followers capitalized on the distractions of the war and reconstruction and public inattention to its message (Mohr 1978, 147–170). They exerted pressure to oust dissenters and abortion practitioners from state medical societies, appropriated the role of policymakers in public and professional politics, and effectively organized a political agenda that controlled the public debate from a minority position.

Producing a document that focused on undermining the significance of quickening as a sign of fetal life (Mohr 1978, 156), the physicians' campaign proved to be the most forceful advocate for the fetus in the abortion debate. A woman's safety having been so considerable a focus of the common law thinking on abortion up to 1840, it would take substantial effort to displace it by an emphasis on the fetus.[20] Even as late as an 1858 commentary by Chief Justice Henry Green of the New Jersey Supreme Court (State v. Leonard Murphy), it was clear that the state's interest "was not to prevent the procuring of abortions, so much as to guard the health and life of the mother against the consequences of such attempts. It is immaterial whether the foetus is destroyed, or whether it has quickened or not. In either case the degree of the defendant's guilt is the same. The only gradation . . . is made to depend upon the effect of the act upon the mother, viz. whether she dies in consequence of it" (quoted in Mohr 137). Linked to such thinking, the nineteenth-century assault on woman's immunity in committing self-abortion and on submitting or giving consent to an abortion rested on a woman's inability to resist coercion or seduction; if she cannot resist, then she must be prevented from harming herself.[21] Intended as an incentive, making the woman culpable was looked upon as a way to decrease the threat to women posed by the prevalence of abortion where it could not be curbed by penalties against the abortionist. Once all that could reasonably be done in the name of saving a woman from herself or others had been done, antiabortion efforts could focus on the fetus. In this light, the demise of the quickening distinction[22] made sense, particularly when a statute made the death of the fetus an offense comparable to the death of the woman and established feticide as a statutory felony.[23]

Taking up the cudgel on behalf of the physicians' campaign, the *Atlanta Medical and Surgical Journal* in 1857 made the claim that the fetus is itself "entitled to protection in its possessions" (quoted in Siegel 1992, 288). It based its claim on the pseudo-medical assumption that the fetus possessed autonomy, the essential quality of human life. To attain that autonomy, Storer identified the fertilized egg as a separate entity, holding that it is only the unfertilized egg that is part of the woman. He entreated women to regard the fertilized egg not as an "embryonic man" (quoted in Siegel, 288) but as a suckling infant. For Storer, the independent egg was only dependent upon the mother for subsistence when it reached the "nest"—the mother's womb—much like the kangaroo in the pouch.

To soften the campaign's appeal to married women, Storer acknowledged that husbands provoked repeated abortions by pressing their natural marital rights. He counseled husbands to adopt a sense of duty and refrain from sensual pleasures: "to increase her health, prolong her life, extend the benefits she confers upon society— in a word, selfishly to enhance her value to ourselves" (quoted in Mohr 1978, 168). Beyond the appeal to a woman's sense of duty to her fetus and to her responsibility to serve her husband's sexual needs, women were told that the physician, rather than the woman, had authority over their reproduction, on behalf of the community to which they owed the duty of bearing children (*Nashville Journal of Medicine and Surgery*, 1876, in Siegel 1992, 296–297). One physician advocate described the process in 1874 in starker terms: "the Almighty, in creating the female sex, has taken a uterus and built a woman around it" (H. L. Holbrook 1874, quoted in Smith-Rosenberg and Rosenberg 1981; Siegel, 292).

In its transformation of the abortion debate, the physicians' campaign constructed the abortion debate as centered on married, native, middle-class women, a function of the kinds of patients that "regular" physicians were likely to see in their practices. The prevailing stereotype upon which the physicians depended maintained that immigrants outbred natives, Catholics outstripped Protestants; urban abortions were far more numerous than rural abortions, and married women made the greatest use of abortionists. The consciously sponsored idea by the end of the Civil War that married women had become the most frequent seekers of abortion and that their ranks were growing was a question of perspective and interest as well as belief.[24] This view was hardly descriptive of the number of indigent and marginal women who were part of the larger flux of society attended by irregular physicians, if they were treated at all, given the incidence of self-abortion (Scholten 1977, 438). Indeed, abortion services were widely distributed across class, religious, and geographic boundaries. Whereas the cost of private physician abortions was not inconsiderable, commercialization had leveled prices for irregular practitioners.

A kind of grassroots family planning had arisen that had escaped the control of both the medical profession, insofar as it could be called one, and the moral mentors of the nineteenth century. This development made resistance to the campaign even more difficult. The physicians' campaign was thus motivated to eliminate advertisements and to pull druggists and peddlers out of the market as a means of disrupting the economic efficiency of what the campaign considered an immoral marketplace (Mohr 1978, 98–100). The first ban on public advertising occurred in Massachusetts in 1847, with the loophole provision that the act be committed "knowingly" to procure an abortion; eleven states and two territories followed from 1849 to 1875.[25] The proscription of public dissemination of information about abortifacients became the most broadly supported and widely agreed-upon of the antiabortion regulations. The advent of mass newspapers in the 1830s had opened up the possibility of commercialization of abortion to all classes in a wholesale way (Olasky 1992, 94). In 1839, the New York Sun advertised pills "so strong that they should not be taken during pregnancy [as they would]. . . produce an a . . . . . n"; an ad in 1840 by a Dr. Vandenburgh promised "an effectual remedy for suppression, irregularity, and all cases where nature has stopped from any cause whatsoever" (quoted in Olasky 94). Madame Vincent in the New York Herald in 1841 advertised, somewhat disingenuously, "lunar pills. . . . [whose] effects are truly astonishing . . . are always certain, and therefore pregnant women should not take them" (quoted in Olasky 95). Playing on the appeal of foreign medical practice in France and Germany, ads like one in the Boston Daily Times in 1845 for lunar pills announced that "these powders was [sic] long used in Europe before their introduction into this country, and have been extensively used in this city with unprecedented success" (quoted in Mohr 54). A special appeal to the potentially deeper pockets of married women in one ad in 1845 led to the recommendation that "married ladies had best consult personally, as a suspension of medicines is at some time necessary as contained in the directions" (quoted in Mohr 54).

The Massachusetts bill of 1847 represented an early statement of the type that would lead to the later Comstock law passed by Congress in 1873 (Mohr 1978, 130). Designed to address obscenity, Comstock included a provision on abortion that prohibited advertising, the sale, possession, or giving away of any print material, "instrument, or other article of indecent or immoral nature, or any article or medicine . . . for causing abortion, except on a prescription of a physician in good standing, given in good faith" (quoted in Mohr 196). In addition, it linked abortion and contraception in the same bill, a move intended to address the declining birthrate of the 1840s as it forbade "causing or procuring the miscarriage of a woman pregnant with child or [of] preventing, or which is represented as intended to prevent, pregnancy" (quoted in Mohr 130).

The ban on advertising was clearly an item high on the physicians' campaign agenda, both to control the access of irregulars to the public marketplace and to curb the commercialization of what physicians considered a medical matter. The ban drew the circle tight around all participants in the act of abortion—as an 1867 Vermont law identified them, "any merchant, druggist, peddler" (quoted in Mohr 1978, 211). An added benefit to such laws would be the improved state of the practice of medicine and "the protection of the public against medical imposters" (Maryland 1867, quoted in Mohr 213). Indeed, Maryland in 1868 and the Colorado territory in 1867 were both sufficiently friendly to the cause of medical regulars that they included provisions that, in the first case, allowed doctors to manage abortions for patients who had experienced botched abortions or accidents and, in the second case, allowed therapeutic abortions to save the life of the woman so long as they were conducted under the advice of a doctor (211, 214).[26]

Once the forces of scientific rationality and moral uprightness partnered to support the antiabortion movement, it became uncomfortable for women's groups to endorse the right to abortion, particularly when abortion began to be looked upon as a practice of women's networks in which participants closed ranks against husbands and fathers to share information and keep secrets (Mohr 1978, 103, 106). Moreover, as James Mohr reports, leaders like Elizabeth Cady Stanton "and the vast majority of feminist spokeswomen were unwilling to condone abortion or encourage its practice" (111). Their eyes were on the prize of enfranchisement; neither birth control nor the abortion issue would be allowed to distract them (Siegel 1992, 305). The woman's movement pinned its hopes on Storer's suggestion that husbands could agree with their wives to allow them more control over conception by abstinence in the bedroom (Mohr 112–113; Siegel 305). A strategy emerged that would build on the newly emancipated rights of southern slaves. Women asked for the right to refuse their husbands' sexual advances and be free from being treated as "chattels personal to be used and abused at the will of a master" (quoted in Siegel 308), as one speaker at the national Women's Suffrage Association expressed in 1871. In support of that view, the suffrage newspaper *The New Northwest* (August 15, 1873) challenged "the expropriation of women's domestic labor in marriage" (quoted in Siegel 306). It may well have been that rising abortion figures and a shift toward more married women aborting their pregnancies reflected an expanded desire for family planning among both men and women in the nineteenth century. But supporting abortion as a right did not appear to be a position that significant women's groups could pursue to good political effect.

Run by an elite movement of professionals intent on developing the cultural authority of allopathic medicine, the abortion campaign was part of a larger nineteenth-century debate about the way in which political power would be distributed in the post-war years (Starr 1982, 102ff). The state, it was argued, ran the risk of "miscegenous decay" as immigrants, the lower classes, and newly emancipated slaves were in a position to wrest power from the "native" American classes (a code for white, Protestant, middle-class Americans [Siegel 1992, 299]). Citing the threat of reverse Darwinism, a physician in *The Peninsular Journal of Medicine*, 1874, spoke of "the ignorant, the low lived and the alien" outbreeding native American stock until "the Puritanic blood of '76 will be but sparingly represented in the approaching centenary" (quoted in Mohr 1978, 167).

The physicians' campaign thus fit into a much larger picture of racial and reproductive politics. Reva Siegel (1992) concludes that "Laws against abortion and contraception fused concerns about reproduction of the social order with concerns about the physical process of reproduction, thus resembling anti-miscegenation laws and other eugenics legislation adopted in the postbellum period." In the same way that anti-miscegenation laws had proved important to institutionalizing the dominance of one gender, "laws that criminalized birth control helped maintain a particular regime of gender status" (318). In these terms, racial and gender developments paralleled each other, both influenced by the spread of social Darwinist views on human heredity and reproduction of the social order (320).

Slavery, in retrospect, had created conditions for American blacks that, while they initially fed procreation, subsequently informed social efforts to support sterilization. As long as slaves were deprived of their civil rights and reduced to what constituted civil death in order to support and serve their master's way of life (Davis 1997, 63), the slave society of the South encouraged the propagation of slaves. Once African Americans attained liberty and asserted equality to enable their own autonomy, establish their own affiliations, and make their own moral choices, however, their reproductivity became a threat. It inspired a coercive state to counter with anti-miscegenation laws, sterilization campaigns, and black codes that made their offspring once again "stolen property," this time by making them wards of or apprenticing them to their previous masters through Jim Crow laws (226–227).

In one reading, the nineteenth-century racial story of abortion is a story of historical genocide tied to sterilization and birth control. People of color had heard the physicians' campaign and knew it meant them. Even more pertinent was the influence of the eugenics movement. In the 1930s, Margaret Sanger, speaking for the

American Birth Control League, volunteered that "Morons, mental defectives, epilectics, illiterates, paupers, unemployables, criminals, prostitutes, and dope fiends" (quoted in Davis 1981, 214) should be sterilized. In 1939, she organized a Negro Project that became identified with the words of W. E. B. DuBois, who held that "the mass of ignorant Negroes still breed carelessly and disasterously, so that the increase among Negroes, even more than the increase among whites, is from that population least intelligent and fit, and least able to rear their children properly" (quoted in Ross 1998, 171).[27] Indeed, DuBois' words were often attributed to Sanger herself.[28] Fearful that the word would get out "that we want to exterminate the Negro population," Sanger coopted black ministers to "straighten out that idea if it ever occurs to any of their more rebellious members" (Davis 215).

The motive for the physicians' campaign was, finally, three-fold: concern for the unborn, control of rebellious middle-class women, and the felt need to address the threat of teeming immigrant and racial populations. The effect the campaign had was to radically alter existing abortion legislation, so that the post–Civil War years became massively important to the antiabortion movement. By 1880, Mohr (1978) reports, twenty-one states revised existing legislation, and thirteen others outlawed abortion for the first time (314–315). The majority of legislation now controlled abortion before quickening; a number of laws penalized women; many banned contraception. Therapeutic exceptions to abortion law would be largely in the hands of the medical profession. The earlier practice of prosecuting those who administered abortions while male sexual partners largely went free and pregnant women were considered victims was long past. Indeed, the physicians' campaign represented a wholly new story in the progress of abortion rights in American culture, signaling a change that meant one could no longer legitimately claim that history presented a "seamless web" on abortion.

Conclusion

A historically disjointed and contested scene had presented itself in America (Smith and Hindus 1975, 549, 559) that would inform abortion politics well into the twentieth century. The seventeenth and nineteenth centuries were better described as periods of restraint and control, whereas the eighteenth and twentieth centuries functioned as periods of breakdown and resistance. The changes in American society from a rural community to a modern society went through Puritan, Enlightenment, Victorian, and modern and postmodern forms of social organization over four centuries. Those forms of organization can arguably be represented as cyclical patterns of integration, disintegration, and transition. The stories of abortion that developed over those centuries reinforce that discontinuity. The seventeenth-century story is one of man's sin reflected in the body of the pregnant woman and the fetus, which he tries to conceal, asserting his will on an unwitting female victim with the aid of a knowledgeable outsider. In the eighteenth century, the female victim becomes herself agentive and sinful, a marginal figure from the lower classes, indigent, a servant, an African or Indian, or a repeat offender, a woman separated from middle-class women of established families. The male sexual partner no longer assumes culpability, although the accomplice in the abortion is still directly accountable. In the nineteenth century, the white middle-class female is placed under the control of medical authority mediating between her and the state, to which she is said to owe a reproductive duty. Social welfare takes a dominating role, both in its concern for innocent life and in its support of woman's role to protect marriage, family, motherhood, and community but also to preserve social order and the welfare of the state. Social Darwinism, the religious value of life, and patriarchal authority converge with the professionalization of medicine to insert reproductive law into the larger picture of nation building.

As we have seen, pressures on abortion regulation were created by falling birthrates,[29] scandalous cases of abortion deaths, public advertisement of abortifacients, and the physicians' campaign. They were supported by the growing specialization of the legal profession and efforts not only to professionalize it but to model American criminal trial law on rules of evidence and proof that originated in the more established tradition of British criminal trial law. These developments in legal procedure were to affect the treatment of abortion as a crime by clarifying evidentiary requirements and closing legal loopholes. Requirements that a party have an "intent" to abort or to "knowingly" advertise were, for example, progressively removed from the statutory language. Language that required a prosecution to establish that a woman was actually pregnant was eliminated in an 1869 Massachusetts statute, and language was added that referred to a woman who was pregnant, or not, or who was thought to be pregnant. The requirement that an abortive remedy be demonstrated to have caused the death of a fetus was addressed in an 1845 Massachusetts statute by making an abortionist guilty of having "attempted" to abort a fetus. The difficulty of determining whether a quickened or unquickened fetus had been aborted—in order to affix the appropriate misdemeanor, manslaughter, or felony penalty—was resolved by eliminating the distinction and assigning a single penalty for both acts. Problems of the value of the pregnant woman's testimony, given her insecure legal status as both an accomplice and a victim before the bar, were addressed by enhancing her status as a witness. To facilitate the prosecution of abortions in cases where the abortion had not been advised or recommended by a physician, therapeutic exceptions were incorporated.[30]

In sum, the qualifications in the law that were eliminated, added, or modified appear to have largely been calculated to assist in successful prosecution of the crime. Those features of the law that did not affect successful prosecution were, as a result, largely left alone. The range of state penalties for abortion suggests that they were not much stricter after quickening as opposed to before it. There was little difference in penalty whether the abortion was merely "attempted' or effectuated. Nor was there much distinction between a felony, manslaughter, or a misdemeanor penalty (they were largely in the range of one to ten years and up to $1,000 in fines).

The issues that arose in the historical process of formulating abortion law centered on several key features that combined to create a complex, often incoherent picture. A central concern was clearly the health and safety of the pregnant "victim," which accounts for the introduction of felony murder charges for abortion providers. A provider's culpability was, however, complicated not only by whether the mother survived but by therapeutic exceptions for abortions made for a woman's health and safety as well as by questions of a woman's agentive ability in terms of giving consent, her vulnerability to coercion by other parties, the felt need to protect her from injuring herself, her own culpability in self-abortion, and whether that culpability was more than a misdemeanor. The relative guilt of providers could depend upon whether they administered poisonous substances or used instruments and whether the abortion occurred before or after the quickening of the fetus. The level of guilt—whether it was a misdemeanor, manslaughter, or a felony—depended upon determining whether the act constituted an assault as opposed to a function of supplying materials or giving advice to procure an abortion. Each of these considerations shifted back and forth over time and from state to state.

Consideration given to the fetus, even after quickening, lacked clarity as well. Even as the life status attached to a baptized child dropped out of the legal process, the child's birth still had to be distinguished in some way. Denied the status of a rights-bearing entity unless born alive, the fetus had to be declared stillborn or born alive, and if declared dead, a direct causative connection had to be drawn with the act of abortion. Some degree of intent had, as well, to be determined, including actual knowledge of a pregnancy and an attempt to abort. Moreover, prosecution had to demonstrate that blocked menstrual flow or spontaneous, natural abortion was not implicated.

To be successfully prosecuted, an abortion had, in addition, to be considered in light of social perceptions. Chief among these were humane exceptions for abortions necessary to the life or health of the woman, which were only imperfectly addressed by therapeutic exceptions built into the law. The public's desire for individual autonomy in private reproductive acts, reflected in the declining birthrate and expanded commercialization of abortion, acted as a brake on support for abortion prosecution. On the other hand, the public had an interest in an orderly process in the law that responded to its desire for a punishment that fit the crime as well as for the certainty of punishment for a crime that offended public morality. Certainly, public interest in safe medical care by qualified experts made abortion regulation a contentious issue whether one supported regulation or was opposed.

Historically, abortion law was a complex entity. It was informed by powerful cultural interests whose pressures created a hodge-podge of regulations across many different states, each with its own interests. Abortion would, in spite of the ability of nineteenth-century laws to hold well into the twentieth century, remain an open question capable of tugging at the national psyche. Old wounds would reopen in twentieth-century abortion law, restarting the chain of discontinuity that had characterized it from the seventeenth through the nineteenth centuries. Indeed, Justice Blackmun in *Roe v. Wade* (1973) was to hold that in most of the nineteenth century women had a broader right to abortion than they did in most states at the time of his decision. The prochoice brief of 281 American historians in *Webster v. Reproductive Services* (1989)[31] contended that abortion was not only not illegal at the time of the adoption of the Constitution, but it was widely established as a practice in most of the nineteenth century and well into the twentieth century. Moreover, nineteenth-century restrictions by gender and race would be either inapplicable or impermissible in contemporary Constitutional law, whereas Ninth Amendment rights are retained by the people.

Still, history and tradition can be used to serve a number of different readings as a roundtable on the *Webster* historians' brief at the American Historical Association demonstrates.[32] Social practices and beliefs of a given historical period, according to Sylvia Law (1990) who submitted the brief, should not be constructed to limit rights today to those recognized in the founding of the country. Whereas certain social practices and beliefs are ascribed continuity and certain time periods are privileged to count in a story, the aberrational antiabortion period of the nineteenth century should not, in this case, be one of them. A second contributor to the brief, James Mohr (1990), claims that rights and privileges are "less easily erased, if they can be demonstrated to have been part of the 'history and traditions' of the people" (24). Clearly they are more defensible in a constitutional sense if they can be determined to have been the original intent of the framers. They would be of even greater consequence if they have been continually maintained, socially supported, and regularly enforced. But times change, the Constitution does not enumerate every right, and the people of today have needs that could not have been anticipated two centuries ago.

Estelle Freedman (1990), the third contributor to both the roundtable and the brief, holds that it should thus be possible to acknowledge that abortion was not common through the seventeenth century; it was not a pressing issue for the framers of the Constitution since economic and social conditions discouraged its use, and it only became more common as women entered the work force in the nineteenth century and sex became separated from reproduction (30–31). Colonial America, in her construction, showed tolerance for abortion and the Constitution. It neither condemned nor accepted but was silent on it. By contrast, criminalization in the nineteenth century represented an aberration tied to demographic and economic changes. Discontinuity rather than continuity must be said to have prevailed historically, as "it is tricky to claim abortion as an inherent and original right given that feminists of the nineteenth century condemned the practice" (31). The lesson in Freedman's story is that history and tradition should be used to inform changes in the law and not to justify original intent. In an extension of that position, we find Kathryn Kolbert arguing in *Planned Parenthood of Southeastern Pennsylvania v. Casey* (1992) oral arguments that the Court cannot merely "look at whether abortion was illegal in 1868, that is at the time of the adoption of the Fourteenth Amendment" (in Friedman 1993, 316) and thereby judge the intent of the framers of that amendment. Indeed, the fact that abortion might have been illegal then should not be used to accord status or lack of it to the right, since, along with other rights—to travel, to vote, to be free of racial segregation—"State legislators have acted to inhibit those rights at the time of the adoption of the Fourteenth Amendment" (317). She goes on to contend that the Court would be in an "anomalous posture" if abortion was legal at the time of the Constitution, as she contends it was, and yet illegal at the time of the adopting of the Fourteenth Amendment. One could, equally, argue that original intent at the time of the founding of the Constitution might not itself be dispositive, given the subsequent adoption of the Fourteenth Amendment. Moreover, if the right to abortion is not historically continuous, neither is its denial in the second half of the nineteenth century continuous.[33]

The antiabortion story is no less welcoming of some ways of reading nineteenth-century history, tradition, and law on the abortion question. The prolife story put forward by Joseph W. Dellapenna's amicus brief for the Academy of Medical Ethics[34] on behalf of the state of Pennsylvania in *Casey* tells a story in which it is not antiabortion statutory law that breaks with tolerant common law history and traditions. Rather, it is *Roe v. Wade* that breaks with a consistently antiabortion common law broadened and codified by nineteenth-century statutory law. The major purpose of that presumably consistent body of law was not to protect women but to protect fetal life.[35] In the medical brief story, the growth of nineteenth-century laws was not a question of the organization of medical practitioners against their competitors. It was a question of battling the legal immunity of new technologies (in particular, intrusive surgical abortions) so that they could not escape the law and of ensuring that different stages of pregnancy were equally regulated. The issue in this story was thus not whether abortion is a crime but whether the crime is a misdemeanor or a felony.

The antiabortion story in legal argument had to demonstrate that the physician's campaign, patriarchy, and racism were not the prime movers in the growth of nineteenth-century abortion regulation. Moreover, it had to claim that they did not stymie the popular will expressed in the growing demand for and commercialization of abortion services in the nineteenth century. If it was going to clarify its appeal, the antiabortion story would have to resolve which audience was most affected by abortion. If it was middle-class women, then abortion threatened white, middle-class, and largely Protestant social dominance. If it was the poor and the outcast, then abortion presented itself as a form of racial genocide of black women or associated itself with such marginalized groups as prostitutes and radical feminists, neither likely to appeal to mainstream Americans. The antiabortion story had either to make a more compelling identification of abortion and infanticide or develop its case against abortion as a unique practice in its own right. Its salience as a story required that it separate abortion from other reproductive practices, such as contraception, which were generally accepted to be rooted in privacy rights.

An influential version of the historical antiabortion story provided by Marvin Olasky (1992) tries to develop a consistent construction based on two distinctive lines of development. The first line holds that abortion occurred most frequently not among mainstream Americans but among several peripheral groups. The first is prostitutes, the "most abortion-prone members of the population" (78). The second includes practitioners of free love, among whom are included spiritists, feminists, and members of other "radical movements" who practiced adultery and experimented with love outside of marriage, in one case identified as "the fashionable and intellectual communities" (the *Cincinnati Lancet and Observer* in 1867 [quoted in Olasky 62]). The last group is made up of serving women of the poorer classes without social safety nets (37). Asserting that "most American women were very unlikely to have an abortion" (82), Olasky's version supports the position that "abortion was never part of the American mainstream," but, rather, that "it was a recourse of those adrift on particular sidestreams: victims of seduction, prostitutes, and spiritists" (289). This version was nevertheless compromised by a variation in the antiabortion story featured prominently in the nineteenth-century physicians' campaign. The campaign had held that abortion infected the social body as a whole, having most insidiously infiltrated native white Protestant middle-class culture. This position raised the specter of that culture being overwhelmed by immigrant, non-white, and lower-class breeding practices. The latter story line accused outsider groups and the "impure" of out-breeding established families, while established families were pictured as those most at risk if they practiced abortion.

The second line in the Olasky version holds that respectable nineteenth-century physicians of substance based their objections to abortion not only on their medical ethics, fetal science, and their religious beliefs but also on their recent experience in the Civil War with death and with slavery (1992, 113, 121, 128). Their influence, as he tells the story, was minimal in the second half of the nineteenth century, following the establishment of the AMA. At that time, both abortions and the practices of abortionists thrived in spite of their risks to women (292). Olasky objects to the portrait of the AMA as a stalking horse for discriminatory male patriarchal views of family values that subordinated women and subverted their access to abortion, considering such a portrayal a myth and an oversimplification (109ff). According to

Olasky, physicians in his telling were unable to build an organization sufficiently powerful to challenge all irregular competitors and exert authority over all medical practices. Allopathic physicians were constrained by the opposition of alternative medical movements, by the wishes and demands of their patients (124), and by the support of some within their group for providing abortion services. Moreover, many favored legalizing prostitution (prostitutes having been linked to abortion by the presumably greater numbers of this group who sought abortions), a position represented in this story as the moral equivalent of legalizing slavery (127).[36]

Twentieth-century American abortion stories did not, as a result, agree on the legacies of history, tradition, and law from the colonial period through the nineteenth century. No common narrative was likely to be consented to, nor was any sense of community likely to be reached on this issue. The abortion debate was thus to remain a wide-open field in the twentieth century, a field open to a broad range of constructions—political, legal, and cultural, written and visual, instrumental and artistic—to which the remainder of this book shall devote itself.

Notes

1. The relevant line in the Hippocratic oath has been variously translated, largely in two different readings. First, the oath was translated as limited to a particular kind of abortive remedy (the use of a suppository, or pessary); and second, it was translated to prohibit abortion completely. Riddle (1992, 7–10) considers the former the accurate translation. He attributes to Scribonius Largus, a Roman writer of the first century A.D., the erroneous reading "not to give to a pregnant woman a kind of medicine . . . that expels the embryo/fetus" (8). Riddle cites an Arabic translation from 1269 that gives what he considers the correct version: "Nor will I contemplate any pessary which may cause abortion" (8). Riddle concludes, "The literal meaning of the Hippocratic oath as we presently possess its text is that the one taking the oath swears not to administer an abortive suppository. The implicit meaning is that a physician was free to employ contraceptives, oral abortifacients, and the various surgical and manipulative procedures available" (9).

2. Traditional midwives up to the middle of the nineteenth century in the United States were trusted among women not only because they were women and could therefore preserve privacy and decorum for their female patients but because they could provide both birthing and abortion services with a minimum of disruption to a household and maximum confidentiality (Stormer 2000). They were neither beholden to medical associations, as doctors were, nor associated with the extreme and invasive gynecological procedures that physicians were identified with as a means of learning their craft and asserting their medical authority. Indeed, women experienced many gynecological difficulties in the second half of the nineteenth and early twentieth centuries because doctors used ergot and instruments to hasten labor and save themselves time, causing lacerations and inducing puerperal fever. Moreover, doctors were often responsible for carrying infections with them from patient to patient, so that they introduced yiatrogenic infections into birthing rooms (Leavitt 1986). Midwives nevertheless tended to be blamed for high abortion and maternal death rates by physicians who struggled to assert themselves, so that the use of midwives declined by the 1930s and abortions and births shifted out of homes to hospitals and clinics (Reagan 1997).

3. Matthew Hale supports Coke's view in 1682 (*Summary of the Pleas of the Crown*), holding that a child "if born alive, and after dies of that potion, it is murder. The like if it dies of a stroke given by another in like manner" (quoted in Keown 1988, 10); but in a posthumously published work in 1736 (*History of the Pleas of the Crown*), he appears to have denied that abortion resulting in death after live birth is murder (10), although the case in 1327 that is relied upon here is one in which the accused pleaded not guilty and for that reason "the Justices were unwilling to adjudge this thing a felony" (quoted in Means 1971, 337).

4. See, for background, Powers 1966.

5. Given the general concealment of abortion and the difficulties of proof and prosecution (both of actual pregnancy and of aborting that pregnancy), few cases were reported under common law. Until the mid-seventeenth century in England, ecclesiastical courts retained jurisdiction over abortion cases, using the standard prescribed by canon law that human life was presumed to begin at quickening as a fairly bright line that distinguished toleration from prosecution. The shift in British law in the mid-seventeenth century meant that abortions would no longer be prosecuted in ecclesiastical courts but, rather, in common law courts. Moreover, differences would exist between the charge of felony (under ecclesiastical law) and that of a misdemeanor (under common law) as well as in the relative importance given, respectively, to fetal as opposed to maternal life. John Keown (1988), nevertheless, surmises that both common and ecclesiastical law predominantly prohibited abortion to protect fetal life (11).

6. Whereas ancient law failed to protect the fetus or the newborn until some formal or ritual recognition by the parents and community, the Middle Ages prohibited exposure of infants.

7. The Act of 1803 served as something of a model for nineteenth-century American statutory law that was to follow, but it was English common law that established seventeenth- and eighteenth-century colonial precedents. John Keown's study (1988) of abortion law in England suggests that common law from 1200 to 1600 was based on "the first maternal perception of fetal movement" (3), or quickening, which established a bright line between toleration and prosecution. Human life was presumed under church canon law to have begun at that point and for the most part ecclesiastical courts had jurisdiction over abortion cases until the mid-seventeenth century (4–6). Difficulties with proof of abortion in earlier stages of a pregnancy meant that stillborn births or death after birth were more easily prosecuted, partially explaining the rationale for the post-quickening standard and the relatively greater emphasis placed on cases of infanticide as opposed to abortion.

8. The law held that whereas slaves may have been deprived of all their civil rights, they still had the right to life as "men and rational beings" (quoted in Tushnet 1981, 74). A Mississippi case found that killing a slave was indeed murder: "because individuals may have been deprived of many of their rights by society, it does not follow that they have been deprived of all their rights" (quoted in Tushnet, 73). The Supreme Court of Alabama in 1861, nevertheless, acknowledged the difficulty of punishing crimes against slaves, for masters may have been responsible for murder but they were not liable for accidental death when such crimes dealt with those who had no "identity" under the law (Fox-Genovese 1988, 326). Reasonableness was the slippery standard by which such crimes were judged: "Absolute obedience, and subordination to the lawful authority of the master, are the duty of the slave. . . . The law cannot enter into strict scrutiny of the precise force employed [by the master], with the view of ascertaining that the chastisement had or had not been reasonable" (quoted in Fox-Genovese 326, 456 n62).

9. "Hence, the penalties for rape would not and should not, by such implication be made to extend to carnal forcible knowledge of a slave, the offence not affecting the existence of the slave" (T. Cobb, 1858, quoted in Getman 1984, 144). One jury trial, covered by an 1859 law in Mississippi, punished the rape of a female Negro or mulatto under twelve years of age by a Negro or mulatto by whipping or death (Kennedy 1997, 35; 401 n29).

10. The "cardinal rule of slavery in every state that slaves could under no circumstances testify against a white man" complicated the idea of slave agency, making it difficult in practice to hold slaves accountable (Gross 1997, 316). The whole issue of responsibility and culpability on the part of the slave was confused legally so that "just as judges were reluctant to recognize slaves' skills and abilities, so did they fear giving legal recognition to slaves as moral agents with volition, except when it suited very specific arguments or liability rules" (310). The central feature of such law was the distinction made in property law between a thing, or chattel, and a free person, leaving slaveholders continually in litigation over their responsibility for the acts of their slave "property."

11. Dr. Samuel Cartwright of New Orleans produced a series of articles in *DeBow's Review* in the 1850s and 1860s—referred to as a "medical handbook for slave owners" (Gross 1997, 305, 324 n40, n41)—in which he held that blacks were regarded "as medically and mentally inferior to whites" (Savitt 1978, 8). They were considered a separate species immune to diseases whites were susceptible to, so that there was no harm to slaves in sending them under extreme conditions of heat and deprivation to labor in the fields. Cartwright denied that blacks, unlike whites, could be overworked. Indeed, he created a category of diseases peculiar to blacks that included "drapetomania," or running away, "Dysthesia Ethiopia, or Hebetude of mind," or rascality (quoted in Gross, 305) to describe what he considered unreasonable responses to hard labor, both agricultural and reproductive. Diseases of character thus became medically classifiable and were even specified in terms of gender, women being diagnosed in terms of the moral qualities of vice and rebelliousness, which was taken as lunacy (308). Indeed, women were perceived in southern medical thought to be incapable of "taking moral action or having moral dilemmas" (309), so that even attempts at suicide or infanticide were regarded as irrational and rooted in madness.

12. The value of children was nevertheless sometimes mixed from the master's point of view. A balance, for example, of laboring in the fields and breeding was necessary for female slaves on smaller plantations, so that nursing women rushing in from the fields during planting or harvesting were given a small window of opportunity (only a half hour three times a day) to suckle their young (White 1985, 69; Fox-Genovese 1988, 323–324; Davis 1997, 93–94). Household slaves in town, whose time was valuable to their mistresses, would have been required to wean and send their young into the country as soon as possible (Davis 108). On the road in transport, it was not uncommon for slave traders to take a child from a nursing mother and, as an example to other slaves, sell or even give it away, as one ex-slave describes: "The driver would complain of a child's crying and warn the mother to stop the noise. If the crying persisted, the driver would take the child away from its mother and give it away to the first home the gang came across. . . . after one such occurrence, a feeling of horror would shoot through every mother on the coffle, as each would imagine this happening to her" (quoted in Davis 99).

13. Although slave property was clearly valued, owners were conflicted over the most efficient use and maintenance of their slaves, even during pregnancy. In a rare court case that went to the Louisiana Supreme Court in 1842, one slaveowner hired out a pregnant slave only to find she had been beaten and both she and her fetus killed (Schafer 1997, 252–253). The owner was awarded medical costs and days of lost labor at the lower court only to be

reversed at the higher court under the theory that the woman probably died of other causes. Indeed, such treatment of pregnant women was not uncommon. Under the theory that the pregnancy and the postpartum periods were times that encouraged malingering (Fox-Genovese 1988, 322), overseers were encouraged to set an example. One slaveowner's treatment of his slave is detailed in a diary entry in 1855. The slaveowner was indicted for the slave's murder:

> Through a period of four months, including the latter stages of pregnancy, delivery, and recent recovery therefrom, . . . he beat her with clubs, iron chains, and other deadly weapons, time after time; burnt her; inflicted stripes over and often with scourges, which literally excoriated her whole body; forced her to work in inclement seasons, without being duly clad; provided for her insufficient food; expected labor beyond her strength; and wantonly beat her because she could not comply with his requisitions. (Quoted in Fox-Genovese, 189; 436 n77)

14. Illinois, New York, Ohio, Indiana, Arkansas, Iowa, Mississippi, Alabama, Maine, and the territory of Missouri.

15. The status of early laws suggests that laws were generally designed to address cases involving unmarried young women, the largest number of cases prosecuted up to 1840 (Mohr 1978, 43–44; see Brodie 1994).

16. The additional states that passed abortion laws were Massachusetts, Michigan, Vermont, California, New Hampshire, Wisconsin, New Jersey, Texas, and Louisiana, and the territories of Minnesota, Washington, Oregon, and Kansas.

17. Colorado, Nevada, Arizona, Idaho, and Montana.

18. We find just such a process used, for example, in Iowa's general territorial criminal code before it was revised in 1843 (Mohr 1978, 142–143).

19. In 1849 in New Hampshire, 1860 in Connecticut, 1858 in Wisconsin, 1872 in California, and 1873 in Minnesota.

20. The earlier prohibition against administering poison was apparently designed primarily to prevent the pregnant woman from becoming a victim, as was prohibition of the use of instruments when it was adopted in New York in 1828, in 1830 in Connecticut, in 1835 in Missouri, and in 1840 in Maine.

21. The earliest revocation of a woman's immunity occurred in New York in 1845, although it was not enforced in that state in the nineteenth century (Mohr 1978, 124).

22. In New Jersey in 1872 (as well as in Nebraska and Minnesota in 1873 and in New York in 1872).

23. Previous post-quickening statutes had included Ohio in 1834 (where the post-quickening death of the fetus was made a felony), Arkansas in 1837, New York in 1845 (where it was second degree manslaughter), and Mississippi in 1839 (where it was manslaughter).

    Posner (1992) considers that the fetus has not been valued in the same way that an infant has been, based on the different historical penalties for abortion and infanticide. Indeed, the penalty of murder should have attached to abortion before infanticide if the probability of apprehension and conviction had been considered: "abortion should have been punished more severely than killing an infant because it is more difficult to detect" (281). Offsetting this analysis, abortion had, indeed, been consciously tolerated as a social fact of life.

24. Using a comparative cost analysis, Richard Posner (1992) considers that as a general rule the rate of abortion would be "almost ten times higher for unmarried teenagers than for other women" (278) because the costs (psychological, physical, social, financial, and otherwise) of maintaining a pregnancy are significantly higher compared to the costs of having an abortion.

25. In New Jersey in 1849, Indiana in 1859, Vermont in 1867, Maryland in 1867, New York in 1868 and again in 1872, the Nevada and Wyoming territories in 1869, Michigan in 1869, Pennsylvania in 1870, Kansas and Connecticut in 1879, Minnesota in 1873, and Arkansas in 1875.

26 Therapeutic exceptions had been allowed as early as 1828 in New York and in 1846 in Michigan if "necessary to preserve the life of such mother, or shall have been advised by two physicians to be necessary for such purpose" (quoted in Mohr 1978, **129**). New York dropped the two physicians requirement in 1846. Illinois allowed abortions "for *bona fide* medical or surgical purposes" in 1867 and permitted distribution of abortifacients by "written prescription of some well known and respectable practicing physician" (quoted in Mohr 206).

27. Davis (1981, 214) identifies the quote as coming directly from the Negro Project but in slightly different wording.

28. Loretta Ross (1998) asserts that W. E. B. DuBois's quote on black breeding was erroneously attributed by antiabortionists to Margaret Sanger (171; see here, Randall Terry on Sanger [1990], 29; Davis attributes the quote to the Birth Control Federation of America, 214). Ross makes the case that birth control had a very promising beginning in black communities (given Sanger's view that birth control "was linked to social mobility for all women, regardless of race or immigrant status," 170), until Sanger changed her approach under the influence of a growing eugenics movement in the 1930s. (See also, Roberts 1995, 242.) On the relation of abortion and eugenics in the African American community, the antiabortion movement found a useful ally in black churches as they manipulated black fears of race genocide (Ross 166; see also Angela Davis 1981, 213–215).

29. Using a utilitarian analysis, Richard Posner (1992) calculates that since "it takes 1.83 abortions to reduce the population by one . . . an abortion kills, as it were, only half a child" (282). He considers here the replacement effect of aborting a deformed fetus as well as the fact that abortion is used not to affect the number of births but their timing. By contrast, without the option of abortion, he concludes that contraception would also be likely to decrease.

30. In such places as New York in 1828, Michigan in 1846, and the Colorado territory in 1867.

31. No. 88–605.

32. Subsequently published in *The Public Historian* (1990), the roundtable proceedings featured three contributors to the *Webster* historians' brief: Sylvia Law, James Mohr, and Estelle Freedman; see also Colker (1990).

33. The historical story of American traditions told by the Means (1968, 1971) and Mohr (1978) versions of abortion in the Blackmun opinion and the *Webster* amicus brief, respectively, has several distinctive features. Abortion, first, has to be widely practiced in the general population and either generally accepted, ineffectively regulated, or not morally or legally condemned. Here, the story incorporates not only married women and established families to demonstrate mainstream involvement, need, and acceptance but victims such as abandoned women, the poor, and seduced servant girls to call upon society's sense of fairness and its compassion. Legal regulation of abortion has to be partial, protective, and on behalf of women and has to leave loopholes to express tolerance or flexibility. Thus, the story requires provisions that outlaw the use of a poisonous substance—as part of a more general prohibition against widely abused medications—apart from other abortive remedies; that prosecute the party who administers the substance but does not prosecute the pregnant woman (indeed, regards her as a victim rather than an active agent); that deal with intent and willfulness rather than the actual effort of aborting a fetus, to leave open

the loophole of ignorance; that make a distinction between the quickened and the un-quickened fetus, to avoid a direct challenge to other lives than that of the pregnant person; and that ban what is dangerous to a woman's life and health rather than protect the life of the unborn, in order to sidestep ambiguous moral questions. When abortion regulation becomes harsh and absolute, it is represented as an aberration in a chain of acceptance and the work of an undemocratic elite or professional force which fails to respect the values or the will of a culture and its people. Thus, a politically conscious organization of individuals (the AMA)—with a motive to drive competition out of a profession and thereby establish itself as authoritative—or a discriminatory bias on the part of a "superior" racial group (prosperous white Protestants), or a dominating gender perspective (male patriarchy) would qualify. In this story, continued strong mainstream demand for abortion services and a tradition of compassion for widows, orphans, and abandoned women demonstrate the aberrational nature of the antiabortion campaign and the desire of a culture to preserve the ability to look the other way.

34. Nos. 91–774 and 91–902.

35. The antiabortion historical story depended upon whether abortion was considered illegal in common law, which itself depended on resolving whether abortion before or after quickening was a misdemeanor or a felony, a cause for whipping, a fine, imprisonment, or execution. Equally, the antiabortion story depended upon the moral value given to the fetus. Debate over that value was itself a continuing issue in common and statutory law, just as it was in scripture and sermons in colonial times. John Calvin's doctrine, in particular, agitated in New England Presbyterian and Congregationalist churches to the effect that the unborn child "though enclosed in the womb of its mother, is already a human being [not to be] rob[bed] of the life which it has not yet begun to enjoy" (Olasky 1992, 33).

36. On medicine and abortion, see Annas (1992), Joffee (1995), Jordanova (1989), Newman (1996), Butler and Walbert (1985), Callahan and Knight (1992), Appleton (1985), Schoen 2000, and Holmes and Purdy (1992).

CHAPTER TWO

Rosaries v. Ovaries: The Rhetorics
of Abortion

The proliferation of alternative abortion narratives may threaten the legitimacy of Supreme Court abortion decisions, but it also makes the study of cultural and legal constructions of abortion stories a necessary rather than a merely useful exercise. "Because the world as it 'is' appears in the language in which it is represented" (686), as Drucilla Cornell (1990) reminds us, we modify our world through the constructions by means of which we represent it.

Legal and political rhetorics create the impression that there might be one true discoverable text that, in effect, "translates the tongues of Babel into a common language" (Dimock 1996, 3). They offer ways of knowing abortion that promise to produce an agreed-upon narrative that will deliver a sense of community. But the rhetorics of abortion also threaten community, leading to "contiguity disorder" or "agrammatism" (White 1987, 15; Fisher 1987). In such a case, they prove incapable of endowing events with a propositionality that can transcend historical contradictions.[1] Fredric Jameson (1981), for one, resists the use of dominating propositions, or what he calls master codes. He considers them "containment strategies" (54) that enforce formal unity on represented objects, and he rejects the production of a narrative form with the "function of inventing imaginary or formal solutions to unresolvable social contradictions" (79). Wai Chee Dimock, speaking of the "axiomatic conception of justice" (5)—a master narrative of its own—resists the "unitary given" (8). She looks for "the ground of disagreement rather than the ground of commensurability" (9). Centering the different domains of thought that do not collapse into one another, she looks for the losses that appear in translation, the residues of conflict resolution for their "eloquent dissent" (10). These "politics of oppositionality" (Chambers 1991, xi) suggest a disturbance that disallows a superordinate or transcendent "indwelling truth" (Dimock 4). There is, in these terms, never a last word so that there is always some opportunity that "oppositionality can seize on and make use of" (Chambers xiv). It is these ways of knowing—

master narratives, incommensurate narratives, oppositional narratives—that we shall examine here, as we consider in greater depth, and in the public venue, the constructions to which abortion has lent itself. In particular, we shall explore how the legal and political cultures construe abortion and what that means for the prospect of discovering a common abortion story likely to affirm an agreed-upon community of values.

Legal Metaphors

Legal rhetoric has given rise to a series of almost mythic metaphors about women. These metaphors inform the abortion debate as a base line for understanding abortion, having permeated discourse on both sides of the divide. Three constructions will take our attention here: woman as a good/bad Samaritan, as a good/bad mother, and as a slave/slavemaster. In the first representation, the good Samaritan image originated by Judith Jarvis Thomson (1971), a pregnant woman wakes to find herself attached, without her consent, as life support for a talented and desperately ill violinist. The question is whether, if the woman detaches herself, she would be considered a murderer. The parallel drawn between the image of the Samaritan and the pregnant woman argues that in no case is an adult required under law to perform as a good Samaritan to another adult. The question is thus posed, if born life can make no such claim of another, can an unborn life with no standing in the law make such a claim?

By contrast, one can argue against bad Samaritanism based upon two considerations: first, that the violinist would have died in any case as he was terminally ill whereas the fetus was healthy and might have survived out of the womb, and, second, that the violinist does not give up his life to benefit the woman's right to choose, but the fetus does (Foot 1984). The narrative is thus transformed into one of a "child" being asked by a parent to bear an unreasonable burden where the "parent" has a responsibility to protect the child. The fetus is not, in this narrative, an active threat or agent of injury to the pregnant woman; it does not intend her harm, but is, rather, a moral innocent. The pregnant woman is cast as one who is not acting spontaneously but with premeditation, not in justifiable self-defense but consensually and with foreknowledge of the outcome.

An alternate construction arises in the master/slave relationship (Koppelman 1990; Thomas 1984; McConnell 1992). One perspective has the pregnant woman perform the role of a slavemaster who has complete legal control over the fetus/slave, which is reduced to her chattel. This construction construes the fetus, like slaves in early American law, as only a partial human being not entitled to full human status or protection of the law. A related perspective, that of the pregnant woman herself as slave, depicts a woman compelled to carry a child and thereby condemned without cause to involuntary servitude. Compelling a woman to serve involuntarily for the benefit of the fetus creates (as defined in *Bailey v. Alabama*, 219 U.S. 1911) "that control by which the personal service of one man [sic] is disposed of or coerced for another's benefit which is the essence of involuntary servitude" (quoted in Koppelman, 491). By this argument, a pregnant woman is regarded as a reproductive slave not entitled to full human status and forced by the state to bear children.

This construction of the pregnant woman reverts to a perception of women prior to adoption of the Thirteenth Amendment (1865), which ended slavery, a perception that women were not entitled to be free before the law under the presumption that Congress does not have the right to regulate "domestic" slavery (McConnell 1992). Only men were to have the right to create and maintain families under an amendment that never "intended" to regulate marital relations. What was intended was the regulation of the master/slave relationship embedded in the institution of chattel slavery. A distinction was thereby made between slavery that was presumed to be voluntary and non-regulatable (as in marriage) and that which was institutional and regulatable (as in chattel slavery).

Andrew Koppelman's Thirteenth Amendment analysis (1990) positions itself against forcing women to choose between "submitting to servitude or denying a need that almost all human beings find irresistible" (504). Antiabortion regulations (holding that women have no "capacity for moral agency" [506]) are thus just as sexist as peonage laws in the Reconstructionist South were racist (holding "that blacks were lazy and irresponsible" [506]). They limit women to roles suited only for motherhood, just as blacks were reduced to labor in the fields. Because women are "regarded as instruments for satisfying the needs of others rather than as autonomous agents, their dignity as free persons is violated" (507). Indeed, considering the plight of black women in particular, the contemporary pattern of coercive reproductivity is even clearer: "mandatory motherhood and loss of control over one's reproductive capacities were partially constitutive of slavery for most black women of childbearing age. . . ." Abortion prohibitions "consign women to a status of servitude much like that from which the [Thirteenth] amendment was supposed to free them" (508–509). The impact is felt largely by poor women, who are disproportionately black.

Following what he calls the Amistad principle (based on *U.S. v. Amistad*, 40 U.S. [1841]), Koppelman (1990) constructs a story in which, under servitude, "rebellion against such servitude, even if it must involve the taking of life, is only the assertion of a legal right" (513). A woman's best defense against the fetus' "right" to its "life" would thereby be to argue the threat to her own autonomy based on two considerations. First, because the fetus' right to life places one "class of human beings in practical subjugation to another class" (Justice Harlan, 109 U.S. 3 [1883] Civil Rights Cases, quoted in Koppelman, 517), women are compelled to be mothers. Second, the interest in fetal right to life does not necessarily prevail over the interest in liberty. The difficulty here as regards abortion, however, is that the fetus—a party innocent of wrongdoing—is not the agent responsible for the servitude.

The most resonant and widely referenced representation of pregnant women has been in terms of their construction as good/bad mothers. The slavery motif is implicated here, as well, for in effect women are considered responsible for "producing" the community, that is, for giving birth to its future citizens and maintaining the species or race (Tobin 1993; Ehrenreich 1993; Ikemoto 1992; Siegel 1992; Ashe 1992). The good mother accedes to such a construction; she accepts and even contributes to her role of delivering and nurturing the social product assigned to her in this biologically determined division of labor. In this sense, the good mother performs the role of surrogate, carrying on society's genes as the vessel through which they pass. She suckles other people's children insofar as her own child is really designed for the state. The state thereby restocks its labor pool as well as ensures its dominance over other forms of government. In challenges to a woman's limited right to abort a fetus (rarely referred to as "her own" fetus), her non-wage-earning and uncontracted labor are construed as somehow owed (as if the woman herself was working off a debt) to the survival and health of some abstract family.

The good mother is defined as one who does not refuse to be productive by virtue of being reproductive. She is not expected to refuse society its "entitlement" or withhold her services unless, inversely, because she is poor and, usually, a minority she requires an entitlement herself to deliver a child. Nor will she destroy or injure the product of her labor without facing discipline and punishment. This construction is reserved for those, again, poor and usually a minority, who, as in the case of Jennifer Johnson (Tobin 1993), deliver drugs or alcohol via the umbilical cord to the fetus within. The good mother cannot be a Medea either, in the sense of over-identifying with her offspring, as in the case of Mary Beth Whitehead (Tobin; Hartouni 1995). That love which is "too thick" is not hers to give.[2] The good mother, as incubator, will give over her gestational rights to contract rights, as in the surrogacy of Anna Johnson who carried both the ovum and sperm of a couple that wanted to conceive (Tobin), or to the male genetic claim to his property, as with Mary Beth Whitehead who herself had a genetic claim to the fetus, having used her own ovum. By giving over her rights, she gains the additional status of a buffer against social disorder, a preserver of personal core values that reside in the private domain. In line with this argument, the good mother through both her physical weakness relative to men and her maternal function as child-bearer and child-rearer is indelibly identified as the mainstay of the home.

The bad mother, by contrast, is identified with women who vest themselves in the public sphere by working outside the home or with women whose reproduction society has no interest in encouraging (the poor and those outside the dominant social caste by virtue of religious, racial, or ethnic group) (Ikemoto 1992). The bad mother is relegated to the status of an outsider who requires overt coercive control (Ehrenreich 1993), one who is not to be trusted, having rejected the good mother construction that society and its laws have proposed as her model. Operating on the outside of society's preferred construction, the bad mother is the one likely to be surveilled, prosecuted, and punished, pressed into involuntary sterilization, forced pregnancy, coerced cesareans, or forcibly implanted birth control devices (Ehrenreich 1993; Ashe 1992; Roberts 1991). It is, in society's view, the bad mother who is most likely to resist social constructions of her role. At the same time, it is she who is least mystified about the use to which the state wishes to put her body. It is her class, race,[3] or ethnic group that has traditionally been received into this country as an indentured servant or slave class; it is she who most appreciates what it means to be a "designated breeder." It is she who is most likely to experience the material value to herself of her own body through surrogacy contracts or prostitution, she who instinctively understands and most directly experiences the commodification of her sexual and reproductive capacity. These, rephrasing Ehrenreich, are the "bad whores who make good virgins possible" (1993, 584).

Together, the dichotomies represented by the good/bad mother, slave/slavemaster, and the good/bad Samaritan do not provide us with a variety of maternities. Rather, they constrain us to the singularity of one tyrannical notion. As the central role player in abortion stories, the pregnant woman is a contested site on which polarized values play themselves out. Objectified as bad Samaritan, slavemaster, and bad mother, she fails to contribute to a productive reproductivity. Her insistence on "her" right to "her own" fetus is made the equivalent of asserting her right to social destruction and chaos. Her rebellion against a passive social role condemns her to a representation in which she does not deserve her freedom because she is not capable of exercising that freedom in a way society regards as responsible, that is, to support society's desire to reproduce itself. The pregnant woman subjectified is allowed her subjectivity only under conditions that, once again, objectify her: as slave or surrogate mother.

Politics and Rhetoric

In political terms, the abortion "wars" have been conducted to a large extent through rhetoric that allows groups to reach audiences on either side of the debate. Such rhetoric involves the ability to reach out to one's converts or to affect public perceptions by the ways one frames issues for debate. It also offers insight into how abortion is constructed as a public story and provides an opportunity to examine the culturally powerful themes, history, and tradition that inform that story. Abortion rhetoric involves not only the self-presentation of prolife or prochoice camps but also how those camps construct the story of their opposite parts, how both sets of arguments counter each other, and how those arguments progress or develop. The rhetoric of the antiabortion movement receives somewhat more attention in this chapter, if only because it has attracted so much study. Its development speaks to the efforts of a group that considers itself both marginalized by and resistant to the culture it believes dominates on the abortion question. Antiabortion rhetoric has, as a result, forced its perspective onto the national stage in a way that has sponsored a new demand for inclusiveness on the abortion question.

This chapter will examine political abortion rhetoric by providing, first, profiles of the abortion (prochoice) and antiabortion (prolife) camps and their arguments in terms of both historical development and contemporary shifts in style and direction of appeal. Several series of advertisements are also examined. The chapter then considers the creation in antiabortion rhetoric of an originary myth that identifies antiabortion protest with the civil rights struggle, slavery, Vietnam war protest, and the Holocaust and looks at the movement's strategic mining of biblical sources for imagery to justify its "holy war" against abortion. Finally, the chapter considers the roles the antiabortion story constructs for the courts, the medical profession, women, and the "unborn," the key figures in the oppositional tales of abortion rights.

Abortion Profiles

The prolife movement could be described as having essentially rejected secular values for a religious approach to reproductive issues. It has, following the work of Press and Cole (1999), constructed for itself an "alternative culture." That culture contrasts itself to a dominant power structure and culture that has rendered it an outsider group and whose authorities in business, government, the courts, medicine, and the media it considers biased toward a prochoice view. At the same time, prolife is responsive to patriarchal and hierarchical authority, to "traditional" family values, and to a conservative view of male-female relations in which motherhood and the stay-at-home wife are prevailing models for women. Childbearing is depicted as part of a plan for women based on God's will. Part of a world plan in which women are expected to subordinate their needs to male authority, the family, and the social community, it is contrasted to abortion which is regarded as a violation of women's nature. The prolife view opposes a communitarian perspective to putting one's own good above that of the social good and rejects women who give greater priority to their rights over those of the fetus.

As depicted by the prochoice camp (Vanderford 1989), prolife is highlighted as a small but influential political group supported by substantial funding from churches and thereby a threat to the separation of church and state. In its insistence on the rule of a minority perspective and in its disobedience to civil law in preference for religious law, it is regarded as a threat to the democratic process and to proportional representation. According to prochoice, prolife subverts responsible political activity in its extreme and volatile activist tactics against abortion facilities (blockades as well as bombings) and in its terrorist attacks against abortion providers (shootings as well as murders). Prolife is depicted as tyrannical in its insistence not only on physical threats and intimidation but in its legislative plan to require "compulsory" pregnancy and "mandatory" motherhood by limiting, denying, restricting, controlling, prohibiting, or banning abortion rights and services. Finally, prolife is depicted in the prochoice literature as discriminating against women, especially against the poor and the young, through its insistence on eliminating government funding for abortion, requiring parental notification and consent for minors seeking abortions, and rejecting late-term abortions as well as abortions for the psychological and physical health of women.

Prochoice, according to Press and Cole (1999), is a less homogeneous interest group than prolife and is divided along both class and racial lines. In its working-class aspect, it is, like the prolife group, resistant to existing government, legal, and medical authority but without creating an alternative culture based on its own social, political, or religious values. Rejecting a legal system that it feels is unfair and which leaves it vulnerable, the prochoice working class has a strong sense of having to navigate the "system" as an outsider and finds solidarity in its class membership. No friend of the media, the working class is critical of media representation of blue-collar women as disadvantaged. Black working-class women, a proud group, have become embittered and suspicious of the way they are regarded and represented by others. On the one hand, they are intolerant of those among them who, in seeking abortions, make excuses for their lives and refuse to take responsibility; on the other, both black and white working-class prochoice women support limiting government power and challenge the structural obstacles that restrict them in society. This group is considered politically mobilizable and yet has been ineffectively organized on behalf of abortion rights.

Middle-class prochoice women, who reject many of the views held by those of the prochoice working class, have much less in common ideologically with prolife women. They tend to adopt a more forgiving attitude toward those they consider the "unfortunate" and apply a "therapeutic ethos" (Press and Cole 1999, 102–103) that expects people to improve themselves based on individual supportive interventions. The prochoice middle class is thus less likely to challenge the structural inequities of the status quo or to critique social norms and more likely to accept the middle-class authority of the professional class. It is strongly committed to individual rights as opposed to a communitarian perspective, attaching to that commitment an overtly feminist ethos: that women should be autonomous and have control over their own bodies, that they should make their own decisions and resist identifying womanhood with motherhood. The only one of the groups to experience a conflicted sense of its position, middle-class prochoice advocates both defend a political and abstract right to abortion as it relates to others and question personally and in a concrete sense the appropriateness of abortion in their own lives. Moreover, reluctant to be perceived as judgmental, they make subtle distinctions about the moral problematics of abortions for those who have used poor judgment in relationships or failed to use birth control. This is the prochoice group that has been most effectively mobilized and is most active on behalf of abortion rights.

In the prolife literature, prochoice has been depicted as wealthy and powerful beyond its numbers, massively out-resourcing the former's efforts. Prolife believes that the government provides aid and comfort to abortion rights through its use of the people's taxes without their consent. It claims that biased media and sex education programs in the schools sell prochoice abortion views to communities and to their children. Citing Communist China, prolife warns of the threat of coerced abortions and identifies choice advocates with racism in eugenics policies that sterilize blacks. Opposing selfish personal individualism, prolife views the choice for women's rights as inconsistent with the interests of husbands, potential or unborn life, and social values supporting the "sanctity" of life.

In spite of these differences, Press and Cole (1999) identify several shared perspectives that are evident between the prolife and prochoice sides. Like prolife, the prochoice working class sees itself as an outsider without representation in the system. Equally, the prochoice middle class may share with prolife a conservative communitarian ideology, but it maintains its own sense of community values. It expresses concern for relationships that leave children open to abuse and neglect and exerts a protective role in guarding individual rights. Indeed, prolife itself defends individual rights but not in defense of a woman's right to choose; rather, individual rights are the foundation of its argument for fetal rights. Other shared themes suggest that prolife and prochoice both identify with themes of racial justice as well as with calls for more responsible sexual behavior. Many prochoice women join with prolife women in maintaining their identification with the role of mother, if only to supplement identification with their careers as working women. The solidarity and singularity sponsored in prolife thought are, as well, replicated to some extent in the black prochoice working class's solidarity within its racial group. By contrast, the deep heterogeneity of the prochoice middle class is evident in its singular support for individual women's free choice in decisions that are personal.

This review of abortion and antiabortion groups suggests that their profiles express considerably more complexity and greater overlap than might otherwise have been expected.[4] Both groups work within the parameters of a relatively restricted number of social options and roles. They experience what are sometimes felt to be broad and deep differences that seem impassible and infinitely non-convergent. Although they do not often seem so, such differences may, in the nature of things, be more skin deep than irremediable. As a result of this kind of complexity, a variety of splinter groups have emerged, some divisively extreme and others muted or marginalized.[5] This is not to say that the abortion fault line is likely to become a fiction rather than a fact but that shifting tectonics might require greater flexibility than has previously been seen in either group. The abortion issue—while it might not go away—might have gone as far as it can in either direction. It might now offer the opportunity of a continuing back and forth motion between groups to replace the explosive potential of a seismic face-off between opposed camps.

Choice and Life Arguments

Before its legalization, abortion was constructed in prochoice rhetoric in fairly limited and extreme terms (Condit 1984, 1990). It appeared as a ghastly experience that arose out of a need dictated by socioeconomic distress. It occurred in limited circumstances where necessity prevailed (in cases of incest, rape, the threat a pregnancy posed to a woman's health or life, or a deformed fetus). Abortion happened to unfortunate women who were victimized by quacks and unlicensed butchers. This tale of illegal abortion among helpless victims played on the fear of disease and death that such abortions risked and argued for legalizing abortion under limited circumstances in the face of a powerful emotional narrative. What the narrative neglected, however, was that 90 per cent of illegal abortions involved married women and were conducted by doctors using sterile procedures. The further implication of the narrowed argument was the implied promise that legalizing abortion would not increase the number of abortions. Moreover, it would not only legalize an existing practice while eliminating disease and death, but it would do so without risking a negative effect on public morality. It would address the discriminatory lack of access to safe abortions experienced by the poor who, both when abortion was legal and when it was illegal, were often less likely than middle-class women to receive an abortion from their family doctors. Such an argument had the benefit of an incremental strategy whereby the demands made did not require society to move too far or to accept too much too fast; at the same time, it ran the risk of promising too much and maintained too sanguine a view of the implications of legalizing abortion.

In the late 1960s, the prochoice argument developed steam and a number of states seemed likely to legalize abortion. The demand expanded from limited circumstances like rape to include a more general right to an abortion not dependent upon exigent circumstances. The theme of avoiding unwanted children was added to address the serious social problems of delinquency, child abuse, and the cycle of poverty, which, it was presumed, would diminish with the availability of abortion. Having argued within existing social conventions that affirmed a woman's role as mother and the value of family life, the choice argument now began to assert a woman's right not to be discriminated against reproductively and to have reproductive rights equal to those of men.

By the early 1970s, according to Condit (1984, 1990), prochoice foregrounded a woman's right to control over her own body and repudiated the dominant ideology that identified women by their child-bearing role of mother. Here it introduced the positive right of choice to replace the negative discrimination-against-women argument; it offered an alternative model of a style of life and a concept of family that challenged conventional social ideas. Prolife responded, first, by attacking the rising number of abortions, arguing that numbers had expanded well beyond the "good" reasons for abortions that prochoice had originally proposed. Second, and most significantly, prolife capitalized on fetal imagery made available in photography (and later in sonograms) and on developments in fetal science to advance the forceful proposition that the fetus was a human life; it likened the fetus to a child by focusing on anecdotal stories about late-term abortions. The 1973 *Roe v. Wade* decision synthesized the prochoice and prolife perspectives in a ruling that rhetorically accepted the principle of the life potential of the fetus but not its humanity, or personhood, and accepted the characterization of motherhood as a potentially oppressive social role for women but without accepting a woman's absolute right to choice. It essentially concluded, as Condit put it, that abortion within limits was a necessary, if distasteful, element of social life.

By the late 1970s, abortion to some extent having been naturalized in the social landscape, arguments on both sides appropriated elements from each other, fragmented to reach new allies, or differentiated to refine their appeal. Prochoice, for example, referred to the need to protect the "life" of the woman, while prolife associated "choice" with the decision to have sex, not to take the life of the fetus. Prochoice found allies among conservatives on issues of freedom from government interference and on a commonly shared belief in individual rights. Prolife appealed to liberal protectionism on issues of race and gender, extending that protection to the general value of all life, including fetal life. Identifying with Catholics and liberals on an appeal to humanity and with fundamentalists and the right wing on traditional values of family, home, and children, prolife expressed the more unbending religious message of a sacrifice of self for the sake of the fetus, based on love of one's neighbor and all humankind. Prochoice, by contrast, had some difficulty with its argument demanding control and rejecting oppression, which not only carried a strongly self-interested cast to it but which made its own characterization of the family appear harsh and negative.[6] The call for choice and freedom from the "old order" failed to provoke a sufficiently attractive sense of an alternative "new order" to be sufficiently appealing. At the same time, separation from the ideal of "motherhood" proved to have a minimal appeal, even within the prochoice camp, alienating a faction that identified women with a nurturing role. This kind of alienation suggested further the need for an appealing image of an alternative order where women could be identified as both career oriented and nurturing in their relation-ships. The shifts and refinements in both prolife and prochoice camps revealed that three themes needed to be balanced or harmonized: preserving family, protecting women, and acknowledging the value of fetal life. Any consensus view on abortion would have to include protecting women's right to abortion while minimizing fetal deaths within a socially acceptable context that valued both the nurturing woman and the family.

In its initial efforts at building abortion arguments to tell the story of either the prolife or the prochoice camp, rhetoric tended to create purposes that were cultu-rally potent, using strong examples rather than subtle cases. Women were depicted, on the one hand, as making a choice against children and against motherhood and, on the other, as facing circumstances that left them victims who did not fit ideal-ized images of motherhood. Keeping the focus on illegal abortions in the beginning proved an easier prochoice sell than later lines of argument that put women in competition with men for their equality. A liberated line of argument left women vulnerable to being cast as less than innocent sexual actors who "chose" to make their own fetuses pay the price of their pregnancies in order to escape the conse-quences of their own freely chosen acts. A more compelling story was thereby put forward. The new role was that of a "good" victim, an ordinary woman with whom the general public could identify. This woman faced the "evil" of a dangerous and illegal abortion and risked self-destruction under the pressures of difficult personal and social circumstances. This story was more likely to generate a broader base of support than stories relating to the poor and disenfranchised. Moreover, it would evade the harshness of arguments based on opposition to motherhood. Such a story nevertheless carried its own risks, risks that originated not in the rhetoric of the op-posing camp but in reality itself, where the evidence suggests a much greater variety of abortion situations, a more endemic pattern of abortions, and a more complex picture of involved parties that was more threatening to conventional social values and practices. Because it involved multiple alternative stories of differentiated abortion situations, this story would be less likely to build on pre-existing values or to fold into them. Not only did multiple stories threaten to overwhelm a smoothed prototype story, but cracks appeared in differentiated stories. If a woman was having "immoral" pre-marital sex, for example, she seemed to deserve to suffer a preg-nancy, unlike such circumstances as rape, incest, or extreme social conditions. Equally, the presence of the "good" woman (in practice, the middle-class white woman) was critical to any widely adopted abortion tale. Public acceptance of a pregnancy was necessary to any abortion rhetoric that was to be adopted or en-dorsed as a public myth. Thus, for the kind of convergence capable of leading to consensus, situations suggesting a legitimate need for an exemption loomed large as possible themes. Therapeutic abortions, for example, clearly "fit" a rhetorically ac-ceptable construction.

What was becoming increasingly clear as abortion rhetoric approached the nineties, however, was that smoothed stories representing a simplistic reduction of one position's view had become more and more problematic. Reproductive woman could not be essentialized but progressively had to be depicted as encompassing a wide range of factors, including class, "gender, raced and ethnic groups, religious preferences, and sexual orientation, any of which may be more salient in a given context" (Press and Cole 1999, 8). A central or root struggle, nevertheless, did organize thinking about women in the abortion debate. Such a struggle existed in women's attempts to understand their gendered role in society. The conflict between a woman who was mother to her children and mate to her spouse and a woman who was an equal to men and yet different from them (11) had to be resolved. Abortion was presented as the contested site over which that conflict was to be played out.

What Condit (1990) calls the prolife "heritage tale" had many of the same problems experienced by the prochoice "illegal abortion" story. Here, prolife chose a selective view of American cultural history and wrote out all other native traditions, racial or religious, to create a model of self-sacrifice on behalf of the fetus. The model chosen was based initially on a Catholic perspective but was later adapted to a fundamentalist perspective. Recognizing that it needed to reintegrate excluded traditions, the prolife tale subsequently appropriated black and Jewish traditions through analogies to slave history and the Holocaust. It linked them through "sanctity of life" arguments that referenced starvation and sterilization policies in the histories of the two excluded goups. Analogies to slavery placed fetuses and slaves among those who could be killed at will once the general value of life was undermined. Holocaust and eugenics analogies used sanctity of life as their central theme and, like the slavery theme, linked abortion to the subsequent adoption of sterilization, medical experimentation, euthanasia, and mandated breeding practices. Prolife rhetoric in this story juxtaposed pictures of slave coffles and wagons of Holocaust corpses with piles of aborted fetuses. It implied comparisons between the captive fetus in the womb being given birth, the slave in a cage being emancipated, and Jews in death camps being liberated. In each variant, the helpless hostage was dependent upon the social responsibility of "good neighbors" who acted as rescuers. The story thus opposed personal, individualistic murder and child sacrifice with communitarian love and self-sacrifice, modeling its argument on the view that abortion violates the rule of love for one's neighbor (Noonan 1970; Condit 1990, 46–56). This "unified" tale was met by attacks on the prolife religious base for imposing its morality on others and for rewriting American history. Considered by many a "partisan" dogma, it contained story elements that elided, conflated, or otherwise infiltrated the opposed prochoice tale. The prolife tale was quickly becoming a destabilized narrative with little affinity for the groups to which it was meant to appeal.

In the history of both camps, oppositionality and vilification of one's opponent further compounded the instability of stories. They had the effect of escalating controversy and exacerbating differences as well as compromising sanctity, value, and quality of life claims.[7] Renewed oppositionality in abortion rhetoric contrasted motherhood achieved to motherhood denied, subordinate women to dominant men, and the "innocent" fetus to the "selfish" aborting woman. It soon became clear that to generate more broadly appealing stories, both sides needed to avoid an "agon" or contest of rights (Condit 1990, 66). The moment a woman claimed property rights over her own body, for example, opponents could argue that people are unequally endowed with property and that property redistribution was not the law's responsibility. Discriminatory application of abortion rights, it was argued, could not be effectively addressed in a legal way. Prolife feminists contended that prochoice demands to participate equally in the same rights men enjoyed would fail to address discrimination. When women accepted male sexist social norms on male terms, not only was patriarchy reinforced but its discriminatory practices against pregnant women and mothers were enhanced (Press and Cole 1999, 140).

The salience of arguments came into play as well, differing by such demographic variants as family size, income level, race, age, urban or rural residence, and strength of one's ties to a church or religion, among other factors (Adamek 1994).[8] Together with changes in social climate, these factors were, for example, likely to dictate whether concrete, personal, immediate arguments would have greater appeal than more abstract, social arguments. Thus certain groups would find it more difficult than others to avoid the picture called up by one prolife appeal: "When people look at a dead child and they realize that this happens about fifteen to twenty times a day within 20 or 30 minutes of where they live, work, and worship, the reality begins to sink in" (Hunter 1994, 65). Both abortion and antiabortion groups found that a hard physical message was often more salient than a soft social message. Prochoice argued successfully along these lines for abortion in cases of rape, incest, a defective fetus, inability to afford a pregnancy, or danger to a woman's life or health. For its part, prolife argued that the unborn has a right to life and its killing is a murder (Adamek, 72). Agreed-upon themes were generally less subject to variation across sociodemographic categories. These included, predictably, that abortion on demand, at any time, for any reason is not a good idea; that informing a minor's parents, as opposed to parental consent, is a good idea; or that a Human Life Amendment that would outlaw abortion should not be adopted (65–66).

To counter oppositionality, prochoice used rhetorical approaches that avoided excessive confrontation to argue that restrictions on abortion were discriminatory. Women's reproductive rights were featured without assaulting male reproductive rights, and disproportional disadvantages to women who were poor, of color, or young were raised without counterposing those groups to white middle-class women. Such arguments had the potential to rise to a call for universal justice, invoking the need to balance rights or to use a sliding scale of rights that could include the fetus as well. Oblique themes were to prove even more likely to provide "depoliticized language with a lower agonistic charge" (Condit 1990, 31). Such indirection suggested conditions without directly bringing conflicts into play, enabling a case to get heard and opening the possibility of restructuring beliefs. Prochoice, for example, translated its demand for real abortion choices into a demand that government prevent interference in personal decisions of all types. Prolife moved away from attacks on a woman's right to reproductive freedom and adopted an argument that valued children and asserted their right to be protected.

On the prochoice side, in particular, an attempt was made to emphasize a woman's right to have access to "unbiased" information without being faced with scare tactics (such as linking abortion to breast cancer), shock ads (featuring second- and third- term aborted fetuses), or strong language (as in graphic descriptions of "partial birth" abortion procedures). This approach was designed to appeal to people of different religions and backgrounds to allow women to make personal decisions without misleading information or distorted options. Lowering the political charge of appeals and humanizing women who choose abortions became prochoice objectives, targeting a broader appeal to the 43 per cent of women identified as choosing abortion at some point in their lives (see Websites, prochoice.org, 1999; meonline.com, 1998).

At the same time, the choice message was challenged in the media for absenting the actual choice that was being made: abortion (Lomicky and Salestrom 1998; Dolliver 1998; Wolf 1995). The absence of the key word itself became suspicious in clips "set in rural locales . . . [that] tell us that *choice* is as American as apple pie" (Dolliver, 1) and that speak "of belief in oneself, acceptance of responsibility for one's actions, the founding principle of the republic" (2). Unwillingness to use the "A" word created doubt and raised questions about the word's potential "unspeakability." Such messages left audiences potentially as puzzled as they were persuaded.

Reference to choice as a personal "decision" has been challenged as well. Putting it in the context of personal taste (as in a choice of carpeting, for example) (Wolf 1995, 8) rather than a matter of "conscience" (as a matter, that is, of life and death), the term is open to being conceived as for the self, or selfish. Balanced against a slogan like "Abortion stops a beating heart," the "choice" argument pits a personal dilemma against an incontrovertible fact in a contest it is bound to lose. The prolife countermessage exposes the "choice" for self over the welfare of an other in stark terms: "In order to terminate a pregnancy, you have to still a heartbeat, switch off a developing brain and, whatever the method, break some bones and rupture some organs" (McKenna 1995, 23). The appeal of choices that, in common parlance, are about "Ten minutes old" (in response to an abortion counselor's query, "So, how long have you been prochoice?" [Wolf 8]) proves vulnerable in the public marketplace.

Thus, the prochoice position loses "millions of Americans who want to support abortion as a legal right, but still need to condemn it as a moral iniquity" when it dehumanizes, reduces, or cheapens the value of the fetus or when it renders its "decision" outside a communal context (1). Once, however, the argument is shifted to an abstract context such as "a matter between a woman, her doctor, her family, her conscience, and God" (8), the message regains its legs. Seventy-two percent of respondents in a *Newsweek* poll supported abortion when the issue was posed as a matter of conscience (8).

While oppositionality began to be muted in mainstream argument and blended arguments became more common, fringe elements, finding themselves outside of where abortion rhetoric was headed, further isolated themselves.[9] Prolife protest strategies of the nineties shifted away from the civil disobedience of clinic protests, sit-ins, lay-downs, and the "Atlanta crawl" (through the legs of police on barricades)[10] and moved to clinic bombings and arson, and from there to the murder of abortion doctors and clinic workers. The rhetoric accompanying the shift depicted the fetus as a victim held hostage within the woman's womb, a child kidnapped and enslaved to the murderous will of its mother. Choosing to break the wall of silence that allows abortions to continue, prolife rhetoric spoke of the necessity of committing a violent act in a "just war" to prevent a greater evil, justifying the murder of clinic doctors to "save the lives" of the future unborn: killing in order to cure as a way of demonstrating the sanctity of life.

Where oppositionality and vilification characterized the abortion debate, it created a backlash, both because it could easily be belied and because it relied on attacking ideas that were often understandable and shared between the two camps (Vanderford 1989). Negative arguments did indeed encourage and sustain activism within a given camp by arousing believer solidarity, but they did little to attract those who were not already converts. The uncommitted were less amenable to the use of fear, hate, suspicion, and socially divisive appeals and more in tune with resolving, healing, and consensus strategies. Appealing to them required encouraging agreement, toning down the level of rhetoric, and emphasizing common ground.

In both prolife and prochoice arguments, low-complexity approaches and those that failed to integrate arguments by considering alternatives proved unlikely "to find resonance with the more moderate majority" (Dillon 1993, 313) on the issue of abortion. But extremism still tended to find itself reflected in the language of relatively moderate voices, so that a bomb-throwing declaration of war against abortion providers found itself responded to in mainstream prochoice fund-raising rhetoric in such language as "a devious sneak attack," "a war we're fighting," "combating ridiculous assaults," efforts to "ambush women" by "fanatical followers" of a "despicable cause," and the need to stand "vigilant" "through every round of the fight." Less threatening rhetoric in the language of moderate prolife politicians tended to be harder to combat as it was less strident and provided more ambiguous grounds for argument. Such language spoke not of ending the right to abortions but of reducing their number, of incorporating a larger "reverence for life," of including fetuses without targeting abortion, and of targeting issues where there is a greater overlap of support between both sides (parental consent and late-term abortion, for example).

In sum, abortion language had shifted so that while it had been attacked on both sides as oppositional and confrontative or as deceptive "doublethink," it had also been evolving rhetorically. Such prochoice language as "Keep your rosaries off our ovaries" or "Keep your cross out of our crotch" (Hunter 1994, 50) might continue to surface in periods of abortion clinic violence but is hardly seen in quieter times. Even a favored slogan like "Abortion kills" is put into moratorium when its overuse leaves it so devalued that one appears to be crying wolf. Hysterical terms, like "abortuary," "feticide," "mandatory motherhood," and "pregnancy policy" (45–67), soon become devitalized (DeMarco 1994, 214), and "un-American" and "discrimination," which may have been terms of choice early in the debate, prove to have less effect as abortion campaigns expand their appeal. By contrast, alternative terms that are easier to hear stay steady or get called into service. Such terms as "therapeutic" and "unborn" stay in the mix largely because they are less harsh and more amenable to the undercommitted or uncommitted audiences that more and more often need to be appealed to. The use of language to victimize, manipulate, or prevaricate (McClerrin 1994, 276–277) might still be in play somewhere in a campaign, but mainstreamed slogans tend to become more neutral and their testiness muted. "Life, what a beautiful choice" is thus matched by "Choice, what a beautiful life" to bring the debate to a more gentle semantic stalemate. Techniques of avoidance lead the prolife to turn the prochoice "fetus" into the prolife "unborn child"; they lead to the prochoice game of "hide the baby," where references to the fetus disappear entirely, and it is referred to only as part of a woman's body (278; Gillespie 1994, 242). Sliding-scale term choices tend to resolve themselves at less extreme points along a spectrum as well, so that the prolife "partial birth abortion" and the prochoice "dilation and extraction procedure" (or "d and x") tend to be described on both sides as "late-term abortion," however inaccurate or misleading that usage may actually be in medical or legal terms.

The Public Media

The abortion debate appears to have moved along, in the public media at least, toward a new, more broadly incorporative standard that avoids many of the excesses of the past. In an end of the millennium gesture, for example, the Pro-Choice Public Education Project, a consortium of 47 abortion rights groups, expanded its outreach to a young audience. It directed its campaign at sixteen- to twenty-five-year-old women, opening in the tri-state New York area as a bus and subway campaign, on college campuses, and in *People* magazine (Lauro 1999; protectchoice.org). The objectives of the new campaign were to offset graphic antiabortion appeals and scare tactics by providing access to informative sex education—resources available from parents, teachers, and health care providers—and to reinforce the message that "Prevention Is the First Choice" (protectchoice.org). In its signature statement, it sidestepped "abortion" (see McClerrin 1994, 276–277) to keep the focus on the more abstract and socially acceptable "choice": "Your American right of choice is under attack—protect your right of choice."

In the campaign for the year 2000, a print ad presents a page from a yearbook; the text reads, "Pick a boyfriend." The visual shows ten yearbook photos, all of the same boy, who is pictured as a prototypical "nerd." The closing text of the ad reads, "Not having a choice sucks, doesn't it?" Taking a humorous approach to a highly charged issue, the ad raises the serious issue of making a choice without the "freedom to choose" (protectchoice.org). Implicitly admitting that its audience might be uncomfortable with the subject of abortion, the ad does not aim to change the viewer's mind but to get her to consider a replacement issue that is less threatening. Thus, it speaks of choice rather than what is actually being chosen, at the same time exploring problems related to lack of choice (Lauro 1999). A comparable approach is taken in a television ad—continuing the theme "It's pro-choice or no choice"—that shows a politician in the shadows changing the choices a girl makes as she selects a soda from a machine and a channel on the television. The voiceover says, "You wouldn't want some guy in Washington to make choices for you. Why let them make the most important choice of all? Fight for your right to a safe and legal abortion while you still have it" (Lauro C13).

Prochoice has not, however, gone completely soft sell in its pitch. The opening salvo in a poster blitz features the headline "77% of anti-abortion leaders are men. 100% of them will never be pregnant"; the headline is superimposed on a visual of a group of "stodgy looking men in suits" (protectchoice.org) with their arms crossed, mouths pursed, and the top half of their heads cut off in the photo. The implied read on this poster is that women should be making the choice of what happens to their bodies, not the brainless men in suits. The most assertive ads—requiring a retro look at and some residual memory of the parade of horrors overcome by the movement—are three that feature the once-ubiquitous prochoice coat-hanger as its central image. The first displays a Volkswagen Beetle, lava lamp, and platform shoes and reads, "Of all the things from the 70s to make a comeback, there's one we'd really hate to see"—an image of a coat hanger follows the text. A second coat-hanger ad features text on a blank background that reads, "When your right to a safe and legal abortion is finally taken away, what are you going to do?"—the question mark is fashioned from the outline of a coat hanger. This ad, intended to run along the long side of New York city buses, created a controversy when Transit Displays, Inc., the advertising arm of NYC buses, resisted approving its use and finally did so only under the threat of litigation. The last of the three ads, without any text, features a freestanding question mark fashioned from a wire hanger. The visual implicitly raises the question, "Before abortion was legal, what did women do?" It implies as well its own answer: they died "from botched attempts to end pregnancies using wire hangers" (protectchoice.org). Aimed at young women to get them to talk about a highly personal issue not often discussed publicly, the PEP ad campaign's intention is to convince its audience that not only is believing in personal freedom and access to options acceptable but that women need not feel guilty about such beliefs.

The ad that most directly addresses PEP's objectives—and the only one available in poster format in both Spanish and English through the Internet—features an off-beat young woman with a nose ring and body tattoo behind text that reads, "Think you can do whatever you want with your body? Think again." PEP's Internet commentary clarifies that the tattoo poster "makes us think—are women really free to make their own decisions concerning their own bodies? Or, are restrictions whittling away at their rights?" (protectchoice.org).

On the prolife side, ad campaigns have made comparable shifts in the direction of humanizing abortion rhetoric to achieve a more civil discourse. The Outdoor Advertising Association of America, for example, incorporated an ad in its public service "God" campaign (part of a $15 million program of ads that appeared nationally in 10,000 spaces), which won the Smith Agency a coveted Obie award for excellence in advertising. In a campaign that included such one-liners as "We need to talk—God" and "Don't make me come down there—God" (*New York Times* July 18, 1999), the abortion variant read: "Before I formed you in the womb, I knew you—God," a reference to Jeremiah 1:2 (Ward 1993, 398).[11]

For its part, the Respect Life Program of the U.S. Catholic Conference offered a campaign with the goal of reinforcing nine personal values: "self-respect, sense of accomplishment, being well respected, security, warm relationships with others, sense of belonging, fun and enjoyment in life, self-fulfillment, and excitement" (Mall 1994, 116). A personal values approach intended to sell an idea just as one would sell soap, this campaign simplifies abortion conceptually, linking a value to the idea being sold. Avoiding the adversarial appeals of previous antiabortion ads and the punishing messages of fetal murder, fear, guilt, and loss, the new approach is neither negative nor highly selective. Rather, it appeals to its audience's sense of fairness, order, and social stability in an incorporative ecumenicism that aims at a spiritual rather than a religious impact. Adopting the overall theme "The Natural Choice Is Life" (repeated at the bottom of each ad), the campaign resonates with positive terms. It appropriates the term "choice" from abortion rights groups to undermine its oppositional force. It announces "life" as a positive alternative to the unspoken but implied death of the fetus, resonating with the antiwar slogan "Make peace, not war." In a final gesture, it capitalizes on the presumed healthfulness of that which is "natural," calling up, for good or ill, the residual message of natural family planning with which previous campaigns associated themselves.

In its series of ads, the Respect Life Program takes a philosophical approach to the problem of life, announcing in one—featuring the familiar Lennart-Nilsson photograph of the fetus in utero—"To be or not to be THAT is the question" (Mall 1994, 139–140). This ad subordinates the moral order to the physical image of the fetus, foregrounding the implied argument of the ad—the right to life of a "child." It seals the humanity of the unborn, giving it the protagonist's role in the philosophical dilemma of being and nothingness. The Program presents a quotation from Matthew 18:5 ("Anyone who welcomes this little child in my name, welcomes me") as text in two other ads. In one, Mother Teresa embraces a child and, in the second, a woman's hand—with a wedding ring on the ring finger—touches the outstretched fingers of a child, an image resonant of Michelangelo's God creating Adam (Mall 136–137). Both ads feature the added line, "1.6 million abortions a year can't be right," negating a woman's "right" to terminate fetal life. In the Mother Teresa ad, the aged figure's nurturing solicitude for the vulnerable child invites modeling behavior on the part of the advertisement's audience, even as it provokes empathy for the very aged and the very young. Reflecting a collective human yearning to protect the weak, it nevertheless raises the question whether a potentially larger audience might have been reached by an equally admired secular figure and an equally impressive secular quotation. The wedding ring in the second ad—suggesting a mother, marriage, and family—reinforces a dominant religious view of a traditional white family and a middle-class stay-at-home mom carrying on the work of God's creation. No laboring poor, single-parent families need apply.

On a more political note, taking a leaf from the activist environmental lobby, a montage of wildlife shots is introduced in one ad with the line "Some life is protected"; the Lennart-Nilsson photo at the bottom and off to the side, as if cast off, is introduced with the phrase "and some isn't" (Mall 1994, 136). In this ad, the fetus is sidelined to allow the moral message to take the foreground. The ad generates the impression that protecting animal life is wrong if potential human life goes unprotected. The message that it is inconsistent to favor lesser creatures over higher creatures nevertheless suggests another conclusion; one might equally well argue that one should prefer born over unborn life. In its fifth and final ad, the Program presents the shadowy image of a pregnant girl in a rocker facing into the sun. It reads, from Matthew 25:45, "Lord, when did we see you a stranger and not come to your help?" More extensive text follows, asking for reader support and offering more information upon request (138–139). But the ad risks bypassing its intended audience, given the absence of signs of distress in the subject to be befriended. Its good Samaritan approach suggests that such intervention might appear imposed and even gratuitous, rather than welcome, in a culture in which people do not routinely take on others' burdens without being invited.

Adopting the soft-sell approach of the Respect Life ads, the Maine Vitae Society of the Maine Right to Life organization broadcast its own local media advertisements in 1999. In a saturation television campaign, it ran two ads in 872 thirty-second slots over a three-month period in the urban media markets of Portland and Bangor (mint.net/life4me/nws-sp99.htm). With an estimated average viewer frequency of thirty-five viewings for an intended target group of women from eighteen to forty-nine, the two ads illustrate the summary phrase "Think About It." The first ad features a middle-aged woman who is represented as having been prochoice until something happened to change her mind. She muses, "When I was pregnant, I finally realized that all this little kid was trying to do was make it, just make it, just like all of us." In the second ad, a woman who has just had an abortion expresses her regret, staring out a window into a black, rainy night: "They said you wouldn't be bothered by a voice calling for you in the night. . . . There would be no trail of cereal through the house, no spills, no stray toys . . . there is still a voice. Abortion changes everything." A woman to woman campaign, Maine Vitae reaches for the soft underbelly of prochoice supporters, humanizing its subjects, expressing its message from a commonly experienced perspective, and working on the inherent grief and guilt that necessarily underlie such a serious act. Nonjudgmental and empathetic, the ads maintain a hands-across-the-world, sisters-under-the-skin approach.

Proabortion and antiabortion arguments thus appear to have addressed a variety of issues and strategies, some more successfully than others. Clearly, it took moving from a bloody hangers strategy to the hanger as an abstract, historical, interrogatory approach on a woman's right to an abortion to keep prochoice arguments viable. By the same token, it took moving away from absented voices, excluded traditions, depictions of an essentialized woman, and religiously imposed messages to gain prolife arguments a broader, less resistant audience. Both camps had to struggle with oppositional messages that pitted mothers against career women, fetuses against their mothers, and women against men as they considered issues related to rights and roles. Questions of who was the victim—woman or fetus—and games of hide the baby, on one side, and render the woman invisible, on the other, left both sides open to attack, even as renarrativizations of the fetus and the pregnant woman kept changing the nature of the playing field. Choice elided into who gets to make the choice, of what, and for whom, ambiguifying further the kinds of questions that needed to be addressed, just as soft cases (easy to embrace) were obfuscated by hard cases (difficult to support) to complicate what each side had hoped to simplify in smoothed constructions that would be difficult to resist.

Both pro- and antiabortion ads found they had to strike a balance between acting as trusted sources of information and arousing emotions. Both recognized that support on either side was based on conflicting beliefs that were mutually exclusive at the same time that they were often mutually endorsed: abortion as a legal right and abortion as morally repugnant. Indeed, the battle—if battle it had to be—was in many ways between being "good" when possible and accepting the "necessary" when one had to. The guilt and regret attendant on such decisions implied the need for humanizing appeals, appeals for decisions made in a communal context that balanced individual, family, and social concerns, appeals to a sense of fairness, and appeals that established boundaries for both personal decisions and outside interventions.

Prolife Rhetoric and Civil Rights

The abortion profiles, arguments, rhetoric, and advertisements examined here provide a strong sense of the nature of the abortion debate in the public media. Nevertheless, without examining the underlying themes that proved responsible for the development of the antiabortion movement—its allusions to the civil rights struggle, the Holocaust, and the Bible, as well as its constructions of medicine and law and the roles it assigns to women and the fetus—it is impossible to access either the deep structure of abortion rhetoric or its place as an expression of a religious revival that has swept across the nation. It is that expression that ultimately lifts antiabortion rhetoric to the status of a larger resistance to the status quo and to an unsettling subversion of public order that will accept nothing but its own terms for social peace.

In the history of the antiabortion movement, two points of reference arise that construct the movement's self-appointed origins: civil disobedience—in particular the abolition of slavery, the civil rights struggle, the Holocaust, and the Vietnam antiwar movement—and the Bible. John O'Keefe, referred to as the "Father of Rescue" (Risen and Thomas 1998, 43–77), found models in Gandhi and the civil disobedience of the antiwar movement of the Vietnam War but also in his favorite book, Martin Luther King's collection of sermons *Strength to Love*. O'Keefe was driven to create a new civil rights campaign in the mid-1970s that was based on making sacrifices to win the civil rights of "unborn" human children. O'Keefe borrowed his line of argument from the Quaker activist Charles Fager's book *Selma: 1965*. Applying the lessons of the civil rights struggle to the antiabortion movement, the message became let "violence be visited on me, not the unborn" (quoted in Risen and Thomas 60). O'Keefe proposed using sit-ins to express solidarity with the unborn and to recruit by demonstrating that unearned suffering on the part of those who participate is redemptive. Activist arrestees in Montgomery County, Maryland, in 1975 capitalized as well on antiwar symbolism by referring to themselves as the "Sigma Six" (a play on the Chicago Seven) (62), and the movement made efforts to attract such peace advocates as antinuclear activists to its cause. The most typical of O'Keefe's approaches, however, was the use of "Strength to Love" placards (seen as late as 1997 in a Connecticut protest), recalling Martin Luther King's non-violent approach.

O'Keefe's influence on the mainstream antiabortion movement led it to model itself on the antiwar and civil rights movements as characteristically American statements of civil disobedience. Sam Lee (an antiabortion organizer in the St. Louis, Missouri, demonstrations in 1982), for example, recalls reading in jail former Supreme Court Justice Abe Fortas' book *Concerning Dissent and Civil Disobedience*. The book taught him how to paralyze the criminal justice system with large-scale sit-ins that fill the jails and the courts. Indeed, the antiabortion movement that emerged from Operation Rescue in the late 1980s through the early 1990s became the largest social protest movement since the civil rights and antiwar protests of the sixties.

The most transparent attempt to identify the antiabortion movement with the civil rights struggle appears in Randall Terry's "A Letter from Jail," March 27, 1989, written in the Parker Center Jail in Los Angeles following his arrest at an abortion clinic protest (Terry 1990). Announced as "Written from a Prison Work Camp," the letter represents the first of three attempts by Terry to associate himself symbolically with Martin Luther King's letter from the Birmingham jail. His second occurred in a lengthy letter he wrote during his stay in the Fulton County jail the following October, 1989—the result of his refusal to pay a fine dating from the 1988 Democratic National Convention in Atlanta. There, Terry appeals to the Operation Rescue membership "to pray afresh about your part in this battle . . . see if your heart does not tremble within you for this country" (as quoted in Risen and Thomas 1998, 303). Even earlier, Terry had introduced his book *Operation Rescue* (1988) as written in jail in Binghamton, New York, as part of his prolife ministry in a mission field of abortion clinics. His mission, he announced, was to save "those scheduled to meet an untimely death at the hands of the abortionist" (11).

Terry assumes the role of a modern-day abolitionist in the struggle against the long history of injustice against blacks in America. Quoting from King, he justifies his war on abortion: "Where the battle rages, there the loyalty of the soldier is proved, and to be steady on all the battlefields besides, is mere flight and disgrace if he flinches at that point" (quoted in Terry 1988, 42). Comparing the churches that fail actively to support the antiabortion movement to churchgoers who owned slaves in the South, Terry identifies antiabortion forces with abolitionist liberators of the kidnapped and enslaved.[12] In his updated abortion version of the underground railroad, unborn children are constructed as captives within their mothers until freed by antiabortion rescuers (33, 125).

Prolife borrows another page from the history of slavery in its representation of a figure in shackles who asks, "Am I Not a Man and a Brother?" (Sernett 1994, 172), replacing the picture of the slave with that of a child-like fetus. Playing on the idea of the powerful exploiting the weak (Gillespie 1994, 235), fetal remains are exhibited just as slaves had been displayed, showing "the scars of the slaveholder's whips on their backs" (Sernett 173). The refusal to give birth to a child who will be abused in a cruel world is compared unsympathetically to the acceptance of slavery as better than being left unprotected in a world for which one is unprepared (166). A more subtle appeal to the slavery image is borrowed from the Lincoln-Douglas debates, from which prolife lifts the line "No one has the right to decide to do what is wrong" (Willke 1994, 330).[13]

The rescuers of the Holocaust constituted another significant reference group with which Terry claimed association. In 1987, when Randall Terry led his first "mission" to blockade an abortion clinic in Cherry Hill, New Jersey (Risen and Thomas 1998, 262–263), he represented the event as a rescue of innocents scheduled to be slaughtered in the death camp "abortuaries" of a new holocaust. He considered himself a Christian breaking the "Covenant of Silence" who knows when to prefer God's law to man's and to risk civil disobedience, suffering, and jail to become a "prisoner for Christ" (1990, 233–234; 1988, 106ff). Doctors, by contrast, were compared to death camp executioners complicit in the murders "of the aged, the retarded, and the insane": "These medical madmen had taken the godless ideologies of Darwin's survival of the fittest and Hitler's master race to their logical conclusions—the murder of the weak and defenseless" (1990, 72). Should they, Terry asked, be excused because they believed Jews, like the unborn, "were less than human?" (72). In a chapter on doctors in his book *Accessory to Murder*—indicatively titled "Hired Assassins and Their Blood-Bought Prophets" (Terry 1990)—Terry refers to Nazi death camps as "research laboratories in which innocent human beings were being used like lab rats for perverse and cruel tortures in the name of scientific advancement. . . . The surviving children were jabbed and poked with needles to test reflex actions; others had their limbs and sexual organs removed without anaesthesia. . . . And who was wielding the knife of cruelty? Doctors" (71).[14]

Antiabortion depictions of the Nazi biotheocracy (Jay Lifton's term, 1986) as the presumed source of prochoice ideology became a preferred way of presenting not only the medical profession but the legal profession as well. Using doctors as their instrument, the Supreme Court is regarded as the architect of a judicial holocaust that itself warrants a trial like those under the Nuremberg Accords: "The judges who voted for *Roe* and upheld it in subsequent decisions opened the door for the death of nearly thirty million babies to date! That's two and one-half times more babies than all the people murdered in Hitler's holocaust" (Terry 1990, 135). Consistent with such rhetoric, an antiabortion billboard advertisement in Pensacola, Florida, reads, "Hitler would have loved it" (Blanchard and Prewitt 1993, xi).

Defying rational discourse by their visceral appeal, analogues to slavery, fetal death, and the genocide of the Jews require neither evidence nor support as a substitute for reasoning but leave prolife rhetoric open to reasoned attack. Connecting abortion, slavery, and the Holocaust with the antiabortion movement, emancipation, and rescue has the advantage, nevertheless, of accepting chattel slavery as the skeleton in America's historical closet (Sernett 1994, 160). As a lingering shadow in the collective memory and a seminal human rights experience, slavery's foundational story of reversing historical injustice gives the antiabortion story moral depth with historical roots. This "cautionary moral tale" (160) argues that, like slaves, the unborn should be included in the Fourteenth Amendment's expansive definition of a person. Lacking the support of the rest of the Constitution (which requires personhood to enjoy protection of one's rights, privileges, and immunities) and even of the Fourteenth Amendment itself (which requires that a "person" be "born or naturalized"), the prolife position is, however, readily rebutted in the prochoice literature; the extension of protection to women is, after all, more appropriate, and legally more supportable along the same grounds than to the unborn.[15] In its effort to reconstruct itself as a force for emancipation, liberation, and rescue, antiabortion offers to extend universal rights to slaves and their unborn counterparts—fetuses— but refuses to extend them to their most logical human heirs—women.

Antiabortion rhetoric had yet another hurdle to overcome. The creation of an originary story that places the antiabortion movement at the historical juncture of slavery and abolition, segregation and desegregation and in a Southern geography where both the Civil War and the civil rights struggle were most definitively contested is unconvincing, if emotionally appealing, on its face. The coalition of Christian conservatives that seeks to appropriate the history of blacks and Jews is rooted in the very same soil as Jim Crow and the Ku Klux Klan, forces that traditionally discriminated against those whose stories are now being coopted. Cozying up to an alien history of passive resistance, peace activists, and abolitionists, the antiabortion movement disassociated from its own more objectionable Reconstructionist past of lynch-law vigilantism and discriminatory laws and traditions. It asked its audience not only to erase memories of endemic racial violence over the period spanning the mid-nineteenth to the mid-twentieth century but also to discount more recent organized campaigns of clinic violence and abortion-provider assassinations that have defined and given sustenance to its identity as a movement.

Biblical Rhetoric

Whereas the antiabortion movement claimed its origins in civil rights protests, antiwar demonstrations, abolitionism, and Holocaust rescues, its most strategic rhetorical reference was the Bible. Formally established in 1988, Operation Rescue was designed to be a front-line force—at one time called a "prolife mafia" and at another "the green berets of the pro-life movement" (Blanchard 1994)—in a war against an "enemy" whose biblical equivalents were the Pharaoh of Egypt and Herod the King (the biblical slaughterer of innocents). Antiabortion activists regard themselves as like Saul in the siege of the city of Jabesh and like Christ placing his body between sinners and the gates of hell. Like Daniel and the three Hebrew lads Shadrach,

Meshach, and Abednego, activists are represented as cast into the lion's den and the blazing furnace. Like the conspirators of the Gideon Project (the Christmas Day, 1984 bombing of abortion clinics in Pensacola, Florida), they are the destroyers of the altar of Baal, "the place of infant sacrifices covered with infant blood" (Blanchard and Prewitt 1993, 138). Abortionists, by contrast, are compared, in the words of the Gideon Project defense team, to "the worshippers of Baal . . . [they] want a victim" (Patrick Monaghan, defense lawyer for Matthew Goldsby, quoted in Blanchard and Prewitt, 144). Addressing church leaders as "Pillars of Jello," Randall Terry (1988, 172) recalls God Himself fighting for the Israelites alongside Joshua, warriors facing the enemy with their bodies and their swords to prevail in the Battle of Jericho. Where the walls fell down in one great shout and with the encircling of the contested site and the great clamour of "noise disturbance," Terry finds the prototype for clinic protests. The same image becomes the banner cry of a march in Pensacola against the Ladies Center: "We will surround the death chambers of the city, as the trumpets sound . . . the people will shout 'Let my children go!'" (quoted in Blanchard and Prewitt, 81). "Rescues," Terry proclaims, "are not merely civil disobedience, they are biblical obedience" (127).

In a chapter titled "Called to the Front Lines: How We Can Confront the Enemy and Win the War" in *Operation Rescue* (1988), Terry talks of confrontation to "occupy enemy territory" (194) in a battle against "the unscrupulous doctors, the greedy clinic owners, the misguided feminists, or the biased media" (212). It is a battle in which one stands his ground as a good soldier, a warrior prepared to sacrifice for fellow soldiers. One takes orders and carries them out to the end, fighting to win, prepared to die, and recognizing that "if they don't defeat the enemy, the enemy will defeat them. There is no stalemate, no neutral ground" (216). Terry's imagery incorporates legs and arms torn off children we love as if heralding a twentieth-century myth of Osirus and warns that "child sacrifice is practiced every day. . . . Because the tiny *victims* are *concealed* within the wombs of their mothers, people never hear their silent screams and rarely see their brutalized remains" (141, author's emphasis). In Terry's vision, Satan receives their blood as human sacrifice.

The rhetoric of the antiabortion movement thus puts on the mantle of holy war, moving through its own stations of the cross from prayer, preaching, and missionary work to soldiers in the cause who engage in picketing, stalking, harassing, blockading, arson, bombing, and, eventually, murder. A large-scale 1990 event in Washington, D.C., called Operation Goliath and featuring a group of protestors who called themselves Lambs of Christ, was announced as "an all-out Holy War on the child-killing industry, one mill at a time" (quoted from an Operation Rescue brochure in Ginsburg 1989, 235–236). An extension of such rhetoric finds the defense team of the Pensacola bombers summing up the antiabortion movement's view of itself as "pure peacemakers. . . . They are preaching the gospel in their own way" (Paul Shimek, defense lawyer for Kaye Wiggins, quoted in Blanchard and Prewitt 1993, 94).

The holy week image of Los Angeles in 1989 becomes a Summer of Mercy in 1991 in Wichita, Kansas, and a Spring of Life in 1992 in Buffalo, New York. The anti-abortion movement moves from a civil disobedience rescue operation based on the rights of "unborn children" to a holy war that sponsors an Army of God (the *nom de guerre* of a fringe group first heard of in 1982—Risen and Thomas 1998, 4): "We the remnant of God-fearing men and women of the United States of Amerika, do officially declare war on the entire child killing industry. . . . Our Most Dread Sovereign Lord God requires that whosoever sheds man's blood, by man shall his blood be shed!" (quoted in Risen and Thomas 351).

Militants in the antiabortion holy war preach an incendiary gospel accompanied by guerrilla manuals (the *Army of God Manual*, discovered in 1993,[16] and Joseph Scheidler's *Closed: 99 Ways to Stop Abortion*, 1985[17]), philosophic justifications of violence (Michael Bray's *Time to Kill*, 1994,[18] Paul Hill's *Should We Defend Born and Unborn Children with Force?*, 1993,[19] and Randall Terry's *Accessory to Murder*, 1990), political treatises such as Ronald Reagan's *Abortion and the Conscience of the Nation*,[20] and an assassination website known as the Nuremberg Files (christiangallery.com/atrocity) run by the American Coalition of Life Advocates. In such a war, abortion protestor Joseph Scheidler's 1985 demonstration placard "Abortion is murder" gives way first to Michael Bray's sign in 1993, "EXECUTE murderers, abortionists,"[21] only to be superseded in 1998 by the Nuremberg Files' wanted posters and death lists on the Internet. Assuming the mantle of peacemaker, sponsoring holy weeks of violence, and annointing lambs of God to wreak its vengeance, Operation Rescue wages war in a rhetorical reading of the Bible that is as close to the Apocalypse as its fanatical followers can take it.[22]

Roles in the Abortion Wars

The Courts

The antiabortion movement has adopted a model of civil disobedience that washes over uncomfortable historical differences and reductionist rhetoric to construct a story of an evil (the death-camp clinic) that necessity requires be met by a lesser evil (rescue of fetuses) and for which agents of rescue shall be persecuted (as prisoners for Christ) and for which they must suffer (being jailed for breaking the code of silence).

In a story of opposed forces clashing in the darkness to capture a holy grail, the legal and medical professions and reproductive woman play inimical roles, antiabortion rescuers supply the needed warriors, and the innocent fetus the prize to be won. At the top of the story food chain, the courts oversee a system of justice in which "guilty" abortionists are extended the protection of the law while "innocent" children are left to die at their hands and "heroic" rescuers are made to suffer police brutality, incarceration, punitive fines, and jail sentences. A placard at a protest in Appleton, Wisconsin, in 1985 addresses judges in terms of "Black Robes/Black Hearts/Red Hands/Dead Babies" while prolife activists defend their own roles at clinic protests in signs that read "Saving Babies Is No Crime" and "No Jail/No Bail/ No Abortion" (Risen and Thomas 1998, 212). Setting a higher standard for a court of justice in which the guilty are sentenced to eternal punishment, Terry contends that those who hand over their children to be murdered (mothers, doctors, judges, and church leaders) might escape justice here and now but not forever: "ruthless criminals may slip through the cracks of *this world's justice*, they will only fall into the *courtroom of heaven*—where *no deals are made*, no crimes excused, no *details hidden*, no lies told" (Terry's emphasis 1988, 152).

Reflected in the title of Terry's chapter on the courts, the judiciary represents "A New Breed of Tyrants" (1990); Justice Blackmun's majority opinion in *Roe v. Wade* is called a "judicial fiat," or, in a quote from Justice White, a "flagrant display of 'raw judicial power'" (quoted in Terry 115). Terry's picture is one of judge-made common law replacing the legislative process and bypassing the will of the people. Just as he considers that abortion providers have betrayed medical principles, so does he consider that Supreme Court justices have betrayed justice, having "substituted their own laws. . . . [and] [r]epeatedly ignored the intentions of the framers of the Constitution and run roughshod over laws and practices of public morality" (117). If the Constitution is what judges say it is, and since judges, in Terry's view, make law "on the ever-shifting sands of *stare decisis*" (legal precedent in case law), it is the courts that have brought "institutionalized anarchy" to America. It is the Supreme Court whose "rulings tear asunder the moral fibre of the nation" (116). On the level of the lower courts,[23] Terry contends that "prolifers regularly are denied fair trials by a jury of their peers." He protests that a "jury is supposed to represent the conscience of the community" (124), and he appeals to juries for jury nullification verdicts that disregard prevailing law to express a moral or political statement.[24] Judges are urged to accept the "necessity defense" (the commission of a lesser crime to prevent a greater one) and award prolife verdicts.

The Medical Profession

Antiabortion rhetoric's critique of the courts is extended to what it considers the courts' instrument, the medical profession. Playing the medical ethics card, the rhetoric argues that "abortionists have betrayed their profession" and "Hospitals have betrayed their callings" (Terry 1990, 72, 74).[25] A sign displayed outside the Pensacola courthouse pictured a garbage can filled with blood-soaked dolls as a reminder of hospital dumping bins for fetal waste. Joseph Scheidler, not one to shrink from realistic street theater, is reported to have retrieved aborted fetuses from a clinic's disposal and displayed them in front of an "abortuary" (*Chicago Sun Times* May 7, 1987, in Terry 110). The Nuremberg Files website calls for the assassination of abortion providers under an equally graphic signature banner depicting fetal limbs dripping blood. Not one to be outdone, Randall Terry visualizes the medical process itself with bloody, if anatomical, precision: "Nurses must account for all the baby's body parts that are scraped from the uterus during the abortion. If a tiny hand or limb is not recovered from the womb, the patient can develop serious problems later. . . . They must continually deaden their consciences to the horrors they experience on a daily basis" (1988, 125). In rallies like one in Pensacola, speeches rhetorically shaped the movement's preferred view of the physician: "I wouldn't mind seeing those heathen doctors' hands cut off and hung on a string for the world to see" (quoted in Blanchard and Prewitt 1993, 84).

Terry attacks the revised post-*Roe* American Medical Association "Principles of Medical Ethics" for its willingness to accommodate murder within the profession (1990, 73). Healers, he holds, have become killers, and hospitals "originally dedicated to healing and convalescing are now also locations of deliberate death" (75). Why, Terry asks, "would we allow the hands that murder a defenseless baby . . . to then deliver our children?" (74). In prolife terms, the "pro-abortion" medical community's only defense is to argue that "they are doctors and they know best" (79), but faced with the growing stigma of abortion, abortion providers "are in many cases now viewed as second-class physicians" (*New York Times*, January 8, 1990, A1, quoted in Terry 79).

Antiabortion rhetoric distinguishes abortionists from the medical profession and describes their role as dissonant with an acceptable medical identity. Abortion is isolated as a solitary, individual, "selfish" choice within a much larger body of actions that expresses social responsibility; it represents a thread of "uncaring" in a larger "caring" fabric. Having traditionally been associated with the principled communal construct from which its privileges and authority emanate and which gives it legitimacy, medicine must expel those who stand with abortionists from its camp to redeem itself. In these terms, abortion is anti-doctor, for doctors who accept it practice against the ethics of their profession, in conflict with their conscience, and inconsistent with "a caring and concerned medical identity" (304), so that "places of healing have been turned into charnel houses" (305).

Reproductive Woman

The third role renarrated in antiabortion constructions, and the agentive figure most central to the abortion debate, is the reproductive woman. In one reading of reproductive woman, prolife rhetoric asserts a natural law of motherhood supported by the Old Testament law of the father. The rhetoric reads "choice" as murder, an act for which disobedient mothers will be punished and for which redemption must be sought under the natural order of male dominance. Women in prolife rhetoric are to be protected from disobedience, from abortion, which has the potential to impose "Disorder upon the world in perpetuity" (Lake 1984, 435). Exemptions from this new law—for rape, incest, the life or health of the mother, or deformation of the fetus—would allow women to escape redemption and thereby imperil redemption of the social order itself. The fetus, by contrast, represents perfect innocence, or the condition that must be restored in the "symbolic moral landscape" of an "innocent" future (438). The continuity of grace or innocence has thus been disrupted by woman's breach of order, leading humankind into a lower condition. Either the transcendent law of prolife rhetoric will reverse that condition or society will risk continuing the slippery slide into eugenics and euthanasia, forms of what antiabortion rhetoric considers social suicide. The fetus—what we have all been and can be, innocent, again—represents a continuity that can be reasserted through "fixed and constant" moral law (Solomon 1980, 59), as opposed to inconstant and shifting human law.

The question raised by such a moral vision is who shall assume the mantle "of societal conscience" and who the role of witness to testify at Judgment Day. Figuring the Apocalypse in lurid sidewalk speech, performances, and acts of violence at abortion clinics, prolife steps up to perform as such a conscience and to call the fetus to testify as witness (Shaw and Spinney 1999, 60–67). Justice is thereby enacted by the innocent on the guilty in response to the earlier act of abortion, authorized by a vigilantism that exacts its own informal, local law based on biblical texts. The image of such justice, in a further rhetorical flourish, is expressed in a controlling "pair of hands sheltering an infant with the caption 'Life is in your hands'" (Solomon 1980, 59–60).

The movement or pattern of the imposed law of prolife rhetoric is thus that of a fall redeemed, that is, of a descent from grace followed by redemption (Lake 1984). In terms of that pattern, clinic violence is an apocalypse necessary to purge evil and clear the way to a redemption that the formal legal order has foresworn. Unredeemed, society will fall to a valueless totalitarian order of which abortion is a sign, a realm of rational utility in which human life is held in little regard. The fetus, as a sign of the future and symbol of life itself, is thus privileged above the woman who, after all, having fallen from grace, is guilty of killing her own offspring.

Because woman in antiabortion ideology is the lynch-pin upon which social order rests, getting her to return to the nurturing role of mother is critical to prolife rhetoric. One attempt to accomplish that appears in Jerry Falwell's antiabortion book *If I Should Die Before I Wake*. . . . Falwell "appropriates a central feminist narrative (women as sexual victims of men and patriarchy, and abortion liberates them) and renarrates it from a born-again point of view" (Susan Harding 1990, 79). His cover page pictures an empty bassinet awaiting the absent child who does not get to be born. Jesus is himself an absented figure, the implied addressee of the title line, He whom the prayer implores should take the soul of His implied "littlest angel." In Falwell's text, choice is reinvented as adoption rather than abortion. As a choice, it still leaves the cradle empty from the biological mother's point of view, but it can be recast to read that the cradle is awaiting the presentation of a birth. The prayer, rescripted for adoption, would then address the mother who disappears her unworthy self for her baby's sake (91–92). The preferred choice here is a surrogacy for Christian couples. The pregnant mother has been reinscribed as herself an innocent victim redeemed by the selfless act of giving her child up to adoption (86). Thus the first, rescued birth of the fetus is matched by a second, redeemed birth of the unmarried teenage girls who constitute the subject of Falwell's text and to whom the text is directed. Among those of the Christian right, teenage pregnant girls are retrieved by overcoming adversity to choose motherhood (Ginsburg 1990, 70–71), reframing pregnancy as heroic choice.

The difficulty of recalling women to the preferred prolife role is summed up by Randall Terry in his reaction to those he considers hard-core feminists: "What do child-killing Marxism, lesbianism, witchcraft, and 'vibrators' (for female masturbation) have in common? You guessed it: the National Organization of Women (NOW)" (1990, 43). Encapsulated in Terry's question are the primary targets of prolife misogyny. They represent the three forces that lead women like Betty Friedan, as Terry puts it, to compare "the plight of motherhood/homemaker to being in a concentration camp" (45). The first is economic independence from men as women achieve the financial freedom that liberates them from their biological dependence on men. Freedom from patriarchy through displacement of the biblical law of the father is the second. The third is celebration of a female-centered existence with feminism as a "Goddess" at its core in a new matriarchy. The exemplars of inimical feminism are identified by Terry as divorce, working women, public schools, socialism, state-run daycare, homosexuality, and extramarital sex.

In Terry's re-narration, the presumed feminist "replacement" order leads to a society in which if a man gets a woman pregnant, "threatening to leave, he tells her to kill the baby. If she keeps the child, she often raises it alone" (1990, 51). Under feminism, children who survive "can neither read nor write; but they can fornicate, rebel against authority, and flounder in the sea of humanist amorality" (49). Nevertheless, because feminists regard their reproductive role as an instrument of repression, "Feminism will always demand child-killing. . . . Abortion is the core of NOW's agenda" (52). Indeed, a woman can span two worlds as a feminist, "retaining both one's femininity (by getting pregnant) and one's feminism (by killing your child)," all in the name of "serving the goddess" (53). The goddess, Terry reminds us, is not only "godless" but associated through the anti-Christ core of feminism with witchcraft. This witchcraft is taught in women's studies courses and feminist conventions and presumably practiced at abortion clinics: "One has to wonder what happens with the blood of innocent children murdered in this killing center"

(56). Antiabortion rhetoric, finally, closes off the possibility that aborting mothers can contribute anything of consequence to a dialogue on children. As Terry says, "Anyone who promoted the wholesale slaughter of children has forfeited any right to talk about the children who escaped your knife" (58).

Another, perhaps more culturally potent, rhetoric—ultrasound technology—comes into play in the construction of reproductive woman. Having to some extent framed antiabortion rhetoric, ultrasound has so conditioned the way the pregnant woman is perceived that the contemporary perspective on a woman as well as a fetus can be said to be mediated by technology (Haraway 1991, 189). Intrusive peeking into the uterus makes the pregnant woman transparent and illustrates the popular prolife expression "if there were a window on the pregnant woman's stomach, there would be no more abortions" (as quoted in Taylor 1998, 37; see Ginsburg 1989, 104). Indeed, this very transparency is used by Paul Hill, the assassin of abortion doctor John Britton in 1994, to justify his crime; his defense-of-others defense merely advises the judge that he "need only watch an ultrasound of an abortion being performed" (as quoted in Taylor 15). A pregnant woman under ultrasound, as a result, not only risks being disenfranchised as a citizen, but she risks the enfranchisement within herself of a citizen with greater rights than she has (Franklin 1991, 201).[26]

The Fetus

The figure held to have the highest value in prolife rhetoric is the fetus. The priority slogans of the antiabortion movement—"Abortion is murder" and "The fetus is a child"—figure the fetus endowed with personhood and, thereby, with rights commensurate with those of the pregnant woman. Secondary slogans tie a fetus' rights to a woman's rights, pointing to a fetus' "right to her own body" (bumper stickers, National Right to Life Committee, in Newman 1996, 19) and to "Equal rights for unborn women" (20). The fetus' rights-bearing humanity becomes the message of an "abortion war" memorial in Fargo, North Dakota. Set beside a war veterans' memorial, it is dedicated to "all of our nation's children who have died by abortion" (Ginsburg 1990, 69). In advertising slogans, the fetus' humanity is adapted to a personal appeal to individual readers or viewers: "This is what *your* feet looked like at 10 weeks old"; "You began as a fetus" (Condit 1990, 90).

Within the variety of slogans and appeals created by prolife rhetoric around fetal images, a distinctive opposition is maintained between two ways of seeing. The first presents plastic fetuses, baby dolls, fetal ultrasound images, and born children meant to capture the image of an autonomous whole entity. One such image, a plastic pocket pet, is provided in a thumb-size version as a promotional device at demonstrations. These fetal dolls are given such names "as Baby Hope, Young One, and Precious Preborn" (Oaks 2000, 92). The second presents the severed limbs of the

broken fetus blasted by abortion to suggest the parade of horrors wreaked on innocent life. The desecrated fetus, the fetus of dismembered or reassembled fetal parts,
is the fetus meant to shock, to provoke horror.

On the abortion clinic site, fetal images and fetal rhetoric have instrumental
value in turning pregnant women away. Protestors, some wearing necklaces of
bloody doll limbs, perform street theater in which dolls are hacked to pieces with a
prop machete (Shaw and Spinney 1999, 62–63); fetal coffins and fetal waste are exhibited, and bloody plastic fetuses are thrust in women's faces. Accompanied by
seven-foot crucifixes and wooden rosaries and by blue and pink balloons, sidewalk
counselors chant such slogans as "Where would you be if your mother chose abortion?"; "Want to see what a picture of a dead baby looks like?"; or "My mom chose
life." To an escort who appears to be the pregnant woman's parent, the counselor
might ask "Was your grandchild murdered today?"; referring to the presumed father
of the fetus, the line might be, "If this man really loves you . . . he won't be taking
you to an abortion clinic to kill your child." In one demonstration (in 1981, Prince
George's County, Maryland, Risen and Thomas 1998, 83), "Save the whales; save
the snail darter; kill the babies" is proposed as an ironic slogan. Considered "a willing participant in her child's death" who therefore must be touched and won (125),
the mother is addressed with such lines as "That's your son or daughter," "That little
baby's heart is beating," "You don't have to kill your baby," "Pray for the babies who
are scheduled to die here today," "You know this is an abortion clinic where they
murder babies?" and "There will be a day when you want to have children" (Shaw
and Spinney 54–55).

The image of the fetus as a whole child, by contrast, is an image designed to in-
spire reverence or awe, a contender that can meet the challenge of competing rights
posed by the pregnant mother. Ultrasound, as it were, gives birth to a fetus lying in
wait to be discovered.[27] The "child" is introduced in a presentation that "shows" the
baby already autonomous. It contains within itself all that is necessary to its being,
commanding from within rather than partnering with its mother. Bypassing the
process that leads from blastocyst and embryo to fetus, the developed fetus expresses
the sense of a finished product, an independent entity separate from the mother's
womb. It has been famously transformed into a new-world traveler, an astronaut
floating free in a fluid amniotic space (Sofia 1984). Umbilical attachments act as a
cord to a mother ship absent from the picture. If the embryo is space child, the
image seems to suggest, the mother must be empty space (Petchesky 1987, 270).
The generative role of the woman is usurped in space by cosmic man as a symbol of
the future, of life, of generativity. The rhetoric suggests here that earth itself is an
embryo whose womb is space (Sofia 57), raising abortion as a metaphor to the level
of planetary extinction. Aborting woman becomes, in this reading, the enemy of
earth.[28] She is useful only as the site of the fetus, as a space pod the walls of whose
womb can be stripped away to peer within, rendering the woman rather than the

fetus invisible to our gaze (Petchesky 276–277). With the erasure of the reproductive female, alternate reproductive possibilities pose themselves, including the ectogenic fetus (gestation outside the body) and the pregnant male (an abdominal pregnancy that puts a spin on the pathenogenic archetype) (Squier 1995, 113, 117, 124–129). Technology itself is raised to the level of generative power as a spermatic tool (Sophia 1984) that sponsors the notion of an extrauterine fetus and, from an interstellar perspective, a deathless embryo capable of independently colonizing intergalactic space. The woman's right to her own body has been superseded in this model by a network of rights belonging to the human collective as a whole. Here, abortion rights and antiabortionism become "discursively intertwined and mutually producing" (Mason 1995, 239), exploding false dichotomies and collapsing their opposition.

In Carol Stabile's terms, "The visual technologies used to isolate the embryo as astronaut, extraterrestial, or aquatic entity have had enormously repressive reverberations in the legal and medical management of women's bodies" (1998, 173–174). The once-utopic womb is now dystopic for the self-generating fetus, "a hostile, infanticidal toxic waste dump" (175). The mother has become a danger from which the government must protect the fetus, enactments of which appear in prosecutions of mothers for fetal abuse. By contrast, the very grounds of fetal personhood in public culture have been changed by the rhetoric of reproductive technology. The public ultrasound fetus is used in an AT&T "reach out and touch someone" ad campaign to focus on a telephone "connecting" its mother and father (Haraway 1997, 176–177); in a Volvo ad in which cars are sold as safe environments, it appears pictured in-utero over the line "Is something inside telling you to buy a Volvo?" (Taylor 1992).

Emancipated as an entity unique unto itself, the fetus is open to being produced as a product of virgin birth (Newman 1996, 2). John Salvi, an assassin of abortion providers, displays the fetus as a Jesus figure on his pick-up truck (referred to in Newman, *New York Times* January 1, 1995, A1). Divinely created without the aid of woman (Sofia 1984, 49), the sacralized fetus is sometimes more than a child; it is a cherub, a homunculus, or a tiny adult. In its most protected guise, it is a newborn's head cradled by a human hand over a slogan that reads "How much does an abortion cost? ONE HUMAN LIFE" (in a Providence, Rhode Island, billboard 1993; Newman, 22). Arising from the hands of some superordinate being, the fetus rises to the stature of Athena birthed from the brow of Zeus. Whatever form it takes, it is disassociated from the mother's womb. It is contrasted to the latter in an opposition that renders the womb a passive receptacle and the fetus an active agent. Once conceived as a "child" endowed with agency, the fetus can lay claim to being a patient in its own right, with its own rights. By implication, if the fetus becomes the patient, the pregnant woman would have no authority over the doctor's treatment of her own body. Indeed, if in the context of fetal therapy and repair, the fetus is a patient for whom an appointment can be made, there ceases to be much of a legal distinction between patienthood and personhood. Once a patient-person, the fetus becomes the cost society is asked to pay for woman's "unnatural" insistence on entering the workplace, competing with men for jobs, and jeopardizing family stability: mothers abort their young. The shift in fetal law then becomes not what harm in pregnancy is done to women, but by them; the former victim has become an assailant; gestation, once natural, is now treacherous (Hartouni 1997, 41).[29]

Historical medical representations of fetal imagery demonstrate how ingrained prolife rhetoric is in cultural images that are already widely accepted. Karen Newman's study (1996) of visual representation of the fetus demonstrates that "increasingly from the mid-seventeenth century on . . . [the fetus] is endowed with seemingly 'gratuitous' detail that exceeds the instrumental function of the obstetrical image. The addition of seemingly innocent minutiae in fetal representation works to render the fetus as 'lifelike' and 'human,' an autonomous individual." The gestating female body is suppressed, and the male role in conception is regarded as formative, "a notion crucial to Aristotelian generation" (44). In a 1973 flyer, the National Right to Life Committee's version of generation appears to have moved little, if at all, from Aristotle's. The appeal raises the question, "Did you 'come from' a human baby? No! You once were a baby" and goes on to ask a similar question about a fetus and a fertilized ovum. Presuming the answer is "no" to all but the fertilized ovum, it concludes that "You were then everything you are today." Nothing, the appeal contends, has been added except nutrition (quoted in Sofia 1984, 56). The fertilized ovum here feeds on a source of food, the mother, with no other relationship between them; the life-giving moment has already occurred in the injection of the sperm that awakens the egg. Always an adult, Dr. J. C. Willke of the National Right to Life Committee asserts, the embryo is not what we came from or become but what we are and have throughout been (Sofia 57). The fetus so delivered is the preborn human, an inverted image of the "postnatal fetus" (Hartouni 1997, 35, 39), a term that Congressman Henry Hyde famously uses to refer to himself on the born side of the birthing divide.

Conclusion

Antiabortion rhetoric's construction of the roles played in the abortion debate by the courts, physicians, women, and the fetus gives rise to an unforgiving oppositional narrative that leaves little room for compromise. The Supreme Court, for example, is modeled as a group of justices with bloody hands who should themselves be tried at a Nuremberg Court of abortion. Their crimes would, in this construction, be most fully addressed at an otherworldly court of higher justice. Held up to an uncompromising light, physicians find they are identified with Nazi doctors, hired assassins, and medical experimentation and are attacked for killing the innocent to cure the guilty. Presented as violators of their professional oath to do no harm, they are depicted not as those who heal but as those who kill. They are accused of adopting an uncaring role within a caring community, a role that is dissonant with their medical identity and which denies their obligation to the fetus as patient. Women fare no better, for they are presented as having violated the very laws of nature, having denied the sacrosanct role of mother and undermined the institution of motherhood. Choice is constructed as choice for self as opposed to family and community, such that a woman who aborts puts her soul at risk. To protect her prospects for redemption and the redemption of society itself—whose order she has undermined by her "choice"—antiabortion rejects any exemptions from its law. It refuses waivers for the life or health of the mother, for rape, incest, or for a nonviable fetus. Woman's choice has, in this rhetoric, become a slippery slope into social suicide, so that justice requires both vigilance and vigilantism. To prevent the larger apocalypse in which mothers killing their young inverts natural law, a lesser apocalypse of clinic violence and abortion-doctor murders is mandated.

Balanced against the negative forces of the courts, physicians, and women, the fetus is pictured standing alone. It is the true standard-bearer of rights-bearing humanity, that which all of us—man and woman—once were and that which, therefore, communally represents all our rights. Dismembered, the fetus invokes the refusal of innocence and the horror of dismantled hope. The rhetoric surrounding its appearance associates it with the bloodied mantle of sacrifice and the suicide of a people and its future. The fetus eclipses in its presentation the value of woman as procreator, supplanting her historically privileged position as a figure of generativity and as a social resource to be revered and protected.

It remains for us to ask what is the potential of such rhetoric. Clearly, women risk being reduced rhetorically to the role of child endangerers and potential aborters, identified as anti-mothers and female monsters in what Anna Tsing (1990) refers to as "the ongoing production and negotiation of gender" (282). In society's efforts to avoid blame for the public tragedy of having failed to protect its young, women may well find themselves at the small end of the funnel, so that any part they play in trying to access their rights or to protect their bodies may come to be criminalized, and infanticide or child abuse (crimes) and abortion (a right) may become conflated throughout pregnancy. Indeed, such a process presently appears to be the intention of prolife efforts in the area of "partial-birth" or "late-term" dilation and extraction abortions.

The legal rhetoric of good/bad mother, good/bad Samaritan, and slave/slavemaster confirms for the abortion debate an oppositionality that has often seemed almost impossible to overcome. But it also reminds us that opposed constructions can represent alternative as well as default positions in a conversation that leads to shared values. Indeed, any discourse that is to pretend to represent the body politic as a

whole is going to have to incorporate both "good" mothers—patriarchal construction—and "bad" mothers—a rights-bearing construction of working women and
those marginalized by class or race. As we take one final look at the rhetoric of abortion and the stakes it poses, the prospect of arriving at a view not only of women but
of abortion rights that incorporates a broader range of common ground and of a social network that embraces a community of values seems not altogether impossible.
There is, after all, overlap between certain critical themes in the debate, and the
possibilities for disagreement are not—in spite of all the noise and heat created at
the extreme ends of it—infinite in either their number or their extent. The greater
flexibility demonstrated in contemporary public relations ad campaigns suggests, indeed, that we may have arrived at a place where there is at least as much light as
there is heat. We may be at the beginning of an understanding on both sides—at
least in the more populous mainstream of the debate—of both core and overlapping
values that can be discussed, tolerated, or shared. The history of the development of
abortion rhetoric, particularly in advertisements, certainly shows that the debate
has moved through hysteria and oppositionality to a point where vilification is less
viable, virulence has been marginalized, and humanity has broken free of its fetters
with a desire on both sides to work for broader and less divisive appeals. The prospect of having to tolerate an underlying extremism on the part of minority-fringe
elements may have to be accepted. That concession in itself is, however, just a part
of accepting that nothing is ever truly settled, just agreed upon until it needs to be
addressed anew.

Notes

1. The failure of narrative authority is itself problematic, for the inability to contain or control conflict allows the noise of chaos and cataclysm to thrive. The seamlessness of func-
   tional narratives cracks as narratives disintegrate into meaningless fragments (Langer
   1991, xi). Cultural values are left unaffirmed and necessity takes precedence over principle. Because narratives in collapse have been argued to exist outside of history, they have
   little hope of recovering subjectivity and community, which are critical to the ability to
   create continuity and to restore a way of "being-in-the-world" (Ricoeur 1965, xv).
2. She must resist overidentifying with her fetus even as a means of gaining her own identity.
   As in *Planned Parenthood v. Casey*, she must merge her story with the story of the fetus and
   balance its interests with hers to claim her rights.
3. On race issues, see Harris (1990), Jones (1993), Peggy Cooper Davis (1993, 1997), Angela
   Davis (1981), Roberts (1991, 1995), and Ross (1998).
4. Faye Ginsburg (1993) acknowledges the difficulty she had representing fairly the antiabortion subjects in her study. By focusing on their interpretations, acknowledging the differences between herself and her subjects, and staying within a historical rather than a political context (165), she was able to preserve a separation of researcher and subject that
   made "sensible challenging cases" (175). Ginsburg, like some others (see Wedam 1997),
   was thus led to appreciate a broader range of ideological positions among antiabortion advocates than she had earlier anticipated. Such a discovery revealed ideological overlaps

between antiabortion and proabortion supporters that she had not expected, including support for women's economic and political equality, rejection of the materialization of human relations, and an acceptance of some degree of feminist thought woven into life choices that were made. Ginsburg's subjects became oppositional largely to legitimate their own choices for motherhood over wage labor.

5. Elfriede Wedam (1997) looks at styles of moral reasoning to distinguish between differing antiabortion positions, concluding that one end of the range posits a morally ambiguous and complex ethic of care while the opposite end endorses a simplistic and absolutist ethic of justice. The latter sponsors a logical consistency and an oppositionality that refuses exceptions and renders all abortion wrong, for only one interest counts—that of the fetus. The former adopts a contextualizing approach that weighs interests and negotiates enriched solutions with the potential to benefit both parties, where possible, keeping a variety of options open. The difference between the two positions is thus reduced to making a choice where one has choices as opposed to having no choice, that is, the difference between multidimensional and unidimensional reasoning. Wedam concludes that whereas the morally complex and more highly ambiguous approach allows an antiabortion group to engage proabortion groups through overlapping areas of agreement, it lacks the clarity and appeal to core group members that simple-issue simplistic reasoning has. Within core groups, absolutist logic thus ensures long-term cohesion.

6. Where the prochoice story of a pregnant woman's rights is one of women as victims of men, the prolife tale in the film "The Silent Scream" (a pseudo-medicotechnical reduction of the fetus-uterus schema to a solitary tale told "from the victim's vantage point" [narrator of film, quoted in Petchesky 1987, 266]) is that of the fetus as a victim of women (Condit 1990, 63; Givner 1994). The prochoice images of the coat hanger dripping blood and of a dead woman naked on the floor—both of which require some sense of distant history to act as emotionally affective signs (Condit, 91)—are met by the more immediate prolife threat to an innocent and vulnerable "child," whose severed limbs and broken body have been thrust immediately before us.

7. Randall Lake (1986) looked at the metaethics of antiabortion rhetoric, concluding that they rendered "compromise unnecessary, unthinkable, and unethical" (479). Such a morality is intuitively derived and "supersedes discursive argument" (495). Lake's subjects support one end of Elfriede Wedam's continuum of antiabortion thought (1997) in their rejection of compromise and refusal to acknowledge differing circumstances and consequences as counterweights to the rightness of their intuition. The proabortion stance is contrasted as one in which no human action is intrinsically right or wrong but, rather, must be contextualized. Lake nevertheless finds within the choice camp a basis of belief that is consistent with what he finds in the life camp: the principle of justice. The application of the principle may differ—so that for the choice camp justice applies to a woman's right to limit reproduction rather than to the fetus' right to be born—but it is the same principle of justice based on an instinctive belief that was adopted in both camps. Lake's analysis suggests, moreover, that it may only be the contextualizing moral ambiguity of proabortion reasoning that prevents more of its adherents from adopting a view as extreme in its "allness" as antiabortion rejection of every abortion (that is, a position that embraces abortion for any reason at any point in a pregnancy). See here as well Kathy Rudy (1996).

8. Keith Cassidy (1994) examines the limits in the abortion debate of rhetoric and ideological positions in terms of "the sources and nature of authority and about basic legitimating principles" (9) in a democracy.

9. Of interest here in terms of fringe advertisements, see Von Rosenvinge Sheppard (1993).

10. A reference to a tactic developed by antiabortion protestors at the 1988 Democratic National Convention in Atlanta, Georgia.

11. Roy Ward (1993) contends that "The most obvious answer to the question of what the Bible says about abortion is 'nothing'" (391). He addresses directly the quote "Before I formed you in the womb I knew you" (398) from Jeremiah 1.2 and concludes that its usefulness to the antiabortion cause is undermined by the Bible's general use of the term "nephesh" or "breath" to indicate the life of a person. On the linguistic evidence, he rejects the idea that in Jeremiah the fetus is regarded as a person before birth and interprets the passage to mean that God merely had foreknowledge before the existence of the person (399).

12. Terry's reference to those who, kidnapped and enslaved, were "rescued" by the abolitionist underground railroad (which he compares to abortion clinic "rescues") ignores the fact that Operation Rescue attracted among its members the Christian conservative Right, right-wing militants, and ex-Ku Klux Klan members. This juxtaposition proved an unforgivable irony to many in the old civil rights community.

13. Many in the civil rights community rejected the analogies drawn by Terry, and black leaders at the Atlanta Democratic National Convention in August 1988 refused to accept Operation Rescue's representation of itself as "the successor to the civil rights movement" (Risen and Thomas 1998, 279). The *Atlanta Journal Constitution* reported, "Civil rights demonstrators fought for rights—access to jobs, housing, voting booths, schools and public facilities. . . . The anti-abortion forces have a much narrower goal: it is to deny women their right to a legal medical procedure of the most personal sort" (quoted in Risen and Thomas, 279). For his part, Terry disassociated himself from operation Rescue's recruitment of Christian conservatives, right-wing militants, and ex-members of the Ku Klux Klan. He defended his refusal to pay a U.S. district court-ordered fine (resulting from an Operation Rescue action in May 1988 in New York) by claiming, "For me to pay fifty thousand dollars to NOW and various killing centers would be akin to asking the NAACP to pay fifty thousand dollars to the Ku Klux Klan or the Jewish Defense League to pay fifty thousand dollars to the Young Nazis" (Terry 1990, 129).

14. A section titled "Primum Non Nocere" (first do no harm, a part of the Hippocratic Oath) begins "Doctors had become executioners and murderous barbarians" (Terry 1990, 71). Terry's remarks on Margaret Sanger, founder of Planned Parenthood, provide, as well, a link between birth control and Nazi eugenics: "She, like Hitler, was determined to build a master race—with perhaps a little less violence" (29). In a reflection of Terry's rhetoric, Paul Hill (who murdered doctor John Britten) considered the murder of another abortion doctor "as good as Doctor Mengele being killed" (March 15, 1993, on the Phil Donohue show, quoted in Risen and Thomas 1998, 345).

15. The slavery story is countered by prochoice rhetoric with the repeal of the Eighteenth Amendment, the prohibition amendment, as well. The repeal provides a precedent for rejecting the invasion of privacy and violation of individual free choice. Failure to provide for the latter characteristically American and constitutionally protected values, prochoice argues, would guarantee widespread breaking of the law and loss of confidence in the legal system.

16. The Army of God, an underground group, produced the *Army of God Manual,* an anonymous work that served as a guerrilla handbook. The manual was passed from hand to hand through an underground activist network and was unknown to the government for years. It was discovered by the FBI in 1993 buried in the backyard of Rachelle Shannon, an activist who was subsequently convicted of killing abortion doctor George Tiller in

Wichita, Kansas. The manual went into its third edition and was ultimately made available on the Internet. Its editors describe its usefulness in their introductory notes as "a How-To Manual of means to disrupt and ultimately destroy Satan's power to kill our children, God's children." Its recommended activities range from blocking abortion clinic toilet drainpipes and vents with concrete, dumping truck loads of manure in front of clinic doors, and sabotaging clinic electrical lines, phones lines, and alarm systems to reclaiming fetal wastes from hospital dumps for reburial. Activists learned not only how to plant pipe bombs under clinics and how to track abortion providers but how to use police scanners and disguises to avoid detection and how to slow down the court system if caught. (See the website armyofgod.com.)

17. Joseph Scheidler established the Life Action Network (PLAN) by 1984 (the date, significantly, of the publication of his manual for clinic protests, *Closed: 99 Ways to Stop Abortion*). The first documented act of violence may have been a March 1986 arson in Eugene, Oregon, at a Planned Parenthood clinic, but the escalation to a kidnapping of an abortion doctor, Hector Zevallos, and his wife in Edwardsville, Illinois, in 1982 (Risen and Thomas 1998, 74–75) and the 319 acts of violence against 238 clinics from January 1983 to March 1985 (114) meant that PLAN emerged at the crest of a wave of hostility against abortion clinics, the highlight of which was the triple crown of three clinic bombings in Pensacola, Florida, on Christmas Day, 1984. Described by Risen and Thomas, Scheidler "appeared to the public to be like the Sinn Fein leaders in Ireland who serve as a political front for the terror squads of the Irish Republican Army" (115). Most critically, Scheidler's book and PLAN gave the movement the strategic ability to turn uncoordinated, local activities that varied from city to city into a systematic nationwide campaign.

18. Michael Bray and his wife were well known in the antiabortion movement. Jayne Bray was a featured player in *Bray v. Alexandria Women's Health Clinic*, 506 U.S. 263 (1993), and Michael Bray not only served time in jail for his role in a clinic bombing in Montgomery County, Maryland, but was one of the defendants in *Planned Parenthood v. ACLA*, 41 F. Supp. 2d 1130 (D. Or. 1999), a case centering on an antiabortion website that advocated killing abortion providers. Released in 1989, he emerged to become a leading figure in the violent wing of the antiabortion movement as a member of the Army of God and as a force behind the most violent activities of the activists: the murder of clinic doctors and the posting of their names on a website targeting them for destruction (Risen and Thomas 1998, 78–100). Bray's *Time to Kill* (1994) opened a new era in antiabortion rhetoric. Based on the concept of a "just war," Bray's war in defense of the innocent was justified by a law of retaliation. Armed with their own version of godly force, antiabortion activists were declared justified in the use of direct action in the following terms: "If death is the penalty for killing the innocent, how much more appropriate to protect the innocent even by the use of lethal force against the perpetrator" (42). The failure of the government to stop abortion offers Bray both his justification and his motivation, for government-approved abortionists were, in his view, the sign of an ungodly society. Their murder is thus justified in the same way that regicide would have been justified in the American Revolution. Indeed, Bray finds in abortion "moral ground greater many times over for a revolution in these times than there was in 1776" (170). The revolution he threatens does not stop with ridding communities of abortion clinics and doctors but extends to a change in the social order itself: "The tool which can be used to prevent a death, cause a death, and punish evil-doers, can also be used to alter or replace governments" (150).

19. Hill, who killed an abortion doctor and his escort in 1994, was the party named in *U.S. v. Hill*, 893 F. Supp. 1044 (N.D. Fla 1994).

20. During the 1983 political campaign the essay "Abortion and the Conscience of the Nation" (published as a book in 1984) appeared as a publication in *The Human Life Review* under Ronald Reagan's name. *Time* magazine made the point that "An essay by a sitting President is rare" (quoted in J.P. Mcfadden, "Introduction," Reagan 1984, 7), particularly on the most controversial moral issue of his presidency. Apart from the questionable authorship of the piece—Reagan's campaign team appears to have been a likely source for the essay—and apart from its presumed Lincolnesque qualities, "Abortion and the Conscience of the Nation" is nothing if not a collation of the primary themes of the antiabortion movement at that point in its history.

21. In an Oklahoma City, Oklahoma, event reported in *Planned Parenthood v. ACLA*, 41 F Suppl. 2d 1130 [D. Or. 1999], 1139.

22. On abortion politics, see McDonagh (1996), McKeegan (1992), Petchesky (1990), Solinger (1998, 1994), Staggenborg (1991), Tribe (1990), Diamond (1995), Blanchard (1994), Blanchard and Prewitt (1993), Korn (1996), Kaplan (1995).

23. Terry preferred the more sympathetic lower courts to the Supreme Court, for there clinic protestors experienced some relief, relying on "Sympathetic judges and juries [who] had repeatedly accepted the 'necessity defense'" (Risen and Thomas 1998, 290; 71–73, 140–146). In Fairfax County, Virginia, General District Court in 1977, for example, Judge Lewis Griffith ruled that the defendants maintained a "good Faith belief that their actions were necessary" and that they "acted to stop what they considered to be a crime" (quoted in Risen and Thomas, 71). A decision by the St. Louis County Circuit Court in August 1989 is also quoted approvingly by Terry as "a beacon amidst the darkness of judicial tyranny": "Their violations of the ordinances involved here were necessary as emergency measures to avoid the imminent private injuries of death and maiming of unborn children which . . . [were] occasioned through no fault of the defendants but occasioned by the operation of a lucrative commercial endeavor. The desirability of avoiding death and maiming of unborn children—persons—obviously outweighs the desirability of avoiding the injury sought to be prevented by the ordinances" (quoted in 1990, 133). The St. Louis decision reflects an interpretation of the law by antiabortion attorney Andy Puzer, who helped draft the Missouri statute ruled on in *Webster* (1989).

24. Like the necessity defense, appeals to juries for jury nullification gave some aid and comfort to the movement. But Terry (1990, 124) suggests that such nullification was insufficient to offset the more widespread pattern of contempt of court citations, detention of those who refused to give the court their names (the Baby Doe strategy), the use of "pain compliance" and nunchucks by police against go-limp and body blanket tactics and Atlanta crawlers, seized payrolls and general operating accounts of local organizations, injunctions, buffer zones, large personal fines, and the threat of conspiracy charges and liability claims against churches that supported the protestors. Operation Rescue leaders had to shift personal assets to family members or bankrupt themselves. Vulnerable to charges of contributing to a "continuing criminal enterprise" (Risen and Thomas 1998, 296), church groups became reluctant to get dragged into RICO, KKK Act, and FACE Act suits, drying up the movement's financial backing. Supporters became scarce once the movement turned more violent and arrests involved the federal prosecutory authority offered by FACE rather than more limited local misdemeanor charges (Samuels 1999, 78).

25. The medical profession struggled itself with the ethics of abortion, both historically and in contemporary times (Joffee 1995, 46–52). In an AMA pamphlet dated 1871—at a time when the medical profession in general and allopathic medicine in particular was seeking to assert itself as the dominant scientific and cultural authority (see Starr 1982; Siegel

1992)—abortion doctors are depicted as "educated assassins," "monsters of iniquity," and enemies within the camp (quoted in Olasky 1992). Prolife physician Dr. Barnard Nathanson argues against what Terry calls a "pro-death party line" (1990, 79) ignoring "massive and still-growing data identifying the pre-natal person as a living, valuable, and fully protectable human being" (quoted in Terry 78). The prolife medical argument concludes that those who are doctors and who perform abortions have undermined medical values and have perverted the "scientific/rationalist" basis of humane medicine on behalf of a coercive dogmatic pursuit "driven by the profit motive rather than by principles of care" (Reicher and Hopkins 1996, 306). As invasive surgery with some risk even for healthy women without pathological findings, the prolife perspective maintains, abortion does inevitable psychological and potentially physical harm and betrays medical principles by violating a physician's duty of patient care.

26. Alternatively, women may well find, as Patricia Mann (1995) proposes, that "the boundaries between our own organic selfhood and nonorganic machines" have been broken down to create, in Donna Haraway's terms (1991), a cyborgean image of persons that makes organic motherhood a thing of the past (Mann, 139). When the organic relation of mother and fetus is uncoupled, social offspring become only incidentally the issue of woman's womb and more directly the result of an act of interpersonal agency, leaving as a residue "the idea that the bodily uniqueness of female procreation may be a historically limited phenomenon, and [women] locate their sense of maternal agency on a continuum with many other forms of interpersonal agency in which men participate on potentially equal terms" (144). Indeed, Haraway already sees woman's body as a construction rather than a given and cyborgs as the only forms that have a chance in a postmodern world (discussed in Balsamo 1996, 32–34), a not altogether unwelcome prospect for feminists who have worked long and hard to disarticulate women from the biology and practices of pregnancy (Stabile 1998, 186). In this scenario, women would find themselves part of a network of relations, a set of connections rather than articulated as unique selves (Haraway 1992; Stabile 187). But they would also be open to being constructed in ways that overwhelm their material bodies and, in circumstances not of their own choosing, with all "the promises of monsters" (Haraway 333).

27. See on technology and ultrasound, Hartouni (1993, 1998), Sandelowski (1994), Stanworth (1987), Rothman (1989).

28. Science fiction films provide the ultimate expression of the abortion conflict as one between planetary and interplanetary forces and among humans, mutants, and cyborgs. Films of importance here include Stanley Kubrick's *2001: A Space Odyssey* (1968), James Cameron's *The Terminator* (1984) and *Terminator 2: Judgment Day* (1991), Ridley Scott's *Alien* (1979), James Cameron's *Aliens* (1986), and David Fincher's *Aliens 3* (1992). Some interesting film criticism has been written on this issue, including pieces by Sofia (1984), Squier (1995), Mason (1995), Cobbs (1990), Hurley (1995), Schemanske (1996), Berenstein (1990), Bundtzen (1987), and Rushing (1989).

29. On the fetus, see Buelow (1998), Daniels (1993), Hakin (1997), Markens (1997), and McDonald (1997). For motherhood and the law, see Fineman et al. (1995).

CHAPTER THREE

Cartooning Crisis: Visualizing
the Abortion Wars

Having considered an expansive range of expressions emanating from history, rhetoric, technology, feminism, medicine, and law, it remains to consider cultural constructions centered on abortion from the expressive arts. Absent the constraints of fact and logic that frame professional and technical discourse, such visual and literary expressions as cartoons, fiction, and poetry offer a freer exploration of the imagery and stories that arise from the material of abortion rights discourse. It is that exercise to which the remaining chapters of this work shall be devoted, beginning here with a transitional form—the cartoon—which offers an opportunity to draw a bridge between such public, professional, and political discourses as medicine and law and such personal and aesthetic experiences as the literary and visual arts.

Women and Abortion in Cartoons

In a review of over two hundred cartoons[1] from the post-*Roe* through the post-*Casey* period, three themes are suggested: the violence done in the abortion debate to women, to the Constitution, and to the Supreme Court itself. Pat Oliphant's 1977 cartoon based on God's creation of humans offers a unique starting point for our discussion, both because it is rooted in the foundational nature of procreativity in cultural terms and because it raises necessary gender issues. Taking a figurative leaf from Michelangelo's Creation of Adam, Oliphant's God (Congress) creates woman (or at least the possibility of woman as a fully functioning rights-bearing entity), offering her "abortion aid" on a bed of fetuses, as if from the bones of aborted fetuses. God's gift is treated as a gratuity from on high, as if the right is His to withdraw at will and not a question of woman's having deserved it or having informed His giving it. Adam, the central figure in Michelangelo's Creation, has been displaced in

Oliphant's version, either because he is not a consequential figure in the abortion equation (he has no rights over the unborn child) or because he has no voice (he has no one to speak in his name). At the same time, God/Congress is a male figure and represents the dominating presence of patriarchy, of which Adam is part and from which he benefits.

In the cartoon, Eve/Adam does not give birth to the fetuses on which she is bedded but takes her life from theirs or, alternatively, she gives death to the fetus. Whereas woman is very much present here—she has not been absented, rendered invisible, or made transparent—she is passive, supine, and on the receiving end, so that she cannot be said to represent herself much less give voice to a perspective. On the other hand, she has clear priority over the fetus and has been both individualized and humanized, as the fetus has not. Moreover, she, like Congress/God, is foregrounded as a singular figure whereas fetuses are jumbled in a pile and obscured by her fleshy body, backgrounded, and made part of an undifferentiated mass of like fetuses. In Michelangelo's Creation of Adam, by contrast, God is surrounded by masses of lively children (Eve is tucked under his left arm as he reaches with his right hand for Adam), who frame him as a giver of life; Oliphant's Eve is framed by moribund fetuses as she is a giver of death.

Having displaced her male counterpart, the cartoon Eve becomes a female Adam, carrying humanity's responsibility for its own recreation. She performs in a double-gendered role whose reproductive burden she shall not escape even as she is granted Congress's gift of abortion aid. In an alternate reading, one has to consider whether Adam has not been re-gendered as a woman to suggest that the traditional order has been upset and that women in a liberated society are the link on earth to the powers that be. In such a society, even as Eve is pregnant, she lies on a pile of discarded fetuses, identifying her pregnancy not with procreation but with a further candidate for abortion. A breeding machine whose connection to a life-giving function has been severed, Eve has become dysfunctional in a biological sense and has lost her sense of connection to both the values and needs of the larger community, clearly an image of a selfish personal as opposed to an interconnected social choice.

In a 1992 cartoon by Anne Kelly (Haraway 1997) that also plays on the image of the creation of Adam, woman again replaces Adam while a computer screen with a fetus in the womb replaces God. Alternatively, as the unborn fetus meets the gaze of First Woman, as Donna Haraway reads the cartoon, the two "confront each other as Adam and Eve did in Michelangelo's version of human creation" (186). The fetus can also be constructed as Eve, not-yet-created. If the fetus is Eve, the computer and keyboard constitute the deity, and the female Adam becomes the computer's effect. By contrast, if female Adam is constituted as God, she may be reaching for the keyboard to author the fetus, her file, which she is writing, editing, or potentially deleting: "Certainly the politics of abortion are implicit in this cartoon. Maybe she is reaching for the 'escape' key, or perhaps merely the 'control' key" (186). There is a question, as well, of whether First Woman is not pregnant but merely viewing the spectacle of an artificial life form in which the fetus is a data structure vulnerable to downloading rather than to birth or abortion. The problem of "ontologically confusing *bodies*" (186, Haraway's emphasis) and not disembodiment becomes the focal issue.

Haraway's interrogation of the Kelly cartoon leads to what she considers one inescapable conclusion, that the original has been undone and the story opened up in unexpected ways. To illustrate, she renders it in yet another reading: "The pregnancy is ectopic, to say the least; the fetal umbilical cord and barely visible placenta go off screen on the display terminal, and the electrical cords wander up and off screen from the whole cartoon with no point of attachment in view" (187). In this reading, the computer terminal is like a metafetus. An extrauterine "abortus," its ripped-out umbilical cords are like those in the Lennart Nilsson photographs. Resected by multiple signifiers, the cartoon leads us to question not only what or who is being aborted, but what we should count as choice, how choice relates to life, and for whom this choice is reserved. This final reading is not judgmental but interrogatory, asking us to try on signifiers in new ways and to question whose story this is anyway.

Pregnant women have more commonly been constructed in the cartoon culture in ways that not only implicate their ability to make appropriate social choices but that dictate they make choices that are class bound. A 1977 Herblock cartoon clarifies the class distinction inherent in legal and regulatory constraints that ensure the rights of private patients while leaving the poor to fend for themselves. Standing in front of a "Private Medical Center," a male figure in a business suit advises a young black girl in pigtails and with patches on her pants, "It's very simple—if you could afford children, you could have abortions." *The Louisville Courier-Journal* (*Editorials on File*, June 23, 1977, 835) drives the point home: "what makes the abortion question harder is that a constitutional right is effectively denied to many Americans if its exercise costs money and they don't have enough of it." Chuck Haynies (1977b) turns biblical on this issue in a cartoon in which a robed figure (a conflation of judge and priest) raises one hand in a combined judgment and blessing while he holds in his other hand a newspaper whose headline reads, "Supreme Court Ruling: The (poor) Woman Always Pays." As a tearful woman walks away counting her pennies, the robed figure declaims, "The law giveth and the law taketh away. Blessed be the name of the law." The cartoon is best understood in the context of a Supreme Court Medicaid trifecta (*Maher v. Roe, Beal v. Doe*, and *Peolker v. Doe*) delivered on June 20, 1977, which, in effect, would, according to Justice Brennan's dissent, "coerce indigent pregnant women to bear children they would not otherwise choose to have . . . this coercion can only operate upon the poor, who are uniquely the victims of this form of financial pressure" (*Maher v. Roe* in Shapiro 1995, 106).

A Haynies cartoon (1977a) adds a footnote to the debate as a pregnant woman in one panel reads from a "Compromise Abortion Law" that an abortion "may be performed if pregnancy results from rape or incest (promptly reported)." In a second panel, the same woman, no longer pregnant, reads "or when the life and health of a politician would suffer severe and lasting damage. . . ." As late as 1995 in a Mike Peters cartoon (1995b), the debate still finds the poor with their pregnancies treated as form of punishment if not a political football. The judge renders his verdict on his female defendant: "You've been found guilty of being poor, female, and raped. And we sentence you to nine months hard labor." "Medicaid," in a Don Wright cartoon of the same year, is, indicatively, corrected on a public signboard by an elephant in painter's overalls to read "Medican't."

In a cartoon world, class is thus a clear obstacle to obtaining access to an abortion where public funding is involved. So is a woman's minority status as a teenager where parental notification and consent laws are concerned. Emanating from state legislatures and opening the way to influence efforts that would dissuade the pregnant woman from having an abortion, counseling provisions are implemented by a nurse in a Wasserman cartoon (1995). Here, a patient asks, "Nurse—should I have an abortion?" "That's a very personal decision . . . ," the nurse responds, "and one that I can't make for you. Your congressman will be right in," in effect, leaving medical informed consent in the hands of politicians.

From the physician's perspective, counseling requirements leave the medical provider open to a "gag" rule when, as in *Rust v. Sullivan* (1991), they control his speech. Prohibited in 1988 by federal regulations from counseling pregnant women about abortion in federally funded medical facilities, physicians were held in *Rust* not to have been discriminated against where the government makes a value judgment that favors childbirth over abortion. Having declined to promote abortion, the government's choice does not violate a doctor's free speech rights. The Supreme Court in *Planned Parenthood of Central Missouri v. Danforth* (1976) had already allowed requirements that patients must provide informed consent; in *Planned Parenthood of Southeastern Pennsylvania v. Casey* (1992) it held further that counseling must use persuasive information to retain the pregnancy, and that physicians must do the counseling themselves. Mike Peters (1995a) envisions such a session as it actually might occur. The physician declaims to an increasingly agitated patient across four panels: "What? You want a birth control device?"; "Are you having wanton *sex* with someone, Miss?"; "Aren't you a little young for that, you hussy?"; "How old are you, you pervert? . . . Sixteen? Seventeen? . . ." In the fifth panel, the patient rushes from the room as the physician continues, "Do your parents know about this? What's their phone number?" Relieved, he expresses his satisfaction in the sixth panel: "I enjoy counseling teenagers."

By 1990, at least twenty-two states had passed a parental consent law (*Honolulu Advertiser*, in *Editorials on File* June 26, 1990, 721), and the Supreme Court had upheld its constitutionality (*Bellotti v. Baird*, 1979) so long as a judicial bypass was available as an alternative; a requirement that both parents be notified was rejected

(*Hodgson v. Minnesota*, 1990). A judicial bypass was not, however, the kind of bypass anticipated by Jimmy Margulies (1990) or Signe Wilkinson (1996), both of whom refer their pregnant teenagers to back-alley abortionists who, as opposed to licensed physicians, are able to announce, respectively, "I said I promise I won't tell your parents" and "Butch's abortions, no parental consent required." Bob Englehart (1995), by contrast, gives us a presumably typical family scenario of a teenager approaching both parents. Her query: "If I got pregnant would I have your permission to get an abortion?" Their response, "No." "Then I'd like to have the baby." Their response, "You don't have our permission for that either." Parental consent or notification in the cultural as opposed to the legal arena resolves little in Englehart's version, leaving the abortion issue for minors in as ambiguous a venue as it was prior to such a requirement. One clarification, however, did work to at least bring some consistency to the health care of minors: "It seems crazy," writes the *Honolulu Advertiser* (*Editorials on File* June 26, 1990, 721), "to live in a world where parental permission is needed for a doctor to perform almost any kind of surgical procedure on a minor, where we say no such permission should be required for an abortion." The medical world of the pregnant minor, in these terms, was the obverse of that of a pregnant adult who, having decisional autonomy on any other medical procedure, finds that freedom denied her with abortion.

The obstacles interposed between a woman and access to her abortion rights are pictured by Schorr in terms of a maze (1992) whose entrance is controlled by a nurse. Her invitation that "The doctor will see you now" is complicated by the labyrinthine paths that lead to the physician. In this "Court Approved" maze, the pregnant woman must nevertheless know how to run the obstacles once she is inside if she is to get through. A second maze cartoon by Don Wright (1992a) offers no such gatekeeper, since all paths dead-end before they reach an abortion provider. The maze image itself suggests that luck or trial and error is required to get one through and that one cannot simply enter and receive treatment as a right with Court approval. Moreover, abortion law is structured so that the pregnant woman is denied the appropriate information to run the maze; in fact, she is required to undergo contradictory (antiabortion) instruction about abortion (the maze) to discourage her from even entertaining it as an option (entering the maze). If the woman enters and cannot get through the maze, then she, like the rat for which the experimental maze was designed, is unworthy of the prize at the other end. Indeed, like the rat, the pregnant woman is engaged in an experiment, a human experiment regarding the abortion decision itself.

Tony Auth's view of obstructionist law (1996) invents a version of clinic blockading in which a newly dug, shark-infested moat surrounds an abortion clinic, replacing pro-life picketers; a complicit shovel-wielding Supreme Court justice beside a pile of dirt addresses a female figure outside the moat; as she gazes wistfully across at the clinic on the other side, he advises, "Quit complaining. You still have a right to abortion." Court-originated restrictions abound in cartoons. An earlier, less lethal version by Ed Fisher (1992a) simply depicts a justice holding a hoop in front of an obstacle course that stands between a female figure and an arrow that directs her toward *Roe v. Wade*. A 1992 Bruce Beattie cartoon shows a justice on the steps of the Supreme Court building who announces, "We've added a few more restrictions. Abortions are available from the third Tuesday of every month at 3 a.m. If there's a full moon." A 1998 Don Addis cartoon adds a restrictive prohibition on interstate transport of a minor, referring to regulations that prevent adults from accompanying teenagers for out-of-state abortions. Here, a police officer at the state line interrogates the occupants of a car: "Any fruit, exotic pets or pregnant teens?" John Trever (1992b), by contrast, offers not an abstract or hierarchical obstacle but the justices themselves physically blocking the doorway of the abortion clinic. Prochoice protesters complain to a police officer, "Hey, they can't block free access!! We'll take this all the way to the Supreme Court!" To which the officer replies, "That *is* the Supreme Court. . . ." The role of mediator has shifted to one of immovable object in the face of a now legally resistible abortion right force.

The woman's perspective, indicating the felt experience of abortion regulations, thus presents women in the passive position of objects moved around a board. They are denied a service or kept off a site; rarely are they active agents influencing events. Criminalized in a Nicole Hollander cartoon (1995), women are implicitly compared to sex offenders in an announcement of the defeat of a regulation that would require "a woman seeking an abortion . . .[to] post notice of her intention on the bulletin of her local supermarket . . . At least 72 hours before the procedure and to leaflet parked cars within a 3-block radius of her own home." The female experience from the perspective of the woman herself is perhaps most starkly represented by the torso of a woman wearing a *Roe v. Wade* badge (Rogers 1992). Her shirt reads, "I survived the Reagan Court." A figure depicted without a head (it does not think for itself) and therefore no mouth (it has no voice), woman has "survived" but only as a truncated torso. Tony Auth's version of a late-term abortion cartoon in 1997 takes an equally morbid turn, borrowing a leaf from an Edgar Allan Poe story as a woman is crushed between two walls, one reading "Obstacles to early abortion" and one reading "Ban on late-term abortion." The caption reads, "Choice—What a beautiful life," a play on the prolife slogan "Life—What a beautiful choice."

Pregnant women are faced in late twentieth-century cartoons with few choices, and those choices are further constrained by burdens allowed by *Planned Parenthood v. Casey* so long as they are not severe or unreasonable. *Casey's* new "undue burden" standard[2] could, in theory, act in combination with the state's compelling interest in protecting fetal life from conception to "justify the complete prohibition of all abortions or at least all nontherapeutic abortions" (Brownstein 1994, 879 n4). Indeed, some commentators consider that, save for spousal notification, there has been no burden that Justice O'Connor, who originated the standard, has not been able to embrace (Estrich and Sullivan 1989, 119, 137ff).[3] Even if we were to separate those burdens that provide a coercive constraint from those that are minimal and relate to a valid state purpose, a plethora of regulations still fall between these extremes (134).[4] So long as they have a "conceivable relationship to health," health regulations that are mere pretexts pass national review (138–139), as do cost and availability considerations, waiting periods, and informational counseling requirements (based on O'Connor's *City of Akron v. Akron Center for Reproductive Health* 1983 dissent).

Considering the pregnant woman's experience, a Hollander cartoon (1996) requires a homework assignment in which a student must illustrate the phrase "Undue Burden": "'Heck,' I said to the Reporter as I struggled toward the clinic door through a crush of jeering lunatics while carrying a battery-powered neon letter 'A' strapped to my back, 'I don't mind the sign . . . I just wish I didn't have to be blindfolded.'" Hollander's writing sample, for all its outlandishness, is no less onerous than the potentially more serious standard to which James Bopp's partial birth analysis would subject women, that is, that late-term pregnancies have "constitutionally assumed the burden of carrying the child to term" (Bopp and Cook 1998, 47); that delivering the head of a child is no undue burden, having already carried the child to term; and that the burden is not one of having a child but of being pregnant which can only be avoided in a late-term pregnancy by infanticide (30). Justice Scalia's dissent in a partial birth abortion case (*Stenberg v. Carhart*, 2000) goes even further than such undue burden analysis to deny that the question is even "whether this limitation upon abortion is undue, i.e. goes too far" (530 U.S. 914, slip opinion 72).[5]

If Justice Scalia would have us balance in *Stenberg v. Carhart* the value of "the life of a partially delivered fetus" (71) against "the freedom of the woman who gave it life to kill it" (71), it remains to Joel Pett (1997) to conflate the two in his ironic comment on discussion in the law that women insufficiently consider the welfare of their own fetus in making the decision to abort. Pett's cartoon contains six panels, each featuring a talking fetus encapsulated in a womb that floats in black space, the prolife image of the fetus as space cadet floating free in outer space disassociated from its pregnant host. Each panel delineates a fetal right: "You have rights," the fetus says in panel one; "You have the right to health care, maybe, and to education, if you have the right address" (rights that obtain for private patients, Pett implies, but not necessarily to those on Medicaid); "You have the right to a machine gun"; "You have a right to all the justice you can afford." By panel five, the fetus is identified as female in a shared-rights scenario where it assumes not only the presumed right to life of the fetus but the reproductive rights of the pregnant woman: "You have the right to grow up and get pregnant." And, finally, in panel six, the fetus is granted the right not to have the decisional right of abortion but to have its female voice represented by an "other": "and to consult an as-yet-unborn politician about an abortion." Not only is the unborn politician, Pett implies, unlikely to be female, but the pattern of a woman's right being usurped is implicitly to be continued in perpetuity.

The female perspective is most pointedly represented in cartoon culture with the introduction of the image of the hanger. In two cartoons, the scales of justice are suspended from a coat hanger, a reminder that a woman's legal right to abortion hangs precariously from the very instrument used to effect historically illegal abortions. In a Wasserman cartoon (1992), the female figure of justice balancing the scales peeks from under her blindfold; in one by Dale Stephanos (1992), the figure suggests that both parties "Start praying," conducing neither to confidence in the objectivity of law nor to its transcendent wisdom.

The hanger's critical implication for "balance" in the law is implicated in a Don Wright cartoon (1989) that suggests a tightrope act. A Supreme Court justice carries the *Roe v. Wade* decision as he tip-toes across the flat bottom wire of a hanger standing on its head. In that same year, the year of the *Webster v. Reproductive Services* decision, Paul Conrad (1989a) transforms the scales of justice into a construction of two hangers balanced on either end of a third hanger. The hangers are held by a robed arm extended from a figure outside the range of the cartoon frame, hardly an image of justice unafraid or of a compassionate legal order. A second Conrad cartoon that year (1989b), on the occasion of a half-a-million-strong prochoice march in Washington, D.C., drapes a justice's cloak from a hanger in answer to the implied question of his caption "What a reversal of Roe v. Wade would" mean or do. A court may very well "balance" its "cloak" from a hanger, but such a decision is in no sense "balanced," nor does it follow the legal rubric that a decision must not only be just but must appear to be just. Three years later, as the Court announces it will hear *Casey*, Conrad updates his use of the hanger imagery (1992a). The caption reads "Bush v. Roe" (in recognition of the federal government's participation in the case in an amicus brief and in oral argument) under an aggregation meant to suggest a balance of eleven hangers fallen into disarray (suggesting, presumably, the nine justices and the two litigants).

The rhetorical *tour de force* offered by hanger imagery provides a female perspective tied to violence against women in the most personal and intimate site of all, the female body. At the same time, its representation in cartoon art occurs at a high level of abstraction, both disassociated from its bloody origins and a haunting reminder of them, at the very moment when the venue for the abortion debate has shifted from the political to the legal. The inverted hanger, the tightrope act, the judicial robe held up by the hanger, and the disarray of hangers suggest a world of law seriously out of kilter with lived experience. Unlike the figure of justice or the Statue of Liberty, the hanger as a symbol of the female perspective resonates with the violence of cold steel, an unforgiving and desiccating image.

The much-anticipated corrective to such imagery, the appointment in 1981 of the first female justice, Justice O'Connor, did not, in any case, do much to provide representation in cartoon art for a female point of view. Tony Auth (1981) may have welcomed her to the "Boys Only" Supreme Court tree house, letting a rope ladder down from the columned building inscribed with the familiar "Equal Justice Under Law." But Don Wright's version (1981) of O'Connor's appointment bears a truer sense of the kind of cultural weight her appointment appeared to carry. O'Connor's ascension is met by ballooned speech emanating through the court-house columns to express how the Court "can hardly wait for Mrs. O'Connor to get here. Everybody knows how the Court feels about women"; a second balloon balances the first, declaring, "Right! We'll get her a cute little kitchen and a brand new vacuum cleaner!" In the 1989 aftermath of the *Webster* decision, the female voice on the Court does not appear to have made much of an inroad in representing the female perspective. Indeed, a Jimmy Margulies cartoon (1989) depicts a pregnant woman who arrives at the maternity ward accompanied by a shotgun-wielding Supreme Court justice. She announces to the nurse, ". . . and this is my Lamaze coach." As *The Seattle Times* (*Editorials on File* July 4, 1989, 765) explains, addressing the Supreme Court decision that inspired the cartoon, for the "Missouri women who will be denied the option of abortion, the court's cold analysis . . . will be irrelevant."

The Pregnant Male

The response of the largely male Court to female experience is reduced in cartoon art to the image of the Supreme Court in the guise of the pregnant male.[6] Here, the justice is caught in a double bind: as a male justice, he is asked to represent a pregnant woman with whose situation he cannot identify; on the other hand, he faces the prospect of conflating the role of the judge with that of the pregnant female party to the case. Paul Conrad (1992d) poses the question "What if?" that is, how might the Supreme Court's position on abortion change if the largely male members of the Court were biologically capable of becoming pregnant. Perhaps, this image seems to suggest, the one who has to carry the fetus should be the one to "decide" (both in the sense of being able to make an unfettered choice and of rendering the Supreme Court's decision). The fetus being "delivered" in this image is the Supreme Court decision itself, which puts the male justice in the same conflicted position as the pregnant woman. The pregnant figure is both a physical part of that which s/he is carrying (having become involved, the Court's legitimacy is at stake) and yet physically separate from it (to retain its legitimacy, the Court must remain objective) at the same time. Nevertheless, the pregnant male is less in a position to resolve the pregnant woman's dilemma by being made pregnant than he is to empathize with her

The Law in Cartoons

assination of abortion doctors is the smoking gun that indicts the lawless-
the antiabortion position, belying its profession of "life" by linking it to
f the most indefensibly violent kind.[7] "Don't believe everything you read" is
e of a Steve Kelley cartoon (1993). Confessing the assassination of abortion
r Dr. David Gunn (because the body is defenseless and lying face down, it
he has been ambushed and shot in the back), the caption contests the
t's tee-shirt, which reads "PROLIFE." Giving evidence against itself, the
 figure is thus a particularly persuasive witness to antiabortion hypocrisy in
oon court of public opinion.

defenseless, ambushed, executed abortion provider is depicted by both Her-
 995) and Schorr (1998). Herblock shows multiple murders by assault rifle,
chorr depicts the gunning down of a starkly isolated body. The serial assassi-
 that Herblock introduces link abortion murders to institutional serial kill-
e those at post offices and schools in recent years. The placards of abortion
ors are, as the cartoon labels them, "Directional Road Signs" leading to the
the clinic and to the dead bodies strewn across its entrance. A different kind
acle" to accessing clinic services, they are equally indicative of a larger-scale
 of murderous rage exhibited by frustrated employees and vengeful students.
 construction contrasts the darkness (death) and light (life) of "conception"
assassination" in a diptych. The first panel is bifurcated by opposed halves of
ontaining the words "Life Begins at Conception") and white (containing an
f a sperm with its trailing tail), matching the second panel's opposed halves
 ("And Ends at Assassination") and white (a body labelled "Pro-Choice
" with a trailing stream of blood). The graphic opposition of the presence
ence of light/life is set off in each panel by a curving yin/yang line that sug-
deeper acceptance of the scene rather than surprise, shock, or outrage.
mimicks Herblock's proposition that in the beginning is the end but with a
n that offsets Herblock's progressive incrementalism, so that readers are pro-
vo paths to the same end.

 cartoon imagery expresses the culmination of a trend in both public and
 bates that puts the antiabortion fringe on the defensive. The history of
iolence in cartoon imagery and in the courts puts prolife extremism in the
 of having to live up to its own worst press, in effect, hoisted on its own pet-
mments made by figures in the movement on the occasion of physician as-
ions do not help their case. Marking the murder of Dr. Gunn by Michael
in 1993, for example, a spokesperson remarked, "While we grieve [for Dr.
. . we must also grieve for the thousands of children he has murdered" (the
s Post Dispatch, March 12), undermining the movement's own appeal for
ympathy. Rachelle Shannon, in jail for the murder of Dr. George Tiller in

condition. He is thereby likely to wrestle more meaningfully with the decision to be
made, leading from an an abstract understanding of the law to an experiential one.
The irony of the pregnant justice image is that the empathic response is just as
likely to make the justice/mother more reluctant to want to give up her "baby" as to
make her more sympathetic to the choice to abort it. In Supreme Court terms, we
are speaking of a reluctance to abandon *Roe v. Wade* as opposed to a decision to reverse it.

The decision to be "delivered" is identified in one variant of this metaphor with
upholding *Roe v. Wade*. In a Dana Summers cartoon (1992), the Choice position's
cry to the pregnant justice "Please don't kill our baby" becomes a paradoxical plea
not for the delivery of a child but for the right to abort. "Don't kill our baby *[Roe]*" is
thereby inverted to read "Kill our baby [the fetus]." Bob Gorrell's version (1992), by
contrast, labels the fetus "*Roe v. Wade* reversal?" so that the delivery threatens to
abort the right to choice. By this reading, one aborts *Roe* by delivering the reversal,
whereas one gives life to *Roe* by aborting the delivery. Another reading of the same
cartoon, suggested by the balloon over the pregnant male justice ("Me? . . . Pregnant? . . . Well, maybe just a LITTLE! . . .") indicates that one can be half pregnant.
In terms of this construction, one can abort *Roe* without aborting it, that is, one can
deliver a reversal without reversing *Roe*. But, just as one is either pregnant or not
pregnant, a fetus is either aborted or it is not aborted, and, by extension, abortion is
either allowed or it is not allowed; that is, *Roe v. Wade* is either reversed or it is upheld (essentially Kathryn Kolbert's position in her oral argument in *Casey* on behalf
of Planned Parenthood; in Friedman 1993, 311–322). Paradoxical in its intent, this
cartoon, more directly than others using the pregnant justice theme, addresses the
instability of compromise in abortion law.

The use in cartoons of the pregnant male image and the fact that it is a male who
is "delivering" the *Roe v. Wade* decision/baby raise issues of gender perspectives in
abortion law that, as feminist legal analysis sees it, speak to the absence of the felt
female experience from masculine jurisprudence (Scarr 1990, 151–152). Robin
West's response is that "men's narrative story and phenomenological description of
law is not women's" (1988, 65). The pregnant male image thus presents men making decisions, presumably in women's best interests, where women are themselves
presumed unable to do so. It responds to earlier depictions like that in 1980 in a
Chuck Haynies cartoon in which one member of a panel of judges addresses a pregnant plaintiff in the following terms: "In order to appreciate our opinion on the
matter, you must understand that, never in its history, has a justice of the U.S. Supreme Court asked for, or received, a free abortion." The cartoon implies that,
whereas female justice has the advantage of experience, only male justice retains
objectivity. The pregnant male image thus offers the best of both worlds—objectivity and subjectivity—even as it expresses an oxymoron.

Whereas a male justice may not have experienced the need for an abortion, he is depicted as similarly situated in a Mike Peters cartoon (1992b) labelled "Night-mares of Chief Justice Rehnquist," in which the Chief Justice visits a clinic for "Back Alley Vasectomies." "Sorry Chief," the medical provider advises him, but "first you've got to get your wife's permission, then your doctor's permission, then your parents' permission, then. . . ." In a situation in which sauce for the goose is good for the gander, the Chief Justice is caught among multiple conflicting roles. Not only is he both judge and physician as the author of Supreme Court restrictions on access to reproductive services, but as a patient he both associates himself with the pregnant female in a presumably analogous circumstance and disassociates him-self in a admission that there is no similarly situated class among men.

Legal forays into the world of medicine undermine the cultural authority of med-icine as an institution and subvert the physician role, just as they impact the pre-sumed objectivity and neutrality of the law. In a Paul Conrad cartoon (1992c), Jus-tices Rehnquist, Scalia, Thomas, and White present to "fix" the patient as medically masked men performing a surgical abortion on *Roe v. Wade*. They invoke the purposefulness of lynch law vigilantes rather than the abstract objectivity of a judiciary. In this depiction, medicine is coopted by law which provides the kind of decision-making that non-doctors in medical disguise might make. This infantiliz-ing image is one that has the justices playing "doctor" with pregnant women. They are about to conduct surgery as unqualified practitioners while those with medical expertise and responsibility are kept out of the picture (real doctors as well as preg-nant women are conspicuously absent from the cartoon). The kind of medical deci-sion, the cartoon suggests, that would "abort" the *Roe* decision is one that only false doctors would deliver.

In another version of "justice" in the guise of the physician (Jimmy Margulies 1992), a sonogram taken by the Supreme Court "physician" on a pregnant President George Bush displays the image of a hanger in place of a fetus. The false physician's independence of judgment is compromised here in a balloon that reads, " It's devel-oping nicely." The Supreme Court physician will deliver the conservative president's "baby" (overturning the right to choice), an event that has been refig-ured as birthing a back-alley abortion. Here, the executive cart is pulling the judi-cial horse; justice, in collusion with politics, pays back as it "delivers" on the abor-tion litmus test that influenced the selection of Supreme Court justices for several Republican administrations.

In their effort to circumscribe abortion rights, the male justices of the Supreme Court have been constituted collectively in cartoons as an obstructionist court. Even as it pretends to experience the female perspective and to represent the interests of women, it carries the burden of its own interest: protecting fetal life. One image of fetal life in cartoons that proves compelling is the fetus considered in the light of Supreme Court death penalty jurisprudence. Wayne Stayskal com-pares "Death Row" to "Death *Roe*" (1992) in a diptych that juxtaposes the death

row inmate in a darkened cell to the spotlighted figure of ɑ the spotlight trails back to its source to create the appearaɪ with an attached umbilical cord. The inmate carries the lal infant the label "no reprieves." This polarizing cartoon pi identifies *Roe* (*v. Wade*) with row (death), abortion with ᴄ thereby murder). It implicitly raises the question "What ᴄ committed to place it on 'death *Roe*'?" in an inversion in ɪ prieved and the innocent condemned. The jail cell and the confinement, but in the first instance it is the perpetrator oɪ cerated and in the latter it is the victim of a presumed crim and the criminal's victim are both absent, obviating the pᴏ priate analogues: pregnant woman and murderer; fetus and ɪ toon as constructed thus ensures that the focus is on the fet jail and that ambiguities related to the pregnant woman ᴀ Mike Luckovich (1992) points up the contradictions inheɾ der" rhetoric in an execution cartoon in which a Court ideɪ "Burn baby, burn!" A conservative Court, he implies, is inᴄ for life. At the same time that it supports both capital punisɦ sition, it endorses a left-wing slogan from the draft–card– which the Right supported the Vietnam War. By implicatioɪ flicts both sides of the abortion debate, for those presumablʏ and with anti-capital punishment movements (both anti-deᴀ (pro-fetal death).

A third cartoon on this theme (Don Wright 1992b) depiᴄ infant on a death chair, saying "If, on the other hand, thiⱤ uncared-for precious little life gives me any trouble. . . ." calls the fetus a "child" to assert its right to life (the state's i fies the child with an adult to assert the right of the state to est in death). On another reading, the same Court that insiⱤ tion issue—when its interest is in social reproduction aɴ values—insists on death on the issue of capital punishment shifts to one of preserving social order and economic stabiliᴛ plied by Wright's cartoon is that forced pregnancy leads tᴏ then crime, and ultimately to the death chair, a chain leadiɪ an interest in life to an interest in death as life itself leads frᴏ This argument achieves an oxymoronic consistency in the ᴄ prolife requires keeping open the option of capital punishmeɪ tion that has little to do with justice and a lot to do with clᴇ details" that a prolife decision would leave in its wake. The ɪ tice who holds the child suggests the appropriateness here of ᴀ a small brain.

1993, wrote to her supporters advising them that "For the Army of God, 1994 was a pretty good year. Paul Hill performed a termination procedure [the murder of Dr. John Britten] on an abortionist and his accomplice. . . . The year ended with a big bang, thanks to John Salvi III [the murderer of two clinic receptionists]" (quoted in Risen and Thomas 1998, 368). Depriving the movement of even the most superficial cover in defense of its claim to moral ground, high or low, the violence-prone wing of the movement risked further opprobrium by its "No Place to Hide" campaign. Targeting "The Deadly Dozen" doctors on "Wanted" and "Unwanted" lists, the campaign provided private information (home and work addresses, phone numbers, physical descriptions, and license plate numbers) and offered rewards for information leading to their "arrest, conviction, or license revocation" (361, 212). The American Coalition of Life Advocates (ACLA) Christian Gallery "Nuremberg Files" website followed, promoting the murder of hundreds of abortion providers under the website's legend: "Black font (working); Greyed-out Name (wounded); Strikethrough (fatality)."[8]

In the cartoon culture, extremism takes on several aspects. It is the face of the presumed cleric tossing a Molotov cocktail into a Planned Parenthood clinic "In the Name of the Father, and of the Son" (Tony Auth 1984) and the grimacing figure dressed in a version of clerical garb that reads in front of a mirror "Abortion Kills" and in its mirror image "Kill Abortionists" (Szed 1994). It is the Operation Rescue "rescuer" striking with his picket sign a prochoice advocate who pleads, "Rescue me" (Walt Handelsman 1992); the bomb-carrying young man who has decided, "I have the right to choose who forfeits the right to life" (Tony Auth 1998); and the armed homeowner gunning for his television who cries out "That's close enough for me" when the TV voice declaims, "I'm not really a doctor, but I play one on TV" (Jimmy Margulies 1995). It is the unibomber passing on his torch (a lighted dynamite stick) from within his jail cell to a waiting hand labelled "Anti-abortion violence" (Margulies 1998b), the guerrilla-garbed masked figure with a bottle-bomb hiding in a back alley (Rob Rogers 1998), and abortion terrorist Eric Rudolph in camouflage in his woodland hideout unable to cash in a winning lottery ticket: "Bummer, I won" (Mike Luckovich 1998).

Antiabortion extremism is constructed as not only the work of religious zealots, ideological terrorists, and survivalists but of an archbishop hacking away at "Health Reform" with an ax labelled "Abortion Dogma" (Tony Auth 1994a) and President Reagan rolling in a missle-loaded tank labeled "To Central America with Love" beside marching prolifers with signs reading "End the killing" (John Trever 1985). Having endorsed an antiabortion amendment to the Constitution, Reagan was addressed as a "symbolic father" by the Gideon Project bombers of Christmas 1984 (Patrick Monaghan's opening statement for Matthew Goldsby in Blanchard and Prewitt 1993, 93).[9]

The new understanding that cultural violence had forced on the health care scene is addressed in a Signe Wilkinson cartoon (1995). In a nest called "Natural Family Planning," a rooster ("Clinic Vandalism") oversees its hen ("Violent Anti-Abortion Rhetoric"), which has hatched a chick nestling a smoking rifle in its wings. A violent generation has bred a new generation to carry on its struggle in terms that will ensure its voice will continue to be heard. The nest has national character as a framing device, for natural family planning policy under these conditions is likely to take on a coerced aspect, under the gun of antiabortion regulators. If Justice O'Connor was concerned in her questioning in the *Webster v. Reproductive Services* (1989) oral arguments that the state might find itself caught between requiring women either to have children or not to have them, then Wilkinson's chickens must give us pause. Cultural violence is very likely to have settled the question in fact if not in law, for if prochoice appears to have won many of the larger battles in the courts, prolife seems to be winning the war on the ground. The significance of violent rhetoric, clinic vandalism, and the sniper's smoking rifle is that a nation lacking the will to enforce its own laws generating access to medical care and public safety is very likely to be reduced to accepting the facts on the ground as they are framed by the guns and bombs of the antiabortion movement, that is, Wilkinson's chickens will rule the roost.

Bray v. Alexandria Women's Health Clinic (1993) tried to address clinic violence by applying a reconstruction statute (the Ku Klux Klan Act of 1871) to control prolife picketing, blockades, and harassment.[10] Designed to redress "civil rights violations inflicted by private citizens . . . on newly emancipated slaves and their supporters" (Eisenberg 1994, 177), the statute was applied to prevent what Justice Stevens' dissent in the case saw as an usurpation of state authority. Stevens found in clinic violence a "striking contemporary example of the kind of zealous, politically motivated, lawless conduct that led to the enactment of the Ku Klux Klan Act in 1871 and gave it its name" (313) but, arguably, leaves citizens' exercise of their rights under the authority of the mob, displacing the protection of the state.

The failed application of the KKK Act was a painful reminder to equal rights and affirmative action interests that mob rule and the violent exercise of speech rights would not be an easy case to make in abortion decisions. Cartoons on the subject of Ku Klux Klan hate crimes find white sheets replaced by black robes in a judicial wiener roast at the site of cross burnings (Bob Jorgensen 1992; Chris Britt 1992a). African American onlookers find "It's worse than white sheets . . . It's black robes" in one cartoon (Milt Priggee 1992a), whereas a KKK leader in another (Bill Day 1992) admits, "I never would have believed we'd be holding a Klan rally to praise the Supreme Court."[11] A Jack Ohman triptych (1992b) features flag burning as the beginning (the past), cross burning as a transition (the present), and the burning of *Roe v. Wade* as the fulfillment (the future) of a continuous process. In a Paul Conrad cartoon (1992b), the burning cross functions as the blackened centerpiece around which images of a swastika, burning flag, and hanger circulate as if it was a magnet or home base for violence and hatred against minorities, dissenters, and morally deviant women.

The iconic view of woman crucified (a figure labelled *Roe v. Wade*) and ignited by the states constitutes the strongest reading of the power of the KKK metaphor. Here, the male figure tossing a match into the gasoline-soaked kindling at the foot of the female to be immolated at the stake proclaims, "Yup! The Supreme Court said burning crosses is constitutional" (Milt Prigee 1992b). Transmuted from a statement of racial hatred into a gender war, this cartoon suggests that a woman who acts on her convictions (claims her First Amendment rights to her beliefs and personal autonomy) is likely to be crucified, burned alive on a fiery cross that has historically bespoken religious and racial hatred and now misogyny. At the same time that it replays the history of lynching, it recalls the history of witch hunting that afflicted New England in the colonial period. The cartoon thus calls forward not only racial and sexual scapegoating and persecution but the debate over the death penalty; here, women who choose to abort must pay the ultimate price of a capital crime. By contrast, the implication is also drawn that the death of *Roe v. Wade* is itself a death sentence for women. In a replay, with a twist, of Justice Stevens' *Bray* dissent, state authority and, therefore, the public safety of women, are all at issue. Usurpation by a disruptive mob is not, however, any longer to be feared; "symbolic" violence is now allowed as free speech. The lawless conduct of the KKK becomes the lawful exercise of state authority so that the law is no longer overwhelmed by violence, having itself become its instrument.

If the Ku Klux Klan Act and civil rights law were not to be invoked, *NOW v. Scheidler* (1994) favored the application of a statute designed to protect against organized crime. RICO (the Racketeer Influenced and Corrupt Organizations section of the Organized Crime Control Act of 1970, 18 U.S.C. 1961–1968) would, however, require a pattern of "racketeering activity" that has an effect on interstate commerce, on the victim's property, or actual or threatened force, not necessarily requiring an economic motive.[12] The defense against applying RICO was the right to free speech under the assumption that such speech is not an act but a form of protected expression. Tony Auth's cartoon (1994b) presents a witness at a line-up that includes three suspects, two of whom are dressed like gangsters and one as an Operation Rescue protestor. The witness identifies a protestor as the guilty party under RICO: "Number three may not *look* like the other racketeers, but he's the one who stalked me, threatened me, harassed me and assaulted me." Wearing a tee-shirt that reads "God is *my* Godfather," the identified suspect sports a halo headpiece and waves signs that read "Abortion is murder" and "Operation Rescue." The dissimilarity of the protestor and his counterparts in the line-up implies the unlikely applicability of RICO to antiabortion activities even as the witness' identification clarifies its appropriateness. The placid aspect of the official supervising the line-up promises a dispassionate use of RICO even as it reflects the general official distaste for prosecuting such crimes against clinic protestors. The very difference in costume and attitude among those in the line-up (the gangsters lack emotion while the protestor is enraged; the protestor declares himself godfathered while one of the gangsters adopts the pretense of an artist carrying a violin case) suggests that antiabortion is a significantly different kind of conspiracy. It is a conspiracy based on wholly different motives, engaging a completely different set of actors, and organized by substantively different kinds of associations and networks. Nevertheless, as Chief Justice Rehnquist's opinion in NOW v. Scheidler made clear, "Nothing more [than an extortion and injury allegation] is needed to confer standing" (256). As Patricia Ireland, speaking on behalf of NOW (the National Organization for Women), contended, Operation Rescue's free speech defense did not protect against violent acts, for "violence has no sanctuary in the First Amendment" (Ireland 1995, 852). Clinic protesters were not protected by analogy to civil rights protesters as Operation Rescue would have them, she argued. For the analogy to apply, civil rights protestors would have had "to burst through the door of the Woolworths, knock people down as they rushed up to the counter . . . call the owner of the Woolworths, threatened him and his family, and finally burn the business and shoot an employee" (851). The better analogy, Rebecca Eisenberg argues in the Yale Journal of Law and Feminism (1994), is between Operation Rescue and "Southern politicians [who]. . . stood in the doorways of newly desegregated schools to prevent African-American children from exercising their constitutional right to desegregated education" (214).

Don Wright's RICO cartoon (1994) has a somewhat different take on the antiabortion response to racketeering charges, suggesting the fecklessness of the antiabortion attitude towards law enforcement in the latter's efforts to control the movement's destructive effects. Wright expresses the arrogance of the movement's seeming impunity as it refused to pay fines levied against both individuals and groups as well as the chilling coolness with which replacement troops were moved up to clinic front lines to replace protestors removed by police. In what could be called a "RICO roll," a free-floating cartoon figure performs a heads-down cannonball dive caught in mid-air under the heading "Operation Rescue's position on the RICO ruling." Don Wright's balled-up figure is pictured in mid-air, its backside exposed in its upside-down view of the legal universe.

If antiabortion's reaction to rulings of the Supreme Court is less than respectful, one can only ask in what condition it hopes to leave the Constitution. Jimmy Margulies answers the question through the cross-hairs of a rifle; its sight is targeted at the Constitution in a spotlight of white against a background of black (1998a). The surrounding blackness suggests the robe of a Supreme Court justice and the white circle a bullseye. The cartoon's heading reads, "Abortion provider targeted by prolife extremists." The first line of the document, "We the People," expresses the cartoonist's larger sense of just what target prolife is aiming at, for a minority tyranny here targets the democratic will of the people. The Constitutional issues, raised in the abstract, do not, in any case, reach to the specifics of equal rights and privacy rights or to free speech and personhood but assault the fabric of the document as a whole. We find just such an assault on the Constitution in a M. Shelton cartoon (1986). Here, a disembodied arm, robed and wearing a surgeon's glove, grasps the Constitution with a pair of calipers. It dangles the document over a disposal can held out by a second set of disembodied hands: "The Supreme Court Upholds Abortion," the caption reads. Offstage and at a distance, the justices not only appear to disclaim ownership of their own ruling but hold the Constitution itself at arm's length in acknowledgment of their shameful treatment of the document.

This assault on the Constitution resonates with Charles Fried's oral argument before the Court in *Webster* (1989) in which he contended that "we are not asking the Court to unravel the fabric of unenumerated and privacy rights which this Court has woven. . . . Rather, we are asking the Court to pull one thread. And the reason is well stated by this Court in *Harris v. McRae*; abortion is different" (10–11; see also Guitton and Irons 1995, 105).[13] Frank Susman rebuts for Reproductive Health Services: "Mr. Chief Justice, and may it please the Court: I think the Solicitor General's submission is somewhat disingenuous when he suggests to this Court that he does not seek to pull a thread. It has always been my personal experience that, when I pull a thread, my sleeve falls off. There is no stopping. It is not a thread he is after. It is the full range of procreational rights and choices that constitute the fundamental right that has been recognized by this Court" (15; Guitton and Irons, 107).[14]

The Supremes in Cartoon

The role of the Supreme Court in abortion decisions has served as a focal point for heated dissent in the abortion debate, leading to personal attacks leveled against the justices themselves. We find, for example, a notice (Buffalo *News*, June 2, 1986) of Justice William Brennan's commencement address at Loyola Marymount Law School in which a plane is reported to have circled overhead flying a banner that read "Pray for death: Baby Killer Brennan" (Blanchard and Prewitt 1993, 258). In the same year, a United Press Syndicate cartoon by Tom Toles (1986) for the Buffalo *News* shows a Right to Life preacher exclaiming in a benediction from his pulpit, "Dear Lord above, please strike Justice William Brennan dead . . . choke, strangle, garrote him . . . annihilate, exterminate, obliterate him . . . butcher him, slaughter him . . . hack, hew, draw and quarter him . . . savage, maul, chop, bayonet, impale, stab, slice and dice. . . ." (in Blanchard and Prewitt, 258).

On the February following the Gideon Project Christmas clinic bombings, "someone fired a bullet through a window of Supreme Court Justice [Harry A.] Blackmun's apartment" (Blanchard and Prewitt 1993, 81). Justice Blackmun alone has served as the subject matter of several cartoons that suggest his central role in the abortion controversy as author not only of the *Roe v. Wade* decision but of five other opinions for the Court on abortion.[15] With the words "*Roe v. Wade*" spotlighted and suspended by bat wings in the sky outside his office window, Justice Blackmun muses in a Jack Ohman cartoon (1992a), "I can't stay on this Court forever. . . ." In a reprise of the last-minute reprieve granted by the *Casey* decision, the sign "Blackmun Returns" is stenciled across his wall. Blackmun's words refer to the coda he attached to his opinion in *Casey* (concurrence in part, dissent in part) in which he poignantly admits to the combined effects of a long tenure and imminent departure: "I am 83 years old. I cannot remain on this Court forever, and when I do step down, the confirmation process for my successor may well be exactly where the choice between the two worlds will be made," that is, between the world of the *Casey* Court's approach and the world of "the Chief Justice and Justice Scalia" (in Friedman 1993, 431).

A figure of stability and continuity, of *stare decisis* in a precedent worthy of upholding, Blackmun's persistence is the counter to Rehnquist's "mad" pursuit of *Roe* in a cartoon (Jim Borgman 1992a) in which the Chief Justice is depicted as "batty." As a bat clings upside down to his outstretched gavel and with his skull cut open to allow a flurry of bats to surge forth representing Court rulings, the mad Chief Justice bellows, "On, my Furies! On to '*Planned Parenthood v. Casey*'!" Associated with the insanity of blood for blood vengeance, the furies in the form of bats represent not merely emotionalism but irrational or "batty" decisions. Justice is merely moving on to hunt down its next victim, forswearing compromise, mediation, and unity as well as case by case justice. Pursuing its own scorched earth policy, irrespective of the merits of a particular case, it tars everything alike with the same brush, holding to some vaguely understood mad agenda.

The relationship between the Blackmun and Rehnquist positions on the Court is addressed in a Chris Britt cartoon (1994) on the occasion of Justice Blackmun's retirement. As the architect of the 1973 abortion decision that legalized abortion, Justice Blackmun empties his office of his belongings, leaving behind a massive volume titled *Roe v. Wade*. Under the surveilling eye of the whistling Chief Justice, whose tapping fingers rest beside the volume, Blackmun remarks in parting, "And don't get any ideas about throwing it out." "Throwing it out" may well have become less likely post-*Casey* than it had been at almost any time prior to that decision. Blackmun himself appeared to have recognized that prospect in moving from his "fear for the integrity of, and public esteem for, this Court" (quoted in Kolbert 1989b, 161, from his dissent read from the bench in *Webster*) to his acknowledgment just three years later (in his concurrence in part, dissent in part to *Casey*) that the 1992 decision was unmistakably "an act of personal courage and constitutional principle" (in Friedman 1993, 414). Indeed, he writes, "just when so many expected the darkness to fall, the flame has grown bright" (413).

If Tony Auth is to be believed, the bright flame of *Casey* may well be Justice Blackmun's lasting legacy. At Blackmun's death in 1999, Tony Auth's visual epitaph celebrates a chain broken by a slip of paper held out in the Justice's hand, which reads "*Roe v. Wade.*" On one end of the chain is an iron ball weighted into the earth. On the other end is Blackmun's legacy, the female sign of a circle and cross floating freely towards the heavens. Certainly Justice Breyer's opinion for the Court in *Stenberg v. Carhart* (2000), the most recent Supreme Court ruling on abortion and the first of the new millennium, suggests that Auth may not be far from wrong: "taking into account these virtually irreconcilable points of view, aware that constitutional law must govern a society whose different members sincerely hold directly opposing views, and considering the matter in light of the Constitution's guarantees of fundamental individual liberty, this Court, in the course of a generation, has determined and then redetermined that the Constitution offers basic protection to the woman's right to choose. We shall not revisit those legal principles" (slip opinion 14).

Justice Blackmun's personal dilemma is, nevertheless, embedded in the Court's disarray, contentiousness, and even dissembling on the abortion issue. If Justices Rehnquist and Blackmun are depicted as publicly positioned on the split Court, Justice Thomas is understood to perform from a hidden agenda that he has carried with him from his confirmation hearings in 1991. Danziger (1992a) pictures him with his hand over his mouth next to Justice O'Connor, deep in thought; a third, partially obscured justice doodles on a piece of paper. Like O'Connor, Justice Thomas shields what he is writing with his hand. The cartoon text reads, "Justice Thomas is fascinated, intrigued, and engrossed by *Roe v. Wade* arguments . . . of course, as you well recall, he's never heard any of this discussed before." The text makes a not-so-oblique reference to Thomas' by now famous confirmation hearing testimony in which he disavowed having ever discussed abortion in spite of evidence to the contrary in his previous speeches and writings (Lubiano 1992, 304; Bhabha 1992, 239). By 1995, the Justice is "outed" in cartoon art by a sign on his desk "Clarence 'Never Discussed *Roe*' Thomas" as he phones Surgeon General nominee Foster with abortion litmus-test advice: "Hello, Foster? . . . You should've told a really *big* lie!" (Joel Pett 1995).

The Court's attempt to step back from the precipice and to begin not only to heal divisions but to reclaim public respect for the Court is evident in a Chuck Asay cartoon (1992c). The *Casey* opinion's authors Justices Sandra Day O'Connor, David Souter, and Anthony Kennedy opine, respectively: "We found in this document [the Constitution]. . ."; ". . . The right of women to take the lives of their unborn children . . ."; ". . . But only in moderation." The tri-authored opinion, the cartoon suggests, straddles the issues of whether the right is found in the text of the Constitution or by interpretation and whether or not it is a fundamental right. The troika is nevertheless portrayed in a cartoon by Templeton (1992) as a still spot of unity at the center of a storm. Their unity comes, however, at the price of being beholden to public opinion polls, which the three justices clutch in their hands. The co-authors suffer as well the loss of their individual identities when they are called to vote by the Chief Justice as an undifferentiated entity: "Where is O'Connor . . . Kennedy . . . and Souter?"

Associated with metaphors that suggest a failed social dialogue incapable of social cohesion, lack of self-contradiction, or consensus, the Supreme Court Justice is constituted as well in the image of Solomon the Judge, once a dominant force of legal authority. A figure of mythic majesty, Solomon is used in cartoons to force the Supreme Court justice to choose between two impossible roles: on the one hand, arbitrary royalty—making a spectacular cut to sever the fetus/child (Jim Borgman 1992b) or, on the other hand, justice fleeing responsibility—refusing to make the needed cut (Ed Fischer 1992b). The Solomon analogy refers us to an act of violence that destroys the sense of democratic wholeness and acknowledges what everyone already knows: no party to the abortion conflict is willing to "give up" its right over the abortion decision to rescue national harmony. Indeed, the very use of the analogy to Solomonic justice prejudges the inconclusiveness of the case. In one reading, the life of the "child" is at issue and the presumption is made that the "true" mother will protect its life at all costs, even to sacrificing her own right to that of the child. In another reading, the Solomon analogy raises the prospect of giving each of the contending parties one half of the prize while destroying the very prize so delivered. If the Court is read as addicted to balancing rights, it is left only two choices: either split the "child" or refuse to choose, neither of which offers a true resolution.

Cartoons using an earthquake metaphor transpose the attempt to balance justice to a balance on either side of a gaping social divide, offering a different sort of test from that suggested by Solomon. In one reading (Brian Duffy 1992), the two opposing sides of the abortion debate are split on either side of a national fault line over which a figure representing the Supreme Court straddles, the only hope of bridging differences. In another pair of readings (Chip Beck 1992 and Mike Smith 1992), the fault line undermines the *Roe v. Wade* decision itself, the "structure" of which has been jolted but not flattened by the shock. Inconsistency in the Court, it is suggested, has led to a seismic crack in the underpinning of the decision ("That musta registered 5–4 on the Justice Scale," Beck). Figures reflecting the "aftershocks still rolling in" (Steve Sack 1992) recall the series of decisions subsequent to *Roe v. Wade* that have chipped away at its holdings. Both sides are shaken in the earthquake metaphor, since nature acts as a destructive force largely outside the control of either party to the debate and threatens the value of any ultimate solution. The earthquake is itself a natural disaster that offers no chance of compromise and only the likelihood of a violent end to the debate, something both sides seem to support in their refusal to step back from the edge of the chasm. The fault line gives clarity to the divisive nature of the abortion issue, its destructiveness, the unbridgable nature of the gap, and the incommensurability of the two sides. Participants in the abortion debate are thus left paralyzed and inactive, waiting for something beyond them to determine their fate. The Supreme Court, regarded in some ways as that mediating "something," is at the same time identified with the earthquake, a force that cannot mediate in spite of being depicted as having one foot on either side of the crevice. Paradoxically, the Court is legitimized only by straddling the fault line that divides abortion and anti-abortion camps, for its ability to mediate is depicted as compromised if it steps on either side of the crevice. Its only hope, apparently, is to ride out the quake.

Constructed as having adopted an aura of indecisiveness and uncertainty in a number of cartoons, the Supreme Court seems to suggest that compromise is less a sign of unity than of collapse of belief. Standing on the middle ground of a pregnancy decision is like being "semi-pregnant," as individual balloons over the heads of the nine justices in a Danziger cartoon (1992b) suggest: "We've made a partial change to *Roe v. Wade*"; "With partial support"; "In a partial manner"; "Giving partial rights"; "To a part of the people"; "With partial restrictions"; "Partially effective"; "In part"; "For the partially pregnant." The indecision of the Court is depicted as endemic among the justices who effectively clone one another in their desire to escape having to make a decision. The mediating role is perceived here as failed decision-making or narrative collapse, that is, the implosion in the abortion law context of a potentially meaning-giving story structure.

The collapse of judgment theme is intensified in a cartoon by Chuck Asay (1992b) in which the justices are depicted as having made a landmark "escape" from the courtroom by way of a ladder through a hole in the ceiling, thereby avoiding either of two doors: one to the left labelled "Right (Constitutional)" and one to the right labeled "Wrong (Unconstitutional)." In retreat through the hole labeled "Semi-Constitutional," the justices have vacated their proper Constitutional role. Asay's cartoon speaks of taking the hard way out (a ladder through a ceiling rather than a door) and implies that, like Solomon in cartoons, these justices fear facing the fire their decision will provoke.

Chris Britt's variation on the theme of escape from judging (1992b) shows us the backs of the members of the Court who flee into the sanctuary of the Court: "So we overturn *Roe v. Wade*," one justice contends, "Women still have a choice." The "choice" to which the justice refers is reflected in falling coat hangers shaken loose from the coat closet by the stampeding feet of the Court. The scurrying justices and the coat hangers in disarray are signs of the state into which abortion decisions have themselves been cast. Another striking version of the theme by David Hitch (1992) depicts the abortion decision as a baby abandoned in a basket by the Supreme Court. The basket is left at the door of a house called "Campaign '92" while cowering politicians peak out from behind the house's curtained windows. From within the darkness of the basket, a child's eyes shine to create an image of a fetus in the darkness of the womb. This image is counterpointed by the wailing mouths of the politicians in the darkness of the house. In effect, each of the immediate parties to the abortion debate has left the basket at the door of the public: the Court has abandoned the fetus in its indecision, prochoice would abort the fetus, and prolife will abandon the child whom the fetus becomes. In the same way, the politicians in the cartoon (themselves fetus-like and fearing abandonment by the electorate) abandon their duty to address the abortion issue responsibly.

The underlying question at issue in cartoons on the Supremes is whether judicial legitimacy as a form of authority can avoid, under conditions of uncertainty, the possibility of each person choosing certain principles of justice in his or her own interests (Dworkin 1993, 192). The elements that positively constitute legitimacy are somewhat more difficult to discern, but clearly imply a sense of fairness, often in terms of what one actually gains as an outcome but even more so in terms of fair treatment procedurally. Legitimacy, in sum, may be said to have been earned by a "principled" interpretation and application of the law (214) and a faithfulness to the continuity of principle in the law. It is just this commitment that our cartoon sample has put under the microscope and which it finds wanting. What legitimacy itself earns a Court, and what the cartoons question, is popular acceptance and justification for its interpretation of a sort that considers a decision a principled one and not a political compromise, inconstancy, or a surrender to expediency (Tyler and Mitchell 1994, 708).

Conclusion

A woman's experience with abortion deals with her relationship to creation—and thereby her assumption of responsibility for procreation—as well as her relationship to her society—and thereby her assumption of responsibility for social reproduction. In both these roles, whenever a woman acts to assert herself as an autonomous, self-representing party, she is held subordinate to, in one reading, the authority of a religious perspective, in another, to that of a patriarchal legal system, and in yet another, to an insecure economic status. The take on women in cartoon art suggests that women's self-assertion threatens to unnerve moral, legal, and social order and to upset the traditional hierarchy that would ensure a woman's service as caretaker of generativity. That service ensures the continued preeminence of a rule of law and a way of life that privileges particular class (middle class), gender (male), and religious (Catholic and fundamentalist) perspectives. Women with the most impacted rights (minors, the poor, the raped) find themselves depicted in cartoon art as unable to effectively represent themselves and cast on the mercy of an unresponsive judiciary. Any woman who wishes to exercise access to her abortion right is presented as met by burdens high and low, due and undue by medical white coats backlighted against the black robes of a controlling justice system (the "whiteface" of medical masks over the "blackface" of judicial roles).

The operable imagery of unbalanced judicial scales, burning crosses, and coat hangers in disarray stand as visual signals in cartoon art of women at the mercy of unequal justice, violence in the medical marketplace, and indecision and inconstancy in the courts. The decision that is both just and has the appearance of being just has been made less likely by the visual winks and nods of male justices who toy with the prospect of pregnancies they can never experience in bodies that are not made to be pregnant. The illusion of an empathic pregnant male justice is less an image of a legal system embodying experience as a legitimate addendum to the law than of an impacted decision unable to relieve itself of a burden that will not heal. Justice is asked to choose between "delivering" a decision or being "delivered" from having to make one, between aborting or bringing to term the abortion right, between birthing woman's true equality or shoring up the legitimacy of the Court.

In terms of the nation's dilemma, the issues and the risks are equally stark. Cartoon art visualizes back-alley bombings of pregnant women as well as death *Roe* and the death chair for fetuses. It presents the assassinated physician trailing blood like an umbilical cord and the Constitution in a sniper's cross-hairs, both targeted for execution. The black-robed justice is variously portrayed, ambiguified in the roles of KKK cross-burners, medically masked marvels, batman and batty-man, and a judicial arm (of the law) extending with calipers the Constitution over a garbage can. Public safety and order are threatened by a disrespect for the law that extends from high clergy taking an ax to health reform legislation to prolifers blithely cannonballing their contempt for RICO rulings. New generations of rifle-bearing assassins are hatched to carry on the threat to the peace of the republic, even as an abortion fault line emerges to sever the nation in a seismic split.

The visualizations provided by cartoon art present stark and graphic images that call up a conflict unlikely to be resolved unless deep differences are directly and forcefully addressed. In one sense, we could refer to the visual images of hangers, scales, earthquake fault lines, crosses, mazes, and Solomon the judge as root metaphors (those images by means of which thought is structured and through which we access our culture), indicating the deep divisions the debate has provoked. In another sense, we could approach the images of cartoon art in terms of their ability to access the cultural fictions, myths, and constructions that have grown up around or conditioned the abortion issue. Not only do cartoons, in both senses, open up possibilities for identifying and decoding oppositional rhetoric, but they open us to the possibility of being persuaded or of growing more tolerant, oppositionality being thereby alleviated and the possibility for an exchange of messages enhanced. If readers are encouraged to respond, either because the comic content of the image invites a response or because it simply creates a less-threatening opportunity for response, dialogue is created. Certainly, the calculated incompleteness of cartoon art is designed to create openings for readers to supply missing material, to complete the image, or to discover its reference in the political realm (Medhurst and DeSousa 1981). Doing so, it invites the participation of readers, welcoming them to enter the game. Moreover, because cartoon art—unlike political rhetoric—exists in a no-man's land where everything is possible and little is excluded, it constitutes an open forum in which we are all equally open to ridicule. It constitutes a great leveling device as well as an affirmation that we each can afford to take ourselves a little less seriously. With all the icons out for display, the possibilities are infinite, both for contradiction and for convergence, suggesting openings for synergy if not for resolution. If only unpacking and decoding happen, the debate is still enriched, for cartoon art will have forced us to leave some of the grossest aspects of our deeply held ideas behind as open to ridicule and will have foregrounded those that are more viable for consideration. Cultural consciousness is likely to be enriched and a larger body of shared meaning surfaced even as different messages continue to resonate more forcefully with different readers. We are, at the very least, however, more likely to establish some consensual ground about the nature of our mutual involvement in the abortion debate. Consensus may occur, even if only to confirm that we are mutually captive in an intellectual bat's cave full of shocks and surprises coming at us out of the dark. Opening up this kind of discussion may not dictate a specific common interpretation, but it may set limits and boundaries for a more human exchange from within the boundaries of a common culture. We may, in fact, have arrived at just such a place in the abortion debate if Tony Auth is right in his 1999 epitaph to Justice Blackmun: the floating circle and cross, the sign of the female, rising high from the severed ball and chain that had rooted it to the earth, broken by a piece of paper held out by Justice Blackmun to signify the legacy he has left in *Roe v. Wade*. Auth has expressed the common limits within which, according to Justice Breyer (*Stenberg v. Carhart*, 2000) we shall, significantly, have to contain the abortion debate.

The use of cartoons as metaphors provides a means of considering whether a situation can be seen through a different prism, a different "set of domain assumptions about the semantic space in which it operates" (Manning 1979, 660). The viewer is then prevented from holding to a singular perspective and discovers that there are different discourses and perhaps, as a result, a need to dialogue. If metaphors see a similarity in difference and then again a difference in similarity, cracks are created within groups and commonalities are created between groups that can prove productive of less oppositional stances. Not only do parties to the debate begin to sense shared values in the other, but they begin to question themselves, doubling what had been one-way tunnel vision. Visualization of a different set of assumptions leaves the viewer in the position of trying on other ways of seeing in short, intense, and directed bursts of insight that possess a quick-strike capacity. Not only does the repetition of advertisements have the ability to wear away resistance, but the surgical precision of cartoons has the ability to interrupt one's hold on a singular idea.

Whatever follows must reconstitute itself based on this disruption to produce new possibilities that viewers must make sensible if they do not want to risk suffering from an even more discomforting cognitive dissonance. The prospect of having encountered an image that jostles us to consider possibilities other than what we have already understood generates an ambiguity that must now be addressed. That which has been semantically frozen is now dislodged, jarred loose, so that the varieties of our world, newly open to our view, are no longer constrained from entering our purview. Hegemonic sets of values are disrupted, and the viewer gets to participate actively in the making of new meaning. What had once been a representation is now produced by active interpretation. Indeed, one approach to the operation of metaphors (Alvesson 1993) takes the position that not only do metaphors leave us open to very different images (115) but that second level, or "hidden," metaphors contest established, or explicit, metaphors. As that contest plays out, it raises doubts about the coherence of our analytical frameworks and alters as well as produces constraints in the political games we play (123). The more enhanced an interaction between first- and second-order metaphors, the more likely the prospect of "metaphorical drifting" (124) in our perceptions of power and politics. Metaphors, as a result, do not prove to be innocent expressions but, rather, become themselves instrumental actors.

If thinking about one's semantic universe is mediated by social milieu and if acquiring new ways of seeing depends upon departing from old world views, then the process that cartoon art has brought into play has the likely ability to sponsor breakaway thinking. Such thinking would reject the self-sustaining orthodoxies and the narrow constraints of taken-for-granted thought in the abortion debate. Basic assumptions would be challenged by alternate ways of seeing, and new alternatives would be created that not only keep the debate alive but ensure it will become more meaningfully lively. This is no more than to say that root metaphors, like paradigms, depend upon the core assumptions that characterize them, so that once these assumptions face images they can no longer explain, they are open to displacement (Morgan 1980). Coherence requires either moving to a new metaphor or accommodating the challenge that has been posed. In this way, cartoon art acts to create awareness that positions can and must change as well as that positions are not received as embedded so much as they are engaged as constructions. Indeed, the mere recognition that one is acting on the basis of one group's preferred metaphor and that different metaphors are capable of capturing a situation in different ways is itself suggestive. It opens up to warring parties the possibility that metaphors exist that have not yet been considered by either group and that may be used to create ways of seeing capable of overcoming the blindspots of those traditionally applied. Cartoon art thus operates as a metaphorical trigger, expanding options, provoking consideration of new ways of seeing, and generating synergies as yet unperceived.

Notes

1. In a review of over 200 abortion cartoons from 1972 to 2000 from *Editorials on File, Repro-ductive Freedom News*, a collection by Christine Marley (1994), and an on-going indepen-dent collection (with reliance on *Newsweek's* weekly and yearly collections and *The New York Times'* Sunday "News in Review" collection), the cartoons in the sample proved over-whelmingly proabortion. The range of issues addressed were limited, constituting a horizon of sorts for this work. Those issues overlapped to a large extent with the issues raised by the politics of abortion (antiabortion violence, class and race distinctions, the role of political lobbying and protests, legal constraints on women, the impact of public consensus and judi-cial indecision on the legitimacy of the Supreme Court) and abortion law (parental con-sent, transport of minors across state lines, undue burden, physician consent, fetal rights) but infrequently accounted for constructions from the antiabortion perspective. Cartoons cited in the work are referenced in the bibliography for further publication information.

2. The undue burden standard appeared first in Justice O'Connor's dissent in *City of Akron v. Akron Center for Reproductive Health* (1983), reappeared in her dissent in *Thornburgh v. American College of Obstetricians and Gynecologists* (1986), and replaced strict scrutiny as a new standard in the plurality opinion in *Planned Parenthood of Southeastern Pennsylvania v. Casey* (1992).

3. According to Alan Brownstein (1994), before viability neither protecting fetal life nor maternal health would represent a sufficiently compelling state interest to allow an abor-tion restriction under what he understands to be a two-tier system: a law that did not con-stitute an undue burden would be given a lower-level rationality review; a law that did constitute an undue burden would be treated under strict scrutiny. Pre-viability would fall under strict scrutiny.

4. In their analysis, Estrich and Sullivan (1989) add that it is not enough that a particular burden, as O'Connor has herself posited, need not affect all women but, they contend further, the burden must be understood from the woman's point of view (134). Thus, the weight of the burden should be considered undue if it is too heavy from the perspective of the experience of the pregnant woman, not a legislator or a judge: "The undue burden test becomes a mockery if it permits legislatures to pass restrictions with little or no appli-cation to people like them, and then to insist that their perspective should govern the scrutiny to be applied" (136). Questions of perspective should not only be critical but de-terminative (137). In the Estrich and Sullivan analysis, health regulations based on phys-ical, emotional, and psychological factors are thus a threat. For O'Connor, they do not rise to the threshhold of "official interference with the abortion decision" (quoted in Es-trich and Sullivan 139).

5. The test itself is referred to "as doubtful in application as it is unprincipled in origin" (quoting from his own dissent in *Casey*, in Friedman 1993, 72); "hopelessly unworkable in practice; ultimately standardless" (from dissent in *Casey* 72); and has continued *Roe v. Wade's* nationally disruptive diversion "by keeping [the Supreme Court] in the abortion-umpiring business" (73–74) over a value judgment rather than what Scalia would take to be a matter of policy or law.

6. Of interest here, see Colker (1994), Johnson (1995); see also on the politics of the Court, Brisbin (1997), Savage (1992b), and Woodward and Armstrong (1979).

7. A piece in *Harvard Law Review* ("Safety Valve" 2000) raises the prospect that Supreme Court cases and clinic access laws closed off the possibility for non-violent antiabortion protest from 1989 on, so that large-scale civil disobedience was forced underground only to

re-emerge as terrorism against abortion providers throughout the nineties (1218–1221). The argument made here is essentially that limiting nonviolent protest is counterproductive since such limits only contribute to increased violence. (See Alexander 1997.)

8. A defendant in a case brought against the website (Portland, Oregon, Federal District Court, *Planned Parenthood v. ACLA*), Michael Bray had himself openly defended the murder in 1998 by James C. Koop of one of the doctors targeted on the website. He referred to the murder of Dr. Bernard Slepian as "justifiable homicide" based on "the right of a person to protect the life of a child by using violence" (Knickerbocker 1999, 1).

   The plaintiff's claim that the "web site amounts to a solicitation to murder" appears to have prevailed over the defendants' contention "that it is a legal information tool" (quoted in Verhovek 1999a, 1, 13; 1999b) . Citing an appeals court ruling, Judge Robert E. Jones determined that the entire factual context of a threat, its surrounding events and reactions to those events, should be considered. Such an approach would counter the defendants' assertion that the website did not specifically advocate murder, although it does link with other sites that do. The critical issue may well have been the listing of personal information about the plaintiffs which compromised the site's status as protected speech. An amicus brief by the ACLU of Oregon appears to have found its contention regarding intent supported by Judge Jones' ruling, that is, that the case centered "not only on the fear the list may have spurred in the doctors, but also on the intent of the abortion opponents who contributed to it" (13). Judge Jones' finding holds that "each defendant acted with specific intent and malice in a blatant and illegal communication of true threats to kill, assault or do bodily harm to each of the plaintiffs with the specific intent to interfere with or intimidate the plaintiffs from engaging in legal medical practices and procedures. . . . I totally reject the defendants' attempts to justify their actions as an expression of opinion or as a legitimate and lawful exercise of free speech in order to dissuade the plaintiffs from providing abortion services" (41 F. Supp. 2d 1154 [D. Or. 1999]). See Knickerbocker 1999; Gey 2000. The Portland verdict was overturned by the U.S. Circuit Court of Appeals in San Francisco on March 28, 2001 (*Planned Parenthood v. ACLA* 2001 U.S. App. LEXIS 4974; Weinstein 2001).

9. As a defender of the Constitution, Reagan nevertheless decried the thirty clinic bombings since 1982 as "anarchist" and promised vigorous steps to stop them (*Saginaw News*, Michigan, *Editorials on File* January 15, 1985, 89), sending mixed signals to antiabortion supporters about his own political opportunism and his ability to maintain contradictory positions. Incorporating such a public figure as Reagan, the movement generated the kind of legitimacy that would raise its issues to the level of national concern in terms of both policy and politics.

10. *Bray v. Alexandria Women's Health Clinic* (1993) represented an attempt to apply the Ku Klux Klan Act of 1871, 42 U.S.C. Section 1985 (3). Justice Scalia's majority opinion had held that racial animus or some other "invidiously discriminatory animus" (268, quoted from *Griffin v. Breckenridge* [1971]) was required and that "opposition to abortion" (269) did not qualify. Scalia had concluded that opposition to abortion was meant to protect the victim of abortion and not to discriminate against women's rights (Eisenberg 1994, 180).

    Justice Souter's opinion concurred in part and dissented in part from the majority opinion. He makes clear that *Bray* turned on two clauses in the statute: the first requiring a conspiracy whose purpose is to deprive a person, or class or persons, of equal protection or equal privileges and immunities of the law; the second requiring a conspiracy preventing or hindering the state from its responsibility to protect the Constitutional rights of its citizens. In his opinion, Justice Souter responds to a comparison of clinic protests with civil rights sit-ins, depicting "small groups of orderly students" (304) whose action to prohibit discrimination in public accommodations would not, according to Title Two of the Civil Rights Act of 1964, "work a deprivation of liberty or property without due process of law, nor a taking of property without just compensation" (305). The sit-ins thus accomplished the equivalent of government action that would have prevented restaurant owners from violating the Constitution by discriminating in providing services on the basis of race.

In a direct riposte to Scalia's opinion, Justice Stevens' dissent in *Bray* accuses him of treating the question of violence "as though it presented an abstract question of legal deduction, rather than a question concerning the exercise and allocation of power in our federal system of government" (309), that is, Congress' intent to protect Constitutional rights from organized violent mobs.

The legal issues raised by the clinic protests were effectively addressed in a federal statute passed in 1994 (FACE, Freedom of Access to Clinic Entrances Act) in reaction to the murder of two clinic workers, nine attempted murders, and "a sharp rise in arson attacks on clinics" (Ginsburg 1989, 237). Tested in 1994 in *Madsen v. Women's Health Center, Inc.*, FACE resulted in a Supreme Court decision supporting an injunction that balances the First Amendment speech and expression rights of protestors with the government's interests in "protecting a woman's freedom to seek lawful medical or counseling services in connection with her pregnancy . . . a strong interest in ensuring the public safety and order, in promoting the free flow of traffic on public streets and sidewalks, and in protecting the property rights of all its citizens . . . [in addition to a] strong interest in residential privacy" (767–768; see Pang 1998/99).

11. In a Beck (1992) cartoon, eligibility requirements to be a Supreme Court justice are described as being met "if the location of this message ["Hate"] on or off your neighbor's lawn is of more concern to you than the message itself." In situations where a legal choice can be made (Asay 1992a and 1992c; Trever 1992a; Ohman 1992b; Conrad 1992b), the Klan or its burning cross is shown to have been legally affirmed. Both Hitler and the Klan are allowed at graduation ceremonies, whereas a religious figure is banned (Asay 1992a); like flag burning, and unlike religious speech in the schools, cross burning is not regarded as a harmful expression (Trever). Asay (1992d) depicts cross burning as a permitted form of "free" expression, along with the swastika, in a comparison with questioned taxpayer "paid" speech (in which an image of Christ in a bottle of urine was exhibited in a show under a grant from the National Endowment for the Arts).

12. By the time of the election of Bill Clinton in 1992, the antiabortion movement had reached a watershed. The *Casey* ruling in the same year was considered by some the final blow for Operation Rescue, a case in which, once again, the Bush administration had—as it did in *Webster*—filed an amicus brief on behalf of overturning *Roe* (Risen and Thomas 1998, 336–337). Indeed, Reagan's appointment of Justices O'Connor and Kennedy and Bush's appointment of Justice Souter to the Supreme Court provided the judicial troika that wrote the *Casey* opinion, with which all nine justices were to concur in one part or another to form a plurality. In 1993, the 6–3 decision in *Bray v. Alexandria Women's Health Clinic* gave new hope to antiabortionists. It found that the Ku Klux Klan Act could not be used by federal judges to control protests, as it had in Wichita, and that Operation Rescue had no "discriminatory animus" against women but, rather, concern for "the innocent victims" (*Bray*) of abortion. The decision had the effect of "expand[ing] the movement's right to use nonviolent civil disobedience" (Risen and Thomas, 343). But this was no longer the direction in which the movement was headed with the collapse in the early nineties of Operation Rescue. Nor was it the direction in which the law would continue in two critical

Supreme Court decisions in 1994. *NOW v. Scheidler* allowed the use of RICO suits and *Madsen v. Women's Health Center* clarified that the new federal FACE statute, signed into law in May of that year, would apply to antiabortion clinic activity. (On *Madsen*, see Pang 1998/99, Neilson 1996; on *Scheidler*, see Lenz 1994; on RICO, see Parker 1996; on *Casey*, see Kairys 1993, Kolbert and Gans 1993, Howard 1993, Benshoof 1993, Daly 1995, Maltz 1992, Brownstein 1994, West 1994; on *Webster*, see Kolbert 1989a and 1989b, Estrich and Sullivan 1989; on *Bray*, see Eisenberg 1994).

13. No. 88–605.

14. Susman's endless thread has resonance as a metaphor, for as the *Legal Times* (Moran 1991, 6) reported the oral arguments, "This is the story of Frank Susman's sleeve. Only figuratively. But in the murky metaphysics of constitutional jurisprudence, rhetorical figures can often bring a clarifying power to legal argument. They can rhyme the law with ordinary life." If Susman's sleeve was "about to get a good hard tug" (6) and if "The right to abortion now hung by only a thread" (Savage 1992a), line-drawing—like thread-drawing—was equally at risk, not just between abortion, the range of procreational rights, and the right to privacy but also between the first, second, and third trimesters. Moreover, Susman had so conflated contraception with abortifacients that "The bright line, if there ever was one, has now been extinguished. . . . We need to deal with one right, the right to procreate" (oral arguments, 16). Susman's assertion of the right to procreate as a whole fabric was anticipated by a moment worthy of notice in the *Webster* orals when Justice O'Connor questioned then-former Soliciter General Charles Fried (allowed to participate in the oral arguments). Her question addressed his introduction of the thread imagery and his subsequent distinction between the abstract "right to control one's body," which he claimed was implicit in *Roe*, and the "quite concrete [state] intrusions into the details of marital intimacy," established in *Griswold v. Connecticut* (1965). Privileging the latter while denying the former, Fried became flustered when O'Connor asked, "Do you say there is no fundamental right to decide whether to have a child or not?" She pursued her quarry, "A right to procreate? Do you deny that the Constitution protects that right?" Once more, she nailed down her own bright line: "Do you think that the state . . . has a right to require women to have abortions after so many children?" To which Fried responded that this would entail the kind of violent intrusion he had disallowed, whereas preventing an abortion merely involved preventing such an intrusion (oral arguments, 12). Susman's fabric held against Fried's thread in O'Connor's questioning, for O'Connor declined to sign onto a concurrence with the Court's opinion in *Webster* and thereby rendered the Court's decision a less decisive plurality (Savage 1992a, 292).

15. *Doe v. Bolton* (1973); *Planned Parenthood of Central Missouri v. Danforth* (1976); *Singleton v. Wulff* (1976); *Colautti v. Franklin* (1979); and *Thornburgh v. American College of Obstetricians and Gynecologists* (1986).

CHAPTER FOUR

The Poetry of Abortion

T he poetry of abortion offers an under-explored opportunity to access the experience of abortion from a woman's point of view. Without denying the importance of history and tradition as ways of understanding the cultural context in which abortion is set; without undervaluing the centrality of legal and medical perspectives to the substantive framing of abortion rights, policy, and practices; and without disregarding the formative influence of abortion rhetoric in informing the public debate on abortion, we have yet to engage abortion through the felt experience of the event itself and the participants themselves, an experience that poetry provides. Some might argue that poetry is hardly the place to look for such an experience, given its exquisite sensibilities and its rarified aesthetic as an art form. But this chapter contends that the several dozen poems it examines, taken from a larger sample of sixty poems, provide an entrée into the hearts and minds of both men and women on abortion and are intimate in a way that is rivaled only by private confessions made to one's most privileged confidant. Like any reading of abortion poetry, this reading faces the plausible objection that it is not fully representative. Its objective is, however, not to experience all the permutations of the abortion experience but to highlight four critical aspects: the abortion itself and what goes into making the decision, the effects of having an abortion, a woman's right to choose whether to reproduce, and the male perspective on abortion.

The Abortion

Anne Sexton's "The Abortion"[1] is an appropriate starting point for reading abortion poetry, if only because it begins with the trip to have an abortion, much as the biblical tale of Abraham begins with the trip to sacrifice Isaac on the mountain. But if the biblical trip only admits vicariously the "fear and trembling" that Kierkegaard admires in the Abraham tale, Sexton's text leaves little room for complaint.

The poem breaks into four parts: the dominating trip south, narrated in the first person (four stanzas), the meeting with "a little man" (one stanza); the return trip north (one stanza); a tracking line in the third person ("Somebody who should have been born/is gone") that repeats to break the body of the poem into three parts; and a coda (one stanza) in a voice that speaks back to the traveler. Initially, imagery of a fertile earth ("the earth puckered its mouth/each bud puffing out from its knot") accompanies the trip as its travelers move through blooming imagery into the southern light. Heading south, the trip is not, however, toward the source of life but toward the ending of life. The speaker has changed her shoes to make the drive, so that it is no surprise when the earth itself changes, the road sinks, and the ground cracks in the dark socket of a Pennsylvania coal mine that has broken open the earth to seize its riches. The trip does not occur in a vacuum, for its object is both presaged in the opening use of the refrain "Somebody who should have been born/is gone" and reinforced by the repetition of the refrain to introduce the speaker's reflection "and me wondering when the ground would break,/and me wondering how anything fragile survives." Tracking the progress of the poem/trip, the third-person refrain not only marks off what precedes it but appears to control what follows it. Suggesting the presence of a second party or a shadow voice for the speaker, it throws the speaker's first-person authority into doubt, both admonishing and provoking a sense of guilt. As if fated, the speaker meets a little man who is not Rumplestiltskin, but who takes the fullness begun by love; distinguished from the children's tale, he does not give back her child. Just as the poem fails to escape its refrain, so is the speaker's anticipation of return of her fullness frustrated by the little man. Thus, the ominous refrain caps a return trip north that is characterized by imagery of a thin sky and flat road that reprise the lost pregnancy, the lost mountainous humps of the trip south. The direction traveled and the import of the event are now convergent, empty of hope in a sacrifice in which one's offspring is not, as in Abraham's tale, returned. Having chosen, the sacrificer must live with her choice and shall not be rescued from it.

The final stanza reprises the imminent doubts of the moment before abortion and turns them like searchlights on the subject herself. What she has been unable to speak is spoken to her, in lines that counterpoise her un-self-reflexive and euphemistic logic with an admission that says what is meant, calling into play a split vision of the self in which the poem exposes its subject's hypocrisy and asks her to accuse herself: "Yes, woman, such logic will lead to loss without death. Or say what you meant,/you coward . . . this baby I bleed."[2] Betraying the coolness with which the body of the poem opened and reflecting the continued warning of the refrain, the coda respects the act of violence represented by saying what is meant, for the speaker must "bleed" to admit her loss. Indeed, bleeding in this sense faces the speaker with her presumed responsibility for birth and the shadow expectation that she ought not to miscarry that duty.

In Sexton's poem, the sight and sound of children are missing as the poet focuses exclusively on the abortion itself as an act of relinquishment. One could read the poem as a denial of the child, an attempt to separate mother from woman just as it separates woman/mother from child. Indeed, the absence of direct reference to the child other than in the poem's last line, "this baby that I bleed," is itself a disappearance that matches that provoked by the cracked and emptied mine. But it is more; it is also a snuff poem in the voice of a detached and brittle figure who is herself emotionally thin and flat.

The way to an abortion is various, for children, as in Margaret Atwood's "Christmas Carols," "do not always mean/hope. To some they mean despair." One woman, pregnant by rape of the enemy, throws herself from a great height. Another's pelvis is "broken by hammers so the child/could be extracted"; ripped like an old sack, she is thrown off as useless, while a third woman, past the age to bear, "punctured herself with kitchen skewers/and bled to death." Atwood's variety of women in distress assumes a limit, although "when" is under question. "Nineteenth-century ditches are littered with small wax corpses/dropped there in terror," and nature continues to present us with the spectacle of the fox mother who eats her young. Indeed, Atwood reflects, both express natural events. By contrast, the isolation of a singular "magic mother . . ./distinct from those who aren't. Which means/everyone else" represents a refusal of actual experience that has been excluded from what we celebrate. If we mean what we say, if we truly believe in the sacredness of motherhood, we must put our money where our mouth is, Atwood advises. Only then will the miracle of every child, a "holy birth," come "down to the wrecked and shimmering earth," for then all children will count. Only when we value the rule (living children) rather than the exception (the unborn) do we truly pay the price of worshipping fruitfulness.

The naturalness of abortion is treated by Atwood as commensurate with that of birth, though it is denigrated socially when compared with a more hopeful motherhood considered sacred. But abortion, too, is motherhood, a dark, broken, and deadly form whose vigilance expresses its despair. Its motherhood is imperfect and not intact, nor is it distinct from nature's savagery. A feature of everyone else's life as "a matter of food and available blood," abortion's motherhood is not worshipped. Its sign is an empty rather than a full belly, a furrow turned back in its rejection of fertility.

Molly Peacock's "Chriseaster" extends abortion's motherhood in religious imagery that compounds the experiences of Christmas and Easter. Thinking herself dead, entombed, and resurrected (under anesthesia), Peacock parallels that experience with delivering in a stable (in her stupor) and aborting in a hospital (in real time). The world itself, for the oxymoronic aborting mother, is both womb and tomb, manger and coffin: having "condensed the birth and death that were/usually separated by seasons as I bled, then closed my eyes sarcophagally." A bleating lamb, a sign of God, stood by "in hunger and terror in the tomb room. . . ." Caught in a singular moment that is both stable and hospital, birth and death, entombment and resurrection, the mother concedes herself to the excess of an archetypal universe that exceeds her experience, swallowing her into itself.

Ai's "The Country Midwife: A Day," a poem in which a mother is routinely de-livered by a country midwife who attends her third birth between abortions, ex-plores abortion as a naturalized phenomenon. A scene of animal smells and sights ("the stink of birth" and her grizzly mate who "rears up on his hind legs in front of me"), the birthing is as mechanical as ice sliding down a warehouse chute and reeks of a deadly potential ("The woman's left eye twitches" as a stain spreads on the sheets beneath her, and the midwife, fingers to her face, acknowledges "I let her bleed, Lord, I let her bleed"). There is no mystery or magic to this birth, just reflex, as if to say that both birth and abortion are indiscriminate, unremarkable, and in some ways indistinguishable.

"An Abortion," by Liz Lochhead, refuses to flinch from such a view, taking us into the animal kingdom itself with the aborted birth of a calf. Lochhead's poem makes a case for the mercifulness of abortion under hard conditions, for the instinc-tive response of the cow is to lick her calf to life. Left alone, the cow would lick ten-derly again and again "at those lollop limbs/which had not formed properly," for they had come from her and she is bound to care for them. She can not bring herself to believe it will not come back to life if she sticks to her loving chore. Still licking, the cow goes quietly with the blue-suited men, as if "she knew exactly what she were guilty of." Through the cow, Lochhead is able to experience the agony of the beast as if it was one with the agony of the human family. Her need to be saved from herself leads her handlers to fit "the quick hoick/of the string loop, the dead thing flopping/to the grass." Instinctively mothering her young, she must be brought by her human handlers to accept nature's harsh verdict on one of its unviable and un-envied creatures.

The title event in Ai's "Abortion," in which a mother wraps her fetus in wax paper for its father to view, is harsh in a less natural way. The father finds the woman in bed, her stomach now flat like a cold iron, having done what she warned she would. With little sense of her maternal relation to the child and no reflection on the risk to herself, she "delivers" her self-abortion and displays it as an emblem of her need or right to commit such an act. She throws it down like a gauntlet, an of-fering proffered before the "man in the house." He responds, still loving her, "what can I say, except that I've heard/the poor have no children, just small people/and there is room only for one man in this house." The aborting woman may appear to be in charge, and the father may seem to be out of the loop. But poverty holds one of the reins that drive the scene and fear of more than "one man in the house" the other. Competing facts condition choice here in the guise of competition for the woman's attention but also in the demands made by family size that affect the ability to provide for a child. The choice is thus neither admirable nor entirely necessary but clearly responsive to the hard facts of a constrained existence, male competitiveness, and a woman's willful choice for self-assertion. He may love her no matter what, but it is a hard love born of a hard life.

The act of abortion in close up becomes the focus of Louise Gluck's "The Egg."[3] In an alternative naming, Gluck displaces the "fetus" of prochoice rhetoric with an unearthly "egg" that requires "enormous hands/Swarmed, carnivorous,/for prey" to dislodge it from a host who, stripped open and dripping, is exposed to cutlery that will operate like a robbery on the body. It tears as if along paper. The victim's protest that the robbery was allowed asks how long it shall go on, as if to speak of the immediate abortion but applying equally to the repeated experience in memory, an oceanic experience that bites away at life. She lacks a safe space, an inlet against a net of bays in a seascape of dismembered fish, flesh, and flies, punctuated by more hopeful "Veronicas of waves." Within this prayerful swelling of waves of waste, "The Thing/is hatching" in the dark. The surgeon breaks through the seascape in a moment of reality in which he catches in a bowl the pieces of the primordial "egg," now named "baby," so that the alienated "thing" is made "child" in a felt real-world abortion.

The subject in another Gluck poem, "The Wound," does not, by contrast, feel robbed, nor does she cast blame. Rather, she watches passively from her bed, as the "air stiffens to a crust," surrounded by paisley walls "like a plot of embryos." Waiting for the kick of her "tenant" as the shrubs bloom and seed and amidst ripe things swaying in the light, she is both fixed and transfixed. Only when it is done does a second figure in another room enter and appear above her, loyally, to cover the scene of the act with sheets. The end has not, however, come: "No end. It stalls/In me. It's still alive." The abortion is a continuing wound to her ripeness, so that at the moment "The prison falls in place," her womb becomes a tomb, without finality. She feels no end; the phantom fetus still throbs with life.

Elisavietta Ritchie's "Natalie" expresses intimacy with its child/fetus, naming it, giving it a sex and life of sorts in the face of the doctor's warning of a fetus that would not grow right, that "would not stick/to my persnickety womb." Giving little hint that she might across the years become some brilliant beauty, the scraped fragments discarded by the doctor's blade are set against another older one, a leftover child without promise or expectation. The shadow of a previous unmourned abortion is reborn in memory, a loss that lacks rituals. Not to be disposed of like hospital waste or dumped alongside strangers in a forgotten grave marked only by tears, the present, female-figured fetus, even in its tadpole state, is hailed: "I wanted you back to inspect, perhaps/preserve in a jar of formaldehyde/. . . like my biology teacher's fetal pig." But the call is regarded as curious by a shocked doctor and occurs too late to be honored. A new ritual, then, more appropriate, is invented; this fetus will fertilize, at its own pace, "a pint-sized plot in the garden."

Brutalized by swallowed Lysol and a stomach pump that "coils like an evil creeper," the fugitive fetus in Dorothy Hewett's "This Version of Love" remains unburied. The mother who cries out to be obliterated, and who hangs by her hair descending into dust, revels in having seen the wonder of her child's glass-like body and her tumbling hair. Touched by this "very shape and effigy of love," the subject hangs back as her fugitive disappears into the rain, across a river, without a footprint. This hallucination of what might have been—called into being by a mother who herself cries out to be erased—frames the poem's more substantial events: conception with a "yank gob" in the hysteria and high hopes of V.E. day; the abortionist's queue, where statues of cupid tumble; and the death of the conceived in the public ward. The "version" of love referred to in the title may have begun in an excess of joy (amid the celebrations of a multitude) and ended in desperation (lonely and castigated by a righteous policewoman who stands beside her bed). But it leaves behind a surreal vision that counterposes those hard real-world facts with a richly sensible effigy figured alternately in a wet shark-skin dress, "wading through the goldfish pools in winter" and "earringed, lying on the lawn" with her bangles clacking and nipples showing through her black lace bra.

The hailed effigy is directly addressed in Lucille Clifton's "The Lost Baby Poem,"[4] once again constructing a future for a lost fetus but adding as well a promise for all its brothers and sisters. The speaker limits her description of the loss of the "baby" to the time she dropped it "down to meet the waters under the city/and run one with sewage to the sea." The image of rushing water is picked up three more times. First, in the speaker's admission of incomplete knowledge, in which she acknowledges she knew nothing about the backflow of waters, about drowning, about being drowned. She matches this admission with her promise in the last stanza that the rivers can pour over her head and the sea can call her one who herself spills the sea if ever she is less than a bulwark for her born children. In the middle stanza, the third use of the image imagines a second loss had the "baby" been born, a loss into strangers' hands, slipping like ice into the winds of Canada, somewhat like the exodus into Canada of resisters from the Vietnam War. The speaker is thus determined to refuse further loss beyond the drowning of herself and her unborn and the potential loss to the war; in her closing oath, she relinquishes her right to bear should she allow such a loss again. If she is ever "less than a mountain," may black men estrange her for their "never named sake." Speaking in a voice out of the black experience, Clifton plays on the flight of Eliza and her child over the ice to escape bearing sons for a master class to use as labor in its wars. Her debt to community is expressed in her acceptance of the black mother's commitment to stand like a rock and refuse to give her children into the hands of strangers.

Speaking to a life of hardship and flight, Clifton makes clear her racial identity in her affiliation with black men to protect their progeny from racial self-erasure. Alice Walker's experience in "Ballad of the Brown Girl" is more literal and direct and is simplified to a third-person story of a pregnant college freshman. An unfamiliar doctor—who doesn't know her name (he calls her whatsyourname), her racial or family history (although he does appear to understand her slang reference to wads of jack)—makes the tolerantly impatient recommendation that she should want the child and that she would be surprised if she told her folks. Without missing a beat, Walker reports the aftermath of the following morning: "her slender/neck broken/ her note short." Critical questions are left un-posed, much less answered: Did she take her doctor's advice? Did her father break her neck? Was the note a suicide's note? Just one question is asked, from her short, cryptic note: "Did ever brown/ daughter to black/father a white/baby take—?"

Walker is clear about the dangerous naivete of a right-to-life physician who assumes all conditions are equal and that all "surprises" are happy ones. His unsympathetic take on the brown girl—who has the money to pay for both college and for an abortion—does not take into account being caught between a rock and a hard place, where there are no good options. But if the reader wants to know who killed the brown girl, Walker does not leave much room to speculate. If the father broke her neck, why the note? If the girl killed herself, why not make clear she hung herself? In a metaphysical sense, the candidate in Walker's gallery who carries the most responsibility for the girl's death is the doctor. A gatekeeper of options, he gets to decide who shall receive and who shall be denied access to an abortion. Closing off the brown girl's ability to retain control over her life means that only the least life-affirming options are left open to her. In this case, there is little mystery what killed her; the brown girl carrying a white child was dead to her race and her family from the moment the doctor made the decision it was not his "right" to make.

The failures that lead to abortion—failures of love, family relationships, the cycle of lives ruined by having babies too young—are addressed from outside the world of women but from within the community affected by abortions in Kenneth Carroll's "The Truth About Karen." From his perspective, rooted as well in the black experience and treating the experience of women who abort, Carroll tells of the secrets and taboos, the women things and the heartbreak whose whispers he should not have heard. Karen's inability to talk to her mother is echoed repeatedly to make clear that her mother had not explained the world to her, while others had told her about the old ways. Karen is left "quietly groping with metal inside her/desperately hoping to avoid the cyclical error of her mother." The speaker, a thirteen-year-old in love with Karen, is not supposed to hear the shame, the secrets, just as Karen gropes "quietly," the brown women whisper painfully and rhythmically, and the shadow of voices promise that a jagged coat hanger will work. The circle of women who speak in whispers are unable to prevent the shame or provide a remedy and are barely able to ensure survival. Karen will live but without having connected to her mother, without being able to face the look of her whose heart must break when she learns the unspeakable. Only the cycle is maintained, the vicious and unending circles that repeat history from one generation to another. Where, the poem asks, "was the water to signal and end/to keep karen from turning to/into her mother." For the speaker, innocence dies, and his love is cursed in a world where a baby is merely an error that is cyclical, an error that signifies a ball and a chain tied to welfare.

Abortion's Effects

Once women move beyond the decision to abort, there is little they can do to avoid coming face to face with the effect of that decision. Gwendolyn Brooks' "The Mother"[5] focuses on women suffering the effects of abortion, their experience of the loss of a child, including their grief and guilt, and how one survives. Beginning with "Abortions will not let you forget" and ending in "Believe me . . . I loved you/ All," the poem moves between these two points through three sets of constructions. The first construction describes in the second person what the mother will never get to do with "the children you got that you did not get": that you will never neglect, beat, or silence them; that you will never wind up their thumb or scuttle their ghosts; nor ever return after leaving them. The second construction, more intimate and direct, speaks in the mother's voice of what "I" have heard, contracted, eased, or said. In the third, the mother directly appeals to the "child" in the conditional terms of if she sinned, if she seized, if she stole, if she poisoned, concluding that, then, one was to believe she had not, at least, been deliberate and that she had loved them all. But if the crime was other than hers, or if she had been insufficiently deliberate, the speaker asks, are her multiple abortions merely what poverty or society has coerced from her? And is the tragic burden of her memories merely what abortions have forced on her? At the same time that Brooks allows us inside the experience of a woman not only engulfed in pain and grief but aware of what, as an agent of destruction, she has destroyed, the blame is implicitly shifted. Moreover, the effects of abortion are experienced not by the fetus but by the mother, that is, the loss is that of the children she will never have rather than their loss of life. The key to Brooks' poem is that the mother's existence as a mother requires that she cannot be identified apart from her relation to her children. This identity yields a mother who has, in effect, been eaten by the children she has been unable to feed.

To truly speak to her children, Brooks' mother must be able to accept her guilt or at least her complicity; paradoxically, to survive, she must escape that very same guilt. But nowhere has the mother accepted guilt. The "children" are treated as that which "you got that you did not get." The act is only conditionally considered sinful, considering only "if" she had stolen their luck, their breath, their reaching out for life. The violence against the children is muted in the speaker's attempts to consider what to say. Terms such as "should," "rather," "but," "what," "how," "only" punctuate the poem with indecision and conditionality. The children never cried or giggled because they were never born, but how that was her doing, in what sense she is culpable, is clouded. To do justice to her children without doing violence to herself returns the mother to the same dilemma from which abortion was designed to relieve her. At the same time, as long as she does not find relief, the "conversation" with her children can go on. In this sense, the mother prolongs her agony; she knows that as long as she remains inarticulate she can retain her tortured memories; she can keep her children alive, if only in her mind and her emotions. The poem is thus both a means of consoling the mother and a lullaby to an empty crib and its non-children.

The controlling term and first word of Brooks' poem, "abortions," provides the rationale for Brooks' evasions and subterfuges, for she speaks not only for one mother (in spite of the specific title "The Mother") but for many mothers, and certainly for black mothers insofar as they are racially "hailed" by the poem. If the background politics of sterilization and fears of racial suicide are read into Brooks' poem, then the mother's multiple abortions, her plea that I loved you "all," becomes a statement on behalf of black motherhood. The lack of deliberateness, the crime that is "other than mine," the stolen births and names, take their place in a larger story written into the history and tradition of blacks in America.

The effect of loss on a mother is not merely race-d as an experience, but gendered. A woman who becomes pregnant is not only condemned to the community of her color but to her biological plumbing and to the attendant trauma and loss of having denied her body, together with the associated survivor's guilt. We find these experiences explored in Diane DiPrima's "Brass Furnace Going Out: Song, After an Abortion." "Brass Furnace" is a poem of lost chances, regrets, bitterness, and the need for forgiveness but also a poem that addresses making contact after death and exploring the life of the child severed from her flesh. A twelve-part poem in first-person direct address, "Brass Furnace" refers to the fetus ("you") in physically graphic details, but the poem does not use the term fetus, baby, or child, even when imagining its life after birth from nine months to age six. Seeking an escape from judgment, the subject asks how she could be said to have failed or even to have understood what she was doing. She seeks, instead, shared blame with the child who "killed" its mother (part one). Here, the poem leaves open the question of what "you" took, even if "I" took life. The speaker herself is unforgiving of the fetus and its father for having given up on her, running out, for failing to be born, for giving up at the first hint of bad news (part two). Communication shifts from sending the fetus with a bitter note in a bottle to its father (part two) to a request for an address or a picture to keep in touch, to send cookies, and to discover whether "you" care what "I'm doing" (part three). Answering the implied question "What happens to the residue of an abortion," the poem slips the fetal remains into the river in a hallucination in which the fetal face dissolves in water like a rotting flower. The fetus is attended by a menagerie of rats, mosquitoes, lion pads, and a giraffe while the mother feeds herself to a flesh-eating snake and chains herself to a tree, awaiting the fetus' end (part four). An abbreviated funeral follows to inter the shadow (part five), and the corpse disintegrates (part six): a fly-infested rotting belly "blown out and stinking, the maggots curling your hair."

In the middle section (part seven), the speaker begins to break down, as if any fate for the fetus—madness, drug addiction, starvation, torture, prostitution—would have been preferred by a mother who can't hang on long enough to cry. Asking for forgiveness in the briefest section of all (part eight, three lines), the speaker does so on her own behalf to preserve herself from dying of thirst should the cosmic waters turn from her. The site of the poem transferred to a shrine (part nine), its images shift from being engulfed in death to calling up life. In this transposed world, the speaker leaves footprints while the fetus is only a shadow; once again at home, she can call up the image of herself pregnant and laughing (part ten). Postpregnancy, the mother imagines the child growing—nine months, age three, age six—in elegant loincloth diapers, teeth sticky with caramel candy (part eleven). This possibility forever closed (part twelve), the speaker anticipates a second chance, although her house is small, if the fetus will appear: "my breasts prepare/to feed you: they do what they can."

DiPrima's subject raises the issue of guilt as if it was not only a two- or even three-way street (mother, father, fetus) but, more importantly, a function of memory, regret, and terror. The abortion has both happened, waging its most terrible effects, and has not happened, leaving open its most wonderful opportunities. That any horror would have been triumphant by comparison is what the speaker cannot bring herself to say. But her trip to the shrine gives birth to new imagery, a transformation of real world hopelessness to an imagined hopefulness. Reliving the opportunities that would never come to be and the child that might have been, the speaker recaptures in bits the life closed to her. Admitting her life's possibilities are now constrained, she nevertheless welcomes whatever she can salvage in her call "will you ever come here again?" This time, she will do what she can, in spite of a courtyard that is gray and absent a view of the sea—this time without illusions.

Ellen Moeller's "ten years ago" explores some of the same territory as "Brass Furnace" but with an acknowledgment missing in the latter. Here, the speaker accepts the trade-off of one life for another, admitting in the opening lines of the poem, and as a condition of her experience with abortion, that had her fetus been born, she would have remained a child. The flip side of that equation is not, however, lost on the speaker, for she makes clear in the very next stanza the instinctive nature of exactly what she has done, to both of them; like rabbits in a drought, new life lasts no longer than a "startle." Stripped of illusions, the speaker is able to admit her action was little more than a reaction, a survival response rather than a reasoned thought.

Without indicating whether her choice actually led to a better life, the speaker nevertheless realizes what it did not lead to, or, rather, what the full price of her choice cost her. She continues to carry the fetus like a question mark and continues to bleed. The choice she faced "ten years ago," as the title indicates, proves a nonchoice, for the departing, ghostly fetus has left her with a forever-unspoken question that did not recede into the timeless as she expected. Still, Moeller's poem is a statement of a woman who was able to say no, who did not herself remain "squinting through my mother's/steamy windows, barely visible/over the sill."

This is not the same choice made in Nancy Shiffrin's "For My Neverborn." Indeed, the speaker of this poem appears to have consciously chosen to treat "The day they sucked you from my womb" as an out-of-body experience. Refusing to shriek, she did not keen her fetus' death nor did she wear black. Refusing to "dig a grave to throw myself into," the speaker maintains the continuing presence of that which she refuses to absent, keeping it for company, talking to her in the silence, looking for her in the light. The ever-present fetus is purposefully embraced; it will not be taken from her in mind and memory as it was sucked from her person in life.

Margaret Gibson provides the ultimate "holding" experience in her "Country Woman Elegy," in which the tale is told of a woman mourning for the seven-month child dead within her. Feeling the weight of the death inside, her love itself was a form of grief. Thus, "she held her loss/. . . until she learned what she needed to learn. Letting go." In "Unborn Child Elegy," by contrast, Gibson examines a maternal connection that allows for the back and forth between mother and fetus as a contest of interests or wills. Indeed, the title is itself in contest with the poem, for this is no traditional elegy; rather, it is more like a dialogue in the process of making a decision. In the sense that it elegizes, it does so for the condition of "unbornness" itself, rather than for the child who is unborn. The speaker's child is a constant demand for birthing that she knows is "there inside/. . . small as a syllable," an entrée to mystery that would "bring me so close to the unspoken I'd shake." But the unborn does not wish merely to be party to a pact in which the speaker would invaginate the world; it wants to be born, a deal-breaker for the speaker who has been told of the pain when pried open by a child. Still, the speaker retains the power to refuse a body to the unborn, a choice that is made easier because she believes in a nothingness that is the breath from whose passion all that lives arises.

One entirely plausible reading of Gibson's ambiguous resolution of her poem is to consider that the speaker wishes nothingness—the "zero"—into being to express her in both birth and death, as if to say that its unbornness must now itself cease its nothingness in order to fill her emptiness. At the same time, however, the speaker resists the convention that a woman is fulfilled only by the life and presence of the born. She finds that which she refuses to bear both alive and present to her even as she denies it a body. Triangulated in a bind that pits her biology, the social construction of woman, and her own, uniquely personal self against each other, the speaker preserves the tenuous balance of zero speaking through ancient stories and the needs of her own voice through which zero must speak to be heard: "Be the zero who speaks for me./Be birth and death, the emptiness/only a child, and never a child, can fill." The child in the opening lines of the poem may be "always unborn," and it may be the speech of "ancient stories," but it is also that whose speech jump starts the world by surprise. To truly experience living and dying, the speaker must allow zero to speak. Thus, this reading suggests, the speaker brings her own emptiness into play, both filling and not filling it as a child both does and does not fill it. She concedes to the desire of the unborn to be born, but it is a concession on her own terms, a concession that aborts the child's unbornness to give it, herself, and the world speech.

An equally plausible, and perhaps more internally consistent reading, suggests that the speaker does not change her position across the poem but reasserts her desire for emptiness and the connection to mystery it brings. She continues to ask the zero to express her emptiness, her resistance to being filled and thereby socially "fulfilled." This reading reconfirms her desire for the continued "unbornness" of that internal grain which is like a seed asleep in the seedbed of her body. Such desire prevents more "of the mystery spilling like salt." Here, the speaker refuses the notion that only a child can fill her emptiness and opts for continued openness to the openness out of which life flows. This position carries with it the irony of refusing birth as a more "creative" alternative than birthing since it keeps alive the larger pool of generativity from which cosmic life must forever replenish itself.

Women and Identity

Like Gibson's "Unborn Child Elegy," Adrienne Rich's "To a Poet"[6] is in many ways a poem of rivalry between woman and child. It is not a rivalry in which art or poetry exists because the child does not, that is, the female poet has not maintained her identity because the fetus gave up its life for her art. Rather, "To a Poet" is an intermingling of three women, or, perhaps, three sides of the same woman—the successful poet who gives us the voice of the poem, the struggling mother who still fights against the current, and the mother who has given up the fight. All these women are in a contest to maintain an identity threatened by abortion and birth. Abortion is used here not to describe fetal murder but the death of the female poet, a case "where language floats and spins/abortion in/the bowl" and small mouths suck life from the poet. Birth is used to describe the giving of life that prevents the suicide of self, but it is a love that landlocks one's life. It is also, more positively, the delivery of female poets who struggle to write in their own words, those whose pens, borrowing from Keats, have "glean'd your teeming brain." Poetry, after all, is that which confers immortality, so that, denied her poetry, a poet is doubly condemned. Whereas birth as love gives rise to poetry (as with Keats) for the male poet, it implies the death of poetry for the female poet, for whom birthing represents society's imposition of a motherhood milk-stained and dragged down. The poet aborted has been killed by motherhood itself, the very institution established to prevent abortion of another type.

The speaker's fear is not for herself nor for the mother who still struggles, "fighting up the falls." Her fear is that another woman will be driven dumb, her words lost, her voice quieted "with loneliness dust seeping plastic bags/with children in a house." It is this other woman to whom the speaker's admonitions are directed, the one whose murder is at issue. But the speaker does not call for a change in social stereotypes nor for institutional changes in motherhood; the cry is not to abort the mother role to control violence against the poet. Neither are writing and childbearing regarded as potentially reinforcing each other. Instead, what is called for is resistance to being overwhelmed by the daily chores of nurturing another life in an implied recognition that the female poet is unlikely either to combine or to separate her two roles. The burden is on woman alone to negotiate the divided and competing demands that will continue to be made of her.

Rich is joined by Anne Sexton and Louise Gluck in her fear that her creative life and her sense of self will be overwhelmed or undermined by giving birth. In Gluck's "Firstborn," the first-person speaker is again caught in the quotidian routine of a kitchen in which "I shelve them,/ They are all the same, like peeled soup cans . . ./ Beans sour in their pot." Of her listless husband, she asks if he misses her care, but then his garden calls and a burst of roses compensates, as when she birthed his son. Though they are all well fed and her "meatman turns his trained knife/on veal your favorite," the speaker ends with "I pay with my life." The male appetite satisfied, the woman subdued yet reproductive, the trade-off in "Firstborn" is clear: present the male with an heir or choose a life that is more individually satisfying. Gluck presses further in "Hesitate to Call," in which the mother's labor is thrown aside by her offspring who had fought inside her like fish caught in a net. Her care done with, she has "lived to see/That all that all flushed down/The refuse. Done? It lives in me. You live in me. Malignant." An abortion metaphor turned on the potential aborter herself, the mother becomes the victim; it is she who has lived long enough to find herself cast aside. Yet the residue courses within her, so that Gluck ends the poem "Love, you ever want me, don't," a warning to the bad seed that has turned her love aside.

"Unknown Girl in the Maternity Ward" is a poem that explores loss that is not the result of an abortion but, rather, that aborts a mother-child relationship postbirth. Here, Sexton reverses the rejection Gluck's subject experiences to ensure that the child who senses the way they belong together will not have long to know her. Recognizing her baby's face, one with her bone for bone, her arms tailored to fit her, she finds relief that "Others have traded life before/and could not speak." The mother in Sexton's poem is troubled by details that suggest the possibility of bonding, and she is aware that her silence harms the child. She is nevertheless able to say there is an end, there is nothing to be done that she will do. Thus, she offers to refuse to respond to her child and to unteach herself motherhood: "I am a shore/rocking you off./ You break from me." She chooses a solitary way and hands off her child. Cast off like Moses from the shore, Sexton's "unknown girl," her unnamed bastard ("Name of father—none") is discarded as her sin, nothing more. Their bond aborted, the castaway is set adrift.

In "Right to Life," Marge Piercy explores in greater detail the dilemma Rich's poem and related female poetry have raised. The right referred to in the title is the right a woman has to live her own life, the right to choose, without which there is no "life" worth speaking of. Taking a defiantly oppositional position, the third-person voice of the first half of the poem argues that women are not a resource to be exploited and that no one has the right to choose for them what they should choose for themselves. Piercy opens with an image in which, given its freedom, a tree would fail the test of the fruit-bearing pear tree "thrusting her fruit in mindless fecundity/into the world." But if its fruit is dropped warm and rotting in the grass, a wild tree at least stretches its limbs high. If a woman is no pear tree, neither is she a basket in which buns are kept warm nor a brood hen, a purse, or a bank, places in or under which one slips eggs or deposits coins to grow in interest, harvest, or sell.

In a repetitive drone, the speaker accuses "you" who transform planting corn and slicing through mountains into an effort to establish rights over a woman so that babies can be pastured to graze or to grow like iceberg lettuce. Picturing the reality of the world as it is lived, the speaker allows no refuge in easy platitudes, exposing the pretense that all is done for the sake of the children. A world in which none are hungry, ill, neglected, or orphaned is posited by Piercy as an ironic test of how dearly children are valued. This is a world in which the poor eat steak and no one coughs to death or eats lead. In contrast, the real world offers disturbing vignettes: a daughter is taken into custody when her single mother dies of an abortion; an unwanted son becomes a pin-cushion for his parents' pleasure. In a more incorporative voice, the speaker reminds the reader that, born of woman, we all suckled from our mothers and that all those who go into the world unloved will return to us with a payment due. The price of "a pain that will/beget pain" is transformed, in the speaker's hysteria, into a synagogue torched, a firing squad, a world burning when someone pushes a button.

Having pictured in close-up how such issues are played out in real life and having tested how such issues are perceived from the child's perspective, the speaker draws home her point. She moves from women's rejection of "mindless fecundity" and from accusations against those who legislate a woman's rights to choosing on one's own what will enter you, what will become of your flesh. She rejects on behalf of women being someone's cornfield or milking cow. She denies that priests and politicians have "shares in my womb or my mind." In a straight transaction that borrows the language of property from those who would use her, the speaker proposes as her last words on the subject the declarative and final "non-negotiable demand": "This is my body. If I give it to you/I want it back."

In a variation on the fecundity theme, Piercy's "The Sabbath of Mutual Respect" presents a plea for respect for others' choices to bear children or not. In defense of lesbian choices, "Sabbath" makes the case that fertility and choice are interdependent; with too much abundance, young growth chokes in the weeds that surround it. Real abundance, moreover, includes the power of choosing yes or no, of opening or closing, of freedom from the fear of poverty and hunger. Respecting a woman's choice, in any case, is not the same as enforcing choice for all women: "when I pledge myself to remain empty/. . . .I do not choose for you or lessen your choice." Choice is thus to choose one's life as well as to rejoice in what one did not choose. The only true error is to allow oneself, like a public conveyance, to be used to bear unwanted children. Remembering that others have paid with their wombs to open doors that give us back our lives, the speaker concludes that "Freedom/is our real abundance."

The Male Perspective

Having considered in women's poetry the act of abortion, its effects, and the choices that are open or closed to women in bearing or not bearing children, it remains to consider the male perspective on abortion and whether either it or the woman's perspective can be said to be a distinctly gendered view. We might do well to use Ben Jonson's "To Fine Lady Would-Bee" as a starting point, given not only the strength of its feeling and the nature of the sentiment it expresses but also the debate it has inspired as an abortion poem.

> Fine *Madame Would-Bee*, wherefore should you feare,
>   That love to make so well, a child to beare?
> The world reputes you barren: but I know
>   Your 'pothecarie, and his drug sayes no.
> Is it the paine affrights? That's soone forgot.
>   Or your complexions losse? You have a pot,
> That can restore that. Will it hurt your feature?
>   To make amends, yo're thought a wholesome
>   creature.
>
> What should the cause be? Oh, you live at court:
>   And there's both losse of time, and losse of
>   sport

In a great belly. Write, then on thy wombe,
     Of the not borne, yet buried, here's the
          tombe.

The poem itself treats the fetus as an ambitious woman's nemesis, answering the implied question "Why would a woman not want to be a mother?" Operating from the assumption that motherhood is a woman's lot, the presumably male interrogator queries his subject directly: Why fear bearing a child? Is it the pain? Is it the loss of your complexion? Will it hurt your features? What is the cause? The speaker supplies his own answers: the pain is soon forgotten; one's complexion is easily restored; you are thought "a wholesome creature"; but your life at court would cost you "losse of time, and losse of sport/in a great belly." Chastening its subject as an unnatural mother, the coda sums up, "Write, then on thy wombe,/Of the not borne, yet buried, here's the tombe." An inconvenient disruption to an idle life, the fetus must pay a hard price. Court life, depicted as at odds with the natural result of love, is in league with the fine lady and her apothecary in making her appear barren, when, in truth, "his drug sayes no." To maintain her social status and without the excuse of an irremediable loss of her physical beauty, she makes the callous and deadly choice to turn her womb into a tomb. With so superficial a motivation, the fine lady has herself become a nemesis and her presumed nemesis her victim.

Her independence at risk, the subject of the poem is here, as in the poems by female poets on the rivalry between the pregnant woman and the fetus, threatened by a double failure: her failed role as a mother and her inability to play an active role in her social world. Jonathan Crewe describes this conflict in men's abortion poetry (1995) in a commentary on an earlier piece by Barbara Johnson on women's abortion poetry (1986). Crewe sees the conflict as a battle between biological and cultural reproductivity, between the maternal reproduction of women and the literary production of men. In her essay, Johnson had examined "a kind of competition . . . implicitly instated between the bearing of children and the writing of poems" (37)—a competition implicated in Rich's "To a Poet," Brooks' "The Mother," Sexton's "The Abortion," and Clifton's "The Lost Baby Poem." Since male poets cannot procreate by giving birth, there is an underlying sense that for them it is their poetry that is "procreative" ("Their poems have been their figurative offspring," Crewe 2). It is not, therefore, "surprising that the substitution of art for children should not be inherently transgressive for the male poet" (Johnson 38). For the female poet, by contrast, the work of art is taken to replace the labor of childbirth, so that "each of these poems exists, finally, *because* a child does not" (36). For women, creation in a literary venue as a trade-off for biological procreativity is the equivalent of denial of life or abortion of the fetus (Crewe 2), that is, it is in some sense "infanticidal" (Johnson 38). Thus, when women become culturally productive, they become biologically un-reproductive (Crewe 2).

Whatever one thinks about the literal correlation of these phenomena, there is something unique in a woman's role in the death of a fetus, just as there is in her role in a child's birth. The presumption thus arises that an abortion, a miscarriage, or a stillbirth is somehow either attributable to a woman or remains a woman's deeper responsibility. A woman is not separate from the fetus in her womb, and when she is separate, in a positive sense, it is because the child gains its own identity—through birth or through the development of a separate persona. Separation that involves a child's death is more problematic, partly because, as Johnson (and prolifers) notes, we have all "once been a child."

It is this dilemma toward which "To Fine Lady Would-Bee" points us. Crewe's commentary on Johnson's essay, however, denies that there is an axiomatic or arbitrary disassociation for men just because they are men. He proposes, instead, that whereas gender differences do exist, there is room for discussion "about the connection—or attempted disconnection—between biological and cultural paternity, literal and figurative fatherhood" (3). Even male poets, he contends, are disturbed by the impossibility of "clear natural-cultural/literal-figurative separations, along maternal-paternal lines" (3–4). It is over the aborted or dead child that this distress becomes apparent.

Both the unborn and the born child are a threat to adult self-fulfillment; at the same time, guilt and anxiety over abortion and child death pose significant counterbalances to that threat. In "To Fine Lady Would-Bee," Ben Jonson draws a bright line for transgressive motherhood (expressed in his "womb as a tomb" imagery) and a clear sense of woman's badness when she rejects her responsibility as a mother. It is a line that he is unable to draw for himself as a father in his poems "On My First Sonne" and "On My First Daughter," each written upon the death of one of his children.[7] Claiming both literary and biological paternity as a means of what Crewe refers to as "self-memorialization" (1995, 18), Ben Jonson exploits his biological paternity on behalf of building a literary monument to himself. Referring to "thou child of my right hand, and joy" and "Ben. Jonson his best piece of poetrie," the poet is never far from seeing himself in his son or from using his son "Benjamin" as no more than a stand-in for a "poetic Tribe of Ben" (18). The child is erased for the man in the same sense that the poet's seed has spilled upon the earth with the child's death. The poet himself "wastes" his seed "in the masturbatory implication of 'child of my right hand,' a phrase in which 'write' hand is also to be understood" (18). If cultural reproduction is the male game, it also includes abortion/erasure. At the same time, it strains to protect male identity by ensuring that the child be an appropriate monument, rather than an obstacle, to the poet's self-preservation. Thus, the male poet no more wishes to have his reproductivity held hostage to his offspring than does the female poet. Moreover, as Crewe indicates, the name of the dead son returns to the father, so that "the poet ventriloquizes his own nomination as father/poet by the dead son" (18).

What we have, in sum, in Jonson's poem is the use value of the son's death to the father as a means of achieving or maintaining his own identity. No such identification is present in Jonson's epitaph "On My First Daughter," where the poet disassociates from his daughter and sees her as not his property but only a gift that diminishes his status by its loss. That her death "makes the father, lesse" has, according to Crewe, the effect of a "father-lesse" poem that is an "attempted benign reconstruction of paternal absence" (1995, 20). The male poet that Jonson exhibits in his poems to his dead children thus allows himself the very escape he denies the woman who refuses her maternal role. If Lady Would-Bee's refusal has given her mobility, both class and sexual, the poet's implied demand that she return to her maternal status would confine her in both ways.

"Epitaph on a Child Killed by Procured Abortion," an anonymous eighteenth-century poem (1740), offers a transition from Jonson's view to that of later male poets. It leaves the stigma of abortion somewhat ambiguous, for it is unclear to whom the poet refers when the fetus is called upon to "Soften the pangs that still revenge thy doom:/Nor, from the dark abyss of nature's womb,/Where back I cast thee, let revolving time/Call up past scenes to aggravate my crime." The abstract "dark abyss of nature's womb" may very well stand for a woman's womb, but it is also an invention that could, equally, place the fetus in the hands of a male force controlling procreation. Two lines of thought converge here. Honor, reputation, and status augur forth as motive forces in the "Epitaph," and the child who is erased has no identity other than as an "outcast of existence and of naught," a "Dire offspring." Male mourning in the positive sense is thereby given less play in "Epitaph" than the negative female motive of vanity in "Fine Lady Would-Bee." Two parties are implicated as "adverse tyrants" in a scenario in which "guilty honour kills to hide its shame." Love without honor and honor without love are the culprits, for "Love, spite of honour's dictates, gave thee breath;/ Honour, in spite of love, pronounced thy death." These twin conspirators are like two parents who conceived life and then ended it: "two adverse tyrants ruled thy wayward fate,/Thyself a helpless victim to their hate." "Epitaph" has not shifted to a position that understands or tolerates abortion, but it has moved toward shared responsibility.

Michael Atkinson's "The Same Troubles with Beauty You've Always Had" updates Jonson's view of the aborting woman with a sympathy that betrays its own times. In a more permissive age, the focus from the male perspective is on the female subject's "troubles with beauty you've always had." Tracing her diminishing attractiveness, the speaker understands both how beauty condemns the beautiful and how, at the same time, beauties use others and are themselves used. The subject is described as a woman who exercises beauty like a playground bully, her beauty being the most important thing about her, her defining and delimiting attribute. But for all the triumphs it has afforded her, it leads her biographer to question how many strikes she has taken and how often she has been date-raped by boyfriends with little patience and the interest of a passing stranger. The subject's lot is not to be a mother but a repeating aborter of the fruit of her encounters. The speaker wonders how many abortions she has had now as he remembers her "walking in like a diva to the cast party" on the occasion of her second visit to an abortionist. She takes a seat among the young girls with their mothers, "each sinner/beside her own avenging angel."

Loving her in silence, the speaker's prize is the perverse reward of being allowed to escort her to such parties; by not bedding him, she has been able to keep him for such situations, her sole remaining friend. The clinic provides the speaker's last firm memory of his subject, eclipsing the annual letters and old photos of herself she sends. In the end, he remembers, better than she, the hatred that filled the faces of the mothers-to-be in the clinic, the hatred of men and children, the refusal to weep or feel shame and the bitter legacy such women passed along with old tissues to their daughters. The beautiful woman in Atkinson's poem, no lover herself of men or children, is less unlike Jonson's Lady Would-Be, finally, than the passage of three centuries might have suggested.

W. D. Snodgrass intensifies Atkinson's update of the mother of multiple abortions in a poem entitled "The Mother." The mother in Snodgrass' poem takes center stage, around her orbiting her young who take on her energy and her light. Unprotected, her young are themselves cast into a dark universe less inviting than her disapproval. Tender only within "a labyrinth of waste, wreckage/And hocus pocus," the mother wreaks havoc, ceasing only when "she has filled all the empty spaces" of her brain with the hallucinated images of her young that she might die righteously, martyred in the world from which her young have been removed. This is a mother who, the third-person narrator represents, needs to be hated. Justified by evil, she finds places in her mind for her feckless young amid the cluttered and precariously strung strands of love through which she moves, hungry, blind, and by habit.

Like a deadly Ariadne, Snodgrass' mother is a figure who threads her way through a maze, leaving no strand of poisonous love unspun, all in her grasp in a realm in which only her thread can navigate the course. In complete and uncaring control where spoilage and breakage prevail, she is at her best delivering up the debris to her young. Community is outside her reach; that is a world over which she has no control and to which she attributes the evil she needs to make her righteous. She is singularly voracious in her vacuous and self-created universe of switched-off reason, a cold and lightless realm of incarnate evil she would have created had it not existed. Snodgrass gives us, in sum, the darkest vision of Jonson's Lady Would-Be as a thing of antique retribution who finds her own identity only in the destruction of her offspring.

William Henry Davies' "The Inquest" pursues a less unforgiving view of an infanticidal mother that finds society complicit, if not in the crime itself, in its toleration of it. The narrator is a juror who takes seriously his oath to inquire without prejudice into the death of one Ada Wright. The knowing child, whose corpse he visits, intimates to him, with a mouth that smiled, "'What caused my death you'll never know—Perhaps my mother murdered me.'" The players in this courtroom drama have made a compact not to see the uncomfortable facts before them—a four-month child of only seven pounds, one foot long, her yellowed eyelid shut. In the court, her mother's evidence reveals only that she was a love-child, accompanied by a smile for the jury's benefit. The coroner catches his cue: "'Now, Gentlemen of the Jury,' said/The coroner—'this woman's child/By misadventure met its death.'/ 'Aye, aye,' said we. The mother smiled." Complicit with his peers, the juror is reminded in a reprise by the four-month babe that the cause of her death will never be known; that maybe her mother murdered her. The community, nonetheless, is satisfied. Label a murder "misadventure" and a problem disappears, except for its victim, whose voice goes unheard. Given voice, she would give the lie to her elders and expose the hypocrisy that allows them to dispose of her case with a wink and a nod.

Shifting from consideration of the woman to a focus on the fetus in male poetry, Frank O'Hara's "An Abortion" addresses abortion as if to suggest that his construction is a generic event more than a uniquely individual situation. The third-person narrator calls upon an unidentified party, demanding that she who "drops leafy/across the belly of black/sky and her abyss" not be bathed in blood. At the pivot of the poem, a couple appears and changes its assent at supper (weeping, to "have her") to a refusal at breakfast ("no"). The narrator turns on a dime to demand that the reader not waste his tears, that the dropping form is monstrous and better murdered in silence. An accommodating shift, the change in perspective transforms the fetus into a threat and promises safety in silence. The choice, made in the light of day and with mutual agreement, is that a monster be removed. The fetus is the spoiler of a way of life that was set and comfortable. It is no longer a helpless victim posed against the belly of the sky. The dropping figure of the opening is thus, in the final lines, "From our tree/dropped that she not wither,/autumn in our terrible breath." The refusal to deliver the fetus into the terrible breath offered in the autumn is a masked kindness. Such kindness hides within it the selfishness of modern love that will neither risk its safety nor explore its nurturing side. Tears shed by such love are false tears and unworthy, but in O'Hara's poem they are not the tears of woman alone; here is a shared selfishness, a shared responsibility, and a shared guilt.

Russell Atkins' "Lakefront, Cleveland" presents the sensible experience of the aborted fetus, describing its demise as a horrifying voyage. In this abortion, a woman has secretly cast her jellied burden into her toilet. Waves reveal a pulp which will be swept into the muck. Calling, "now, then, God, listen," the speaker swears he has heard low "sigh sounds lapse/as from furious determination," a sound of "excruciation/under sepulchral sky." A sensate creature in spite of its lack of form, Atkins' fetus is disposed of in a progress from jelly to pulp to muck, attended by a felt sense of both hysteria and horror but also of fierce struggle set against the grave-like immensity of the sky and a rush of waves that constitute a wake emanating from the city. Its littleness deified by the bigness against which it exerts itself, the disposed-of burden is granted both a power and force that mimics massive natural events in a fitting, if grotesque, farewell.

Advocating on behalf of the fetus and introducing institutional responsibility for its fate, Robert Lowell's "Fetus" targets an abortion surgeon and Harvard lawyers who appear before an accommodating municipal court. The law is a "sledgehammer,/not a scalpel"; an indirect instrument of abortion, it aborts a second time, its victim—justice: the court cannot remediate what it regards as a misstep and so it clears its many killers of killing. Still, the murder of a fetus—too young to qualify for the unsentimental New England strength of a "hope of heaven" belied by a "certainty in hell"—shocks us. The victim, a germ, unregistered and lacking form in flesh, has no way to announce that it lived. With no past, no artistic expression left behind to mark it, no time or place to stir itself, it is caught by the "contradicting rays of science"—the ability to kill or cure.

Shifting to an image of death and resurrection, the speaker entreats that we wrap him but not too close. This age of pretense and hypocrisy is one to which we have not yet awoken. When we do, the poet asks, will our hearts be made larger and will we embrace all men as our brothers, an echo of the prolife claim that the fetus is our brother and, like the slave, must be saved? The loss is not, however, only that of the fetus, already one pound and sucking its thumb. Rather, the fetus is a model, a warning that leaves us questioning at our deaths how much we shall take with us once we learn we have nothing to take. A form of male bonding with its seed, Lowell's poem takes male law and medicine as well as the brotherhood of humankind to task for their failure to recognize the protective role they have chosen to abdicate. "When the black arrow arrives on the silver tray" is a sign of imminent abortion.

Taking one last twist in the final stanza, the poem moves to the first person, an adolescent at the wheel passing stores decorated with billboards for Easter. On one, we find the unfashionable face of a girl from his father's times, one eternally young. She is rediscovered as a two-dimensional poster-board woman, unused and out of date, an afterthought. In the same way, she has been absented from the previous court trial and the moment of abortion itself, much as the female body has been truncated in medical depictions of pregnancy since the seventeenth century and as the woman's voice has gone unheard in centuries of legal abortion decisions. The woman whose place has been taken in Lowell's poem by law and medicine is reintroduced, but as an anachronism. The institutional male voice in Lowell's poem is, however, very much present and entrusted with a responsibility that the poem reclaims as definitive.

Dominating male medicine is given a human face in William Carlos Williams' "A Cold Front," a poem that while it appears to leave the decision to abort ultimately in the hands of the male physician, does so having adopted a woman's point of view and ventriloquizing her voice. The controlling theme is the balancing of lives that is within the province of the physician. Endowed with the role of curing and sometimes of killing to cure, the healer is hooked on the horns of a dilemma. The mother giving birth in Williams' poem is introduced in the first line as a clinical case: pregnant, she is a woman who already has seven children and a newborn. Diagnosing herself, she asks for pills for an abortion, even as her newborn grunts the doctor a greeting. A trade-off is implied in a subsequent juxtaposition of the mother's expressionless look and the baby's grunt. The contest is not only over a contest of rights between the mother and the fetus but between the needs of the born child and those of the unborn. The woman's justification is that of "a cat/on a limb too tired to go higher/from its tormentors." With barely any color left in her face, she tells him she will not bear any more children. Bowing to his patient's need and accepting her right to contribute to a decision about her own care (unlike Alice Walker's physician in "Ballad of the Brown Girl"), the physician draws the appropriate medical conclusion: "In a case like this I know/quick action is the main thing."

Having used up her life to give life, the mother's plea reflects an instinctive understanding of the exchange of life forces. The doctor's intervention to give her back her life is itself a recognition of necessity; circumstances and humanity are his determining motives. Williams' empathy with the realities of motherhood prevents him from disparaging his patient's attempt to escape it, and it does not allow him to accept more than one patient when he is asked to "erase" her unborn. The issue is not one of a woman being held hostage by her fetus nor of a father's reproductivity held hostage by an aborting mother. The doctor has no time to consider whether his actions are transgressive of fatherhood nor whether his patient castrates her husband when she aborts. Questions of female identity through a woman's role as a mother as well as a woman's right to control her own body yield to necessity with an immediate and direct respect for the facts on the ground. The doctor's response may be that of male authority, but it is also incorporatively human.

A doctor-poet like Williams, K. D. Beernick approaches abortion as an abstraction, rather than a clinical case. In his poem "Anonymous: Spontaneous Abortion," Beernick, too, withholds judgment, reflecting the contradictory medical role of a physician-poet caught between the opposed values of life and death. Alternating, he moves from life to death and then death to life across five stanzas; in the sixth and final stanza, he sandwiches life within a doubled treatment of death, much as life is formed from nothingness and returns to it. Beernick contrasts the coldness of death, the brevity of dying, the blackness of despair, and a woman's loud weeping to the heat of conception, the long hours of dreaming, the long years of loving, and the cheerful light of the knowledge of growth. The contrasts are contained within a frame in which conception's silence is like blood and the silence of formless dying is like love, an inversion of the more traditional association of love with life and of blood with abortion.

Arriving at a depiction of abortion in which the mother and fetus are foregrounded and, except for the act of conception, the father is largely absent, Beernick focuses on balancing the points of view of the fetus and the mother. It is the fetus who hears the first premonition of life and senses the cold and starchy white sheets that greeted its arrival. It is the fetus who experiences how "slow the forgetting of all you were to be." But it is the mother who engages in the long dreaming and loving. To her falls the joy, for "cheerful with light were her days in the knowledge of you." Except for the moment of conception, the anticipation of joy falls to the woman and, with the exception of the moment of the recognition of loss, the reality of despair to the fetus. The last stanza seals them together in a moment when their trajectories cross, the moment when the fetus' silent fate ("loud in its silence no infant is crying") meets the mother's noisy loss ("Loudly this night sounds a woman's weeping").

Conclusion

This admittedly selective survey of three dozen poems provides few surprises—abortions are represented as contested, psychologically debilitating, stigmatizing, and the occasion of guilt and regret as well as liberating, the source of greater gender equality, and largely in the province of women to initiate. This reading nevertheless enriches our understanding of abortion with subtle insights that nudge us closer to a middle ground in our perception of the abortion experience. It is difficult, for example, to read these abortion poems without gaining a deeper sympathy for all the players, just as it is difficult to maintain an unyielding position on the political and ideological issues abortion raises.

One theme that is clear in considering the act of abortion is the variety of types and occasions of abortions addressed as well as the variety of motives that lead to an abortion. Abortions are implicated in cases of rape, poverty, inter-racial pregnancy, large families, self-protection, in defense of honor, to pursue ambition, and to retain control over one's body, among other situational determinants. Women are presented as making a calculated choice, as responding to coerced sex, committing a confused act, acting on a suicidal impulse, under duress, or by animal instinct.

In an abortion-related situation like Anne Sexton's "Unknown Girl in the Maternity Ward," the mother recognizes the "fit" between herself and, in this case, the born child, but in self-defense chooses to unlearn her biological mothering instinct. She lacks a defined motive but, rather, makes her decision through an underexamined sense of personal necessity that overwhelms her sense of their belonging to each other. In Sexton's "The Abortion," that vague necessity is displaced in a setting in which the human relation to the natural world is an exploitative one. It is a surprise that anything fragile survives, although the lost one is regarded as someone who should have been or had a right to be there.

Abortion takes on another aspect in Margaret Atwood's "Christmas Carols," appearing natural and, concomitantly, as necessary as motherhood; indeed, it is a form of motherhood along a continuum on which it stands as less Edenic and nearer to nature's neccessity. Dependent as it is on the vagaries of life as it is lived, abortion is not, as a result, worshipped like its ideal counterpart, birthing, on the other end of the spectrum.

If abortion can be understood as one of nature's expressions, it can also have a merciful face to it, as it does in Liz Lochhead's "An Abortion." Here, it is part and parcel of life's exigencies, a rescue of a desperate mother who must be saved from her own maternal instincts when nature itself has determined they are counterintuitive, that is, when nature's harsh verdict has been rendered on the unviable unborn. The same instinctive sense that Lochhead depicts through a cow and her calf is replicated in Ai's "The Country Midwife," in which human reproduction is itself reproduced as an animal scene in which births and abortions exist in an indiscriminate mix of stains and smells in the life of one family. The bullish father and bovine mother are created as parents unlikely to care for their young, so that, life and birth having lost their magic or mystery, birth and abortion become undifferentiated experiences. The brutalizing aspect of abortion takes its toll not only on the fetus but on the mother herself, as we see in Dorothy Hewett's "This Version of Love." The mother cries out to be obliterated, to be herself erased so that her hallucination of the child who might have been and who leaves no footprint constructs abortion as a form of double suicide.

Mothers necessarily differ in their approaches to abortion, just as abortions themselves differ in their nature and effect. The mother in Ai's "Abortion" does not claim to have unsexed herself but to have taken control of her body, assuming at the same time whatever burden flows from her perverse presentation of her dead male fetus as a *fait accompli* to its father. Like Medea in her show of the fetal corpse, yet like Lady Macbeth in her choice for her spouse as the only man in the house, Ai's mother is woman—rather than mother—writ large, the hard case that does not make good law and that writes against the grain as a strong statement of an alternative role for reproductive woman. Ai speaks of an option that would have given the interracial pregnancy in Alice Walker's "Ballad of the Brown Girl" other story lines than the brutality of a girl's life cut short.

Louise Gluck's "The Egg" gives us the mother for whom such an option was exercised for and not by her. Her abortion is experienced as a fetus taken by coercion, as a robbery, an abortion that appears "necessary, if distasteful," given a social life in which alternatives are unsupported or unavailable. The mother in Gluck's "The Wound" accepts as a risk a wounded ripeness in which her womb becomes both prison and tomb, and she herself becomes a prisoner of her lost fertility and haunting guilt. Gluck's wound is an expression of the bleeding that women experience; a sign of revolt, of transgression, of violence, and of sin, the bloody stains mark women as they terminate their motherhood. Commensurately, the cost of the abortion transaction marks a woman's property rights over her own body with a perennial reminder of the recurrent survivor's guilt that plagues women in many of the poems sampled.

If the practice of abortion is one in which a variety of women face a range of experiences, there is less variation in the aftereffects of abortion that the no-longer pregnant woman undergoes. Women are victimized by constrained options or by abortions gone wrong as well as by the effects of regret and guilt in the aftermath of the act. In many ways, however, women's poems speak of self-victimization. The self-reflexive poetry that characterizes much of our sample pleads, like Diane DiPrima's "Brass Furnace," for forgiveness and yearns for a connection that is no longer possible. Living out an unforgiving sentence of life without the possibility of undoing the violence to oneself, one's offspring, or the relationship of mother and child, many of the subjects in the women's poems are nevertheless difficult to empathize with. DiPrima's mother is herself a child whom the fetus must parent, a potentially self-serving and undeserving victim. The poem may offer to heal, to make recompense to the child, but it is even more the attempt of a failed parent to reinsert herself into the life of her child. Her offer, however, comes too late and when all possible damage has already been done. It is the gasp of a woman hungry for a second chance at being a mother when her own act has foreclosed that option.

Moeller's "ten years ago" opens the door to another domain of regret. Hers is a more generous admission of a debt owed to the child who gave the poet life, who gave its life for her life. Moeller expresses a reverse Samaritanism that asks of the innocent and the vulnerable a sacrifice that is not required of those fully endowed with rights. Moeller's poem operates under an exchange of lives theory and adopts the stance of a subject who obeyed her survival instinct and resisted pressure to do otherwise. The question the poem poses is not whether the abortion prevented a loss of life, avoided a suicide, or merely led to a better life for its beneficiary. Abortion led to the possibility of a life for the mother, which was all it was asked to do; what it did not lead to is the possibility of a child.

The nature of the abortion experience in women's poetry uncovers three sources of action or determining forces: structural conditions, agentive actions, and primordial forces. Each is expressed in the sample, although individual women take responsibility and assume guilt in a traditional or conventional sense with much greater frequency than they are determined by the logic of socioeconomic forces. Gwendolyn Brooks' "The Mother," like Alice Walker's "Ballad of the Brown Girl"—poems that address abortion from a race-d perspective (including, from men's poetry, Kenneth Carroll's "The Truth About Karen")—are among the few that look to structural conditions rather than agentive action as a determinant of the abortion experience. Caught in a socioeconomic double bind between doing justice to her children and violence to herself, Brooks' subject is prevented from avoiding harm to either by an oppressive set of circumstances. Margaret Piercy's "Right to Life" expresses a comparable struggle against social determinism but from a feminist position that rejects patriarchy's legislation of its rights over women's bodies. By contrast, Gibson's "Country Woman Elegy" presents a cosmic contest of wills between the forces of the unborn and the world of embodied forms. Gibson's subject struggles from within a primordial experience, offering an atavistic resistance to creation in her desire to preserve the mystery of the cosmos and its powerful openness to creative potential.

Women present abortion as an event largely attributable to their own actions and only partially as a function of circumstances beyond or outside themselves. It is not surprising, as a result, to find that the poetry that deals with women's resistance to the role of mother or the institution of motherhood capitalizes on this agentiveness as the source of that resistance. Adrienne Rich's "To a Poet," for example, extends the logic of an exchange of lives theory to the prospect of reverse termination, in which it is the female poet through her lost poetry who is aborted, rather than the fetus. The implicit question raised by this poem is whether a woman's generativity can or should be fulfilled in the presumably male realm of cultural production rather than through maternal reproduction. Rich's answer is that birthing leaves a woman "landlocked in life." To be, further, denied her art is to leave her murdered by motherhood. As in the majority of women's poems, there is no cry here for structural changes in the institution of motherhood; rather, the individual is herself called upon to negotiate her conflicting cultural and maternal roles and their conflicting interests.

The agentive solution is defended most fully by Piercy in "Right to Life," in which women declare they will choose for themselves and refuse to perform as a reproductive resource for society to exploit. The alternative is rooted in the poem's transposing of the prolife line "We were all once fetuses." The line is intended to convey that whereas we were all once at risk of being ourselves aborted, our mothers made the choice that gave us life. Piercy's reading is that "We are all born of woman," expressing the meaning that a woman is the origin of both life and love and that mandatory motherhood begets unloved children and a violent world. Agentive choice operates interdependently with the abundance of fertility, as Piercy's "Sabbath" makes clear at length. Choice acts not as a master narrative but as an alternative that celebrates respect for others' choices.

The final question raised by this chapter asks whether the male perspective on abortion is gendered, how it differs from the female perspective, and whether, like the female perspective, it is conflicted. Earlier poems considered in the sample of men's poetry, like Ben Jonson's "To Fine Lady Would-Bee," suggest that, indeed, some men attribute to women the responsibility for the "sin" of abortion, regarding it as an unnatural act that turns the life-giving woman's womb into a place of death. The debate over male productivity and female reproductivity indicates the salience of the male view that a productive but un-reproductive woman is infanticidal and that every child never born presents a lost opportunity, attributable to a woman, for the possibility of life.

Our survey of men's poetry on abortion, again selective but not for that reason unrepresentative, suggests that there is considerable differentiation among the views of male poets. Moreover, their approach to abortion is both nuanced and expresses more ambiguity than anticipated in making hard or fast distinctions between the literal, maternal, female role and the figurative, productive, male role. Indeed, men's poetry on abortion is much like women's poetry in its consideration of the counterbalancing of the child's threat to one's identity and the guilt and anxiety experienced over the loss of a child. Such comparability between men's and women's poetry does not, however, eclipse the distinctions between them. The woman poet is unlikely to memorialize herself through her children or to adopt a view of either herself or her progeny as property. Moreover, the child erased is less likely to be seen as a spilled seed. Rather, the loss experienced is that of the maternal connection or relationship. The woman internalizes society's judgment that she is a bad mother if she loses a child, where the male does not suffer from the comparable attribution of a bad father. Whereas the male poet is able to retain his male identity and status with or without children, both personally and artistically, a woman is represented in men's poetry as having to give up her maternal role if she wishes to retain those personal or artistic privileges. Atkinson's "The Same Troubles with Beauty You've Always Had" reinforces Jonson's "To Fine Lady Would-Bee" on this point, for in order to retain her beauty and attractiveness to men, her lot is to be an aborting mother, open to the uses and abuses of men as well as those she brings on herself.

Indeed, in W. D. Snodgrass' "The Mother," the woman who stands at the center of her children's universe is not there to protect her children. Rather, only within a self-created "labyrinth of waste" is she made righteous, only at the cost of her young is her poisonous love justified. Society conspires to protect such a woman in William Henry Davies' "The Inquest," where only the child avoids becoming complicitous when the community endorses its mother's "misadventure." Robert Lowell's "Fetus" is equally cynical, holding that medicine and law conspire to ensure that all "men" are not made equal; the born are more equal than the unborn in a courtroom that sets murderers free with a verdict that repeats the original injustice to a little victim.

Men's poetry expresses as well the hard cases presented by women, which we see in William Carlos Williams' "A Cold Front" and Kenneth Carroll's "The Truth About Karen." The physician-poet Williams provides a decidedly human response to human need, rejecting the lens of sentiment or ideology for that of life experience. Unambivalently, he sides with his one patient, the mother. Having used up her body giving life to her offspring, she now finds her own life at risk. Coldly clinical in his consideration, Williams nevertheless clearly identifies with the perspective of his female patient. The irony of killing to cure (expressed in Lowell as well) is neatly parried by complicating the trade-off of one life for another. The trade is not merely between mother and fetus but between the unborn and the infant already born and chortling at his mother's side, both of whom have need of the same resource and only one of which can effectuate its claim. With equally compelling complexity, Carroll constructs a world of gossip, secrets, and whispers around the pregnant teenager at the center of his abortion poem. Repeated welfare cycles and babies at too young an age speak of the loss of innocence that engages Carroll's soft focus and sympathy.

Men's poetry is thus complicated beyond the easy difference described by "genderized" poetry. Indeed, the almost female solicitude with which the sentient fetus is handled in Frank O'Hara's "An Abortion," Russell Atkins' "Lakefront, Cleveland," and K. D. Beernick's "Anonymous: Spontaneous Abortion" in itself makes a good case for laying oppositional distinctions between men's abortion poetry and that of women aside. As a contest of woman and fetus, a voyage of "furious determination" of the fetus itself, or as a hard case of a mother worn down by giving life, men's poetry may not have the same identification with women that we find in women's poetry or, for that matter, the same stridency about women's need to speak about themselves for themselves. But that is not to say that men's poetry does not struggle over the issues raised by abortion with a comparable sense of anxiety and ambiguity. Men's poetry may struggle with some of its own issues—the relation of progeny and male identity and its view of a woman's identity as a mother, for example—in a way that goes underexplored in women's poetry, but that is not to say that those issues are always addressed without cross-gender understanding or complexity.

Notes

1. On Sexton, see Dessner (1988), Swigert (1991), Dash (1977), Middlebrook (1991), and Johnson (1986).
2. Sexton's "The Abortion" evades saying what the poet means to say until, by self-accusation, she finally confronts herself starkly in the poem's close. For some (McGowan 1998, 129) "The last five words are the true text," and they essentially return the reader to a poem that is of the female and of a female event. In one reading, the trip itself can be understood as "a journey from the female body" through descriptions that "shape the poem into a female form" (129), that is, to figure a woman absent her emotional responses.
3. On Gluck, see Robert Miklitsch (1982).
4. On Clifton, see Madhubuti (1984), McClusky (1984), Ostriker (1996), Johnson (1986), and Clifton (1984).

5. On Brooks, see Guy-Sheftall (1979), Gayle (1984), Dash (1977), and Johnson (1986).
6. On Rich, see Johnson (1986).
7. Of interest here is Stephen Booth's insightful reading of Jonson's epitaphs on his children (1998, 64–120), in particular, Booth's reading of "On My First Sonne" in which he suggests "that a child's death may be divine punishment for a parent's sin" (95). Booth nevertheless objects to the reading that the death of the poet's son in some way signifies the poet's own death (82).

CHAPTER FIVE

The (Short) Fiction of Abortion

We have discussed the national fabric in relation to the abortion wars in our discussions of history, law, and their narrative construction, and we have accessed the culture's varied perspectives on abortion in considering the rhetoric, cartoons, and poetry of abortion. Short fiction offers an exceptionally responsive and untapped resource that ties both together. Working from a base of 143 short works of prose fiction on abortion and a handful of selected longer works of fiction, this chapter considers family and community relationships, race and gender perspectives.[1]

Relationships

At their essence, abortions are conditioned by relationships more than by any other personal element in the abortion equation. Husband and wife, father and daughter, mother and daughter, and other family relationships as well as relationships between the unmarried affect the choice of an abortion in determining ways. Patty Lou Floyd's "The Voice in the Whirlwind" (1987) explores the most traditional kind of relationship, that of the individual to the community, through a tale told by the narrator's grandmother of the tornado of '98. When Sylvie, a local girl, a weak-minded epileptic, "got herself raped" (171), her pregnancy became a matter of concern in a town that "besides being in the Dust Bowl and the Bible Belt, is smack on the center line of Tornado Alley" (167). Who, after all, according to her fellow townspeople, would take care of it; "Us so good to [her]—and what's our thanks? Another idjit, like as not" (172). The day of the landmark tornado, Sylvie refused to take refuge in a neighbor's storm cellar and was met by arms reaching out to draw her in through the uplifted door "like the arms of lost souls reaching up from hell-fire" (195). The opportunity offered by the seclusion of the storm cellar was not lost on the neighbors, including Mrs. Kyle, "one of those women a girl could go to if she got in trouble: 'Brews her own medicine'. . . . 'Uses an ice pick'. . . . 'Common as pig tracks . . . but salt of the earth'" (178–179). The narrator's grandmother regarded Mrs. Kyle not only as a friend but as a woman who provided a service to the town that made it less likely that women, including married women, would have to drop their unwanted newborns in the creek. She did not make the girls bad, and as a midwife she helped many babies into the world. Those who did not need her services might not have understood what she offered, Floyd suggests, but they would have used her if they had. And so, in the storm cellar, in a moment of rare understood agreement, several women held Sylvie down while it appeared she was having a fit, and Mrs. Kyle asked the Reverend for a fountain pen. "Bleeding," she said, and then, "Reverend, the Lord is providing" (190). As they emerged from the cellar into the light, a trade was made between the midwife and the grandmother: a desired dress will be refit in exchange for care that will get Sylvie through without harm. The Reverend, too, did his part in his next sermon, titled "The Voice That Spoke in the Whirlwind," in which "he had put it about that the Lord, in the Whirlwind, had delivered Sylvie of her burden" (1994). Abortion is thereby, in Floyd's view, as much a community's affair as it is an individual's; one gets through life as a result of relationships, casual as well as intimate, intended as well as accidental, that one develops with others.

In "Tiger Bites," Lucia Berlin (1990) takes a more contained view of community in terms of family. Here, a family reunion provides a setting for the potential reconciliation of a daughter, Lou, and her parents. Newly pregnant, the girl has been alienated from her parents by her recent divorce and is contemplating an abortion. Her cousin Bella Lynn meets Lou at the train, both to arrange the abortion and to put a hold on the reconciliation; the father refuses to come to the reunion, and the mother is in the hospital, having made a drunken suicide attempt that she blames on her daughter. At an abortion clinic in Mexico, Lou determines to take charge of her own life. Unlike the other patients at the clinic, she is neither "frightened, embarrassed . . . [n]or intentionally ashamed" (98). In isolation from her family, she discovers she does not "want to have an abortion . . . didn't want an abortion" (99). A resurgence of doubt occurs only as she considers her fitness to raise children and whether her husband will return if she aborts, reflecting the estimation of others rather than her own concerns. In a shared tearful moment, she and Bella Lynn resolve on her decision and proceed to the reunion. Circling the family wagons, the men promise to tear her unsupportive husband "limb from limb" (107). Much like the abortion itself, the family response reasserts control as it isolates an irritant and puts into play an intervention that confirms the importance of a sense of community and the support it provides.

The all-encompassing effects of community and family are extended in short fiction to friends as well. In Nowick Gray's "New Moon" (1992), Jesse and her friend Maria both find themselves pregnant but with different personal agendas. Jesse is alone, tormented by ending the growing life within her and with the regret she feels certain she will face. Maria, a prolife activist, reinforces her friend's premonition of regret. She nevertheless accompanies her friend to an abortion clinic. Settled that she did what was right for herself, Jesse is nevertheless disappointed that Maria, as a good friend, failed to stop her: "I was mad at you for not talking me out of it! I guess I just wanted someone else to blame" (183). For her part, Maria is faced with a spontaneous abortion, the victim of an environmental poison. She admits Jesse had become for her "something less than human" (183); Jesse, by contrast, finds that Maria's pamphlets had accused her of thinking just that about her fetus. Their mutual perspective on the two abortions, one chosen and one spontaneous, is initially that only one of them was able to decide for herself. Ultimately, however, even that recognition is ambiguified in Maria's refusal to confront the party responsible for her poisoned pregnancy. It would be the same, she contends, as Jesse confronting the father who deserted his fetus, "with your aborted baby . . . saying 'Will you make it up to me, Gerry? Will you come back?'" (184). "New Moon" thus presents a scenario in which choice is effectively no choice, as both women are decisionally disabled—Jesse by the fear of desertion, both by the father of her child and by her friend, and Maria by the despair that both attends her loss of a desired child and prevents her from addressing the loss publicly.

The relationship that appears to have potentially the most powerful effect on how a woman regards her choice to terminate or retain a pregnancy is that between the pregnant woman and her mother. In Marshall Klimasewiski's "Jun-Hee" (1991), the title character has gradually and carefully considered her choice: "I had questions, but each day they moved closer to being the questions of how to do this right and further from the question of whether we should do it at all" (26). But it is the appearance of her dead mother in a dream that proves for Jun-Hee the most resolute moment in her decision. Like a "thief in the night," her mother arrives to claim the child. The daughter neither releases the child nor reaches for her; rather, it falls into her mother's embrace in the presence of a small wind: "'That's better', my mother whispered, bent over the child. My mother looked at me—her face was red and swollen with tears" (26). The physician offers solacing words—that this was an "isolated tragedy" and that the couple could try again and have healthy children; her partner focuses on the future—that time past flows "fluidly into the future" (26). But Jun-Hee finds their words eclipsed by the dream moment when she fails to reach out and take her baby back: "I wondered if every woman was tested by her own mother before being allowed her pregnancy" (26). Did her future lay in the hands of the dead as her father believed? Even if her mother forgave her, could Jun-Hee ever know why? What right had the older woman to take their child? Without answers to Jun-Hee's questions, her mother weighs on her as the voice of a tradition that exists to continue the family and to resist its being brought to an end. The relation of mother and daughter is a surety to maintain that continuity. For Jun-Hee, life has reversed itself; she has been usurped in her choice not to have a child by her mother who, in death, now cares for her child. She resists the finality of that dream image, renarrating it in her memory in more favorable terms: "I reached my arms out and I felt the small weight and warmth, supported in my hands. . . . She was falling. I reached out and took her from the air. I took her in and I whispered to her. I held her hand against my chest" (33). For Jun-Hee, the moment must change to bring her relief, but she must also prepare herself to "shed my desire to control" (36). Her baby was gone, like the mother she had not returned home to bury. It had taken "a lifetime to get back to her" (36), and now she had arrived. It was Jun-Hee who had been falling, for fifteen years and a long way from her home. "I know I gave up my child. I'm sorry I let you down. . . . Take care of my baby" (36). Having come to terms with this most important relationship as a precursor to her own potential future pregnancies, Jun-Hee may someday, in some sense, recuperate her loss. Deserted by Jun-Hee, her own mother never had that opportunity. Nor had Jun-Hee, as a child, had the choice to be reclaimed as she was now determined her "birthmate" would be. For Jun-Hee, the reuniting of the three generations reestablishes the familial community that would center her. Couched between the mother she regains in dream and the child of a possible future pregnancy, she would be released from the double burdens of guilt that have disabled her.

A different kind of mother-daughter relationship inflects Bobbie Ann Mason's "Marita" (1989), a relationship in which a daughter does not replace or continue but must share a life with a mother who "lives her life through her daughter's" (54). Marita carries the combined names of two aunts, Mary and Rita, foreshadowing the sharing of her life with her mother. Indeed, the mother "flirts with the guys [she goes] out with," competing as a more beautiful "older sister" (54). Intent that her daughter avoid her own costly mistakes—"two husbands—neither of whom was [the girl's] father" (54)—the mother is angry and disappointed when Marita drops out of college in her first semester. But Marita "always told [her] everything" (58): the silly fabrications that she came back home because she missed her and wanted to do something useful and the, more truthful, revelation that she was pregnant. Having intuited her daughter's secret and seen through her excuses, the mother determines her daughter will have an abortion, with a doctor she has chosen. She "didn't dare offer Marita an out," fearing that Marita might say that "This is what you wished you could have done eighteen years ago" (64).

Having elided two lives into one, Marita is led to thoughts of having been an inconvenience that barred her mother from having a life of her own; at the same time, the mother considers Marita's pregnancy a child-rearing responsibility that would fall on her. The abortion resets the game; the mother, "smiling proudly" (66), gives Marita a party that sets them both free: "I'm lost in pink," says Marita, "lying under my pink cabbage roses, my pink Penny War hanging in the closet" (65), referring to the new peignoir her mother has given her. Just as Marita had run free in high school—bashing the flour baby she had been forced to carry to teach her the responsibility of child care—so she and her mother are now free of husbands and babies and clear of their own mistakes. The two women, Mason reveals, are relieved to have dealt with abortion the way people deal with movies or their dogs on the David Letterman show, not as a choice one makes but as a game one is forced to play in public or lose face. The mother-daughter relationship in "Marita," for good or ill, has not only survived the abortion but has flourished in its presence.

The father-daughter relationship is no less complicated than that of mother and daughter even if the two players often appear less intertwined, more formally related. In Ellen Gilchrist's "1957, a Romance" (1981), the relationship is that of a spoiled daughter and a rich father accustomed to buying her out of scrapes. Rhoda has borne two boys thirteen months apart, both by cesarean section, and is the wife of a man who, she insists, keeps her tethered by repeated pregnancies. Her solution is a periodic run home to her parents to be taken care of and have someone take care of her babies. Hysterical and vain, Rhoda pressures her father into arranging an abortion: "No one knows. I have to do this thing right away. . . . I can't tell Malcolm. He'd never let me do it. . . . He got me pregnant on purpose, Daddy" (81–82). The father predictably falls into line: "As long as nothing happens to her, he told himself. As long as she is safe" (84). Keeping her secret, he provides a cover story that leaves his wife—a practical and gentle woman who is not fooled by her daughter—out of the equation. Having fabricated her story to her father, Rhoda avoids what her physician uncle has advised him: "first you make certain she's pregnant" (87). The doctor who will do the abortion makes a second request for a pregnancy test, which she deftly parries. Continuing to direct the show, her only worry over the past two weeks has been to melt "the baby fat from her hips and stomach [so that] she was pleased with the way her body looked" (89). The abortion complete, daughter and father are restored to the familiar role of caretaker and grateful dependent. Even as her father recertifies that "As long as I live nothing will ever harm her" (86), Rhoda is already harmed, by a willfulness that has likely led to an unnecessary procedure for a hysterical pregnancy. "I think," her uncle advises her, " you imagined you were pregnant because you dread it so much" (94). To Rhoda, real or not, what is important about the possible pregnancy is that it is over: "I'm skinny and I'm beautiful and no one is ever going to cut me open. . . . And no one can make me do anything" (95). Her father, like her husband, is by now well out of the picture; he is supplanted by Rhoda's strong sense of "feeling strange and foreign and important . . . carrying an enormous secret [her family] could not imagine, not even in their dreams" (93).

A different father, in a different ideological geography, Simon Peter Dresser in Sara Paretsky's "The Man Who Loved Life" (1993) offers us a contrast in character. Simon Peter marks a sea change in his life when he realizes his daughter has had an abortion. An official in the prolife movement, he is considered "the rock on which a whole nation of Christians was building its hope of bringing morality back to America" (160). Invited to be keynote speaker before the House of Bishops, he converses with one of the bishops, endorsing the respect children owe their parents and the parents' need, as his father had taught him, to be strong and use force: "That's why you get all these girls going into the abortuaries and letting someone murder their babies. Their daddies or their husbands are just too damned—excuse me, Your Grace—too darned lazy to control them" (162).

Honored by other speakers at the banquet, Simon Peter watches a slide show in which clinic protestors and sidewalk counselors harass abortion clinic patients. One patient sparks a sign of recognition, a girl who headed up the clinic path and whose face Simon knew without seeing. A patriarch betrayed, he turns to his wife and, hissing that she was responsible, exiles her from the headtable. Loss of control over his wife and daughter would lose him credibility within the movement, the slide show in the background reminds him: "One of our failures. . . . We didn't have the resources to give this girl the help she needed to choose Life" (168–169). The memory of his own mother surfaces; she looks on in memory as his father assaults him with a baseball bat. He refocuses to consider his daughter: "He could kill her for this. Kill her for destroying him at the moment of his triumph, for working hand in glove with the old man to get him" (168). The deception of his daughter and his wife are linked to his desertion by a mother who feared to defy her husband. Simon Peter is betrayed on both sides of the generational divide. As his ineffectual mother squeaks at the top of the stairs in his memory, and Sandra mocks him from the screen, Simon Peter shrinks, publicly humiliated by the very women he had most depended upon privately to support him. "The Man Who Loved Life" clearly valued the right to life and his own life in the antiabortion movement over his life with the women he regarded as his personal and ideological trophies.

A presumably enviable solidarity of parents in a positive relationship with their pregnant daughter suggests itself as the subject of Andre Dubus' "Miranda over the Valley" (1988). By the time the eighteeen-year-old daughter Miranda brings home the news of her pregnancy, she and her law-school boyfriend Michaelis have already decided to get married and have the child. Her parents take the news of the pregnancy in stride, the mother convinced that her daughter had been foolish and the father that these kinds of things happen: "don't worry. . . . You're not the first good kids to get into a little trouble" (7). But foolishness and a "little trouble" do not, they communicate to the young couple, have to add up to marriage. Law school, medical bills, the prospect of her dropping out of school or of Michaelis continuing to grow as Miranda is preoccupied with a child are all considerations. The father has an answer if the couple is worried about the "baby"—"That's not a baby. It's just something you're piping blood into" (9). The mother expresses her incredulity at her daughter's protestation that she wants the child and can care for it—"I don't believe you. You mean you're happy about it?" (9). Are they not, after all, just being "foolish"? Whereas Miranda resents being made to feel the situation will simply resolve itself, Michaelis seems alternately relieved and conflicted.

The parents attach a Christmas gift, a free trip to Acapulco, as a consolation prize to the abortion. Having both won and lost, Michaelis' face shows him struggling to deal with both. As time passed after the abortion, his face would heal. Miranda, however, would have difficulty facing him: she had death in her, and "she wished for courage in the past, wished she had gone somewhere alone" (12). She fails to return home at Thanksgiving to be with her parents and Michaelis and drifts instead into a meaningless act of sex with her roommate's boyfriend. Her parents had "saved her" (19), but they would not "get her back" (19). The trip to Acapulco becomes less and less possible as does Miranda's relationship with Michaelis, with whom she would not make love again.

Whereas the parent-child relationship exerts a powerful pull on a young woman faced with an abortion, with mature women it is their partners who play the largest role. Indeed, the most poignant relationship is possibly that between responsible procreators who share their desire for a child but are nevertheless faced with an abortion. In Gish Jen's "Birthmates" (1995), Lisa left her Asian husband, Art, "on a day when she saw a tree get split by lightning" (111). To Art, the tree meant nothing but that "it had been the tallest in the neighborhood, and was no longer" (111). The metaphor of the tree nevertheless became an image of their racial difference and the dissolution of their marriage. Their differences in perspective—his of the stoic use-value of things and hers of experienced joys and horrors—would not allow a house so divided to stand. They had difficulty getting pregnant and had made a joint decision to take infertility treatments, a decision expected to keep them together and for which Art had drawn a decision "tree." The actual experience was more than they had bargained for, "the tests, the procedures, the drugs, the ultrasounds. . . . Giving practice shots to an orange" (117), so that the medical waste produced became itself, as Art discovered, a "souvenir of this stage of their marriage" (117). Three futile pregnancies with genetic aberrations followed, in which he saw hope and she saw loss. She had insisted it was a baby, something she understood with her body; she, after all, had known, loved, and lost the baby, while for him the baby was just something yet-to-be. While she attended grieving class, he dropped out. He felt he had kept his perspective, while she had lost hers until she retreated in her grief "to the horizon of their marriage, and then to its vanishing point" (118). He wanted to call her, years later, too late, to agree it was a baby or would have become one, that mysteriously transparent and perfect-seeming ultrasound boy that, being born, would have broken all its bones. Without insisting on perspective, it was now possible to see "all the children he would never have," a vision that left him "paralyzed. His heart lost its muscle" (114).

The Male Perspective

Many consider that the lost voice in the abortion debate is neither that of the woman nor that of the fetus but rather that of the father. Indeed, the male perspective is critical not only to address the rights and responsibilities of male partners but, equally, to address the effects of patriarchy on abortion rights. What might be regarded as a retrograde male reaction is presented in a sixties timeframe in John Miller's "Bethune, South Carolina" (1993). Here, a college student is faced with an unwanted pregnancy that resulted from a relationship with a soldier. Whereas someone in her dormitory knows an abortionist, the soldier offers to marry the girl as a cheaper alternative to the five hundred dollars an abortion would cost. In his barracks, a fellow soldier reduces the problem not only to one of entrapment ("It may not even be your kid") but to the possibility of infection ("Make sure she hasn't given you a dose of the clap") and to escape ("Drop your load and hit the road") (61). The preferred alternative turns out to be a one-hundred dollar abortion in a hard-luck hotel across from the bus station. Following the abortion, the soldier's thoughts turn to blaming the girl ("Here's another fine mess you've gotten me into") (65), but embarrassment sets in so that several attempts to phone the girl are abandoned for lack of the right words to say.

An unmarried young male's desire to eliminate a problem, to make it go away, represents one aspect of the male reaction to a pregnancy, an aspect that surfaces with equal frequency when it is the father of the pregnant woman who is the focus of a story. The male parent in Greg Johnson's "Little Death" (1996) mirrors the harshness of Miller's soldiers when his wife dies and he discovers his daughter is pregnant. Father and daughter share a house but live in separate worlds, disagreeing on the fate of her pregnancy. The girl is reluctant to give up the only connection she has to her sensitive student lover, who visited her town and departed. Unlike her mother, who gave in to cancer, and her father, who preferred to ignore his wife's illness, the daughter embraces life and struggles to retain her hold on the life within her. Her father's "cold pragmatism" (107) prevails as he removes her from school, escorts "her to the obligatory visit with a counselor" (106), and compels her to consent to an abortion. Linking the "little death" of her fetus to the death of her mother, she seeks solace at her mother's grave following the abortion.

The male perspectives of "Bethune, South Carolina" and "Little Death" appear rooted in what has been regarded as a conventional male reaction to abortion. But the apparent lack of feeling and suspiciousness attributed to such a reaction serve to mask the fact that little has typically been demanded of men in terms of accepting responsibility, becoming intimately involved, or demonstrating genuine support in the event of an abortion. Fiction offers a range of stories from the male perspective that provide highly differentiated reactions from men to an event that proves as powerfully signifying of male identity as the woman's relation to abortion is to female identity.

The father in Joseph Epstein's "Low Anxiety" (1991) is a parent with whom a daughter might be able to share her decision to have an abortion. His sympathy for her ordeal overshadows his own misgivings about her choice. He struggles to imagine how to tell his own mother about the abortion or how he would have approached his father had his father still been alive. Jewish survivors of the pogrom in Poland, his parents had retained an inescapable expectation of horror, so that the abortion would have carried a certain weight with them. A man of some principle, he had no "principled objection to abortion as the taking of a human life" (49); he was more concerned about being forced to think "about the details of his own daughter's sex life, and resented it that he was doing so now" (49). Still, he faces her and they are able to forego feelings of guilt and offers of forgiveness even as he makes it clear he does not like what has happened to her or what she faces: "I can imagine a terrible life for you. A life of confusion and sadness and heartbreak. And it terrifies me" (52). As a father, ultimately, what he wants is beyond reason and beyond his power: he wants her back the way she was before the abortion; he wants his family's life back under his control.

Husbands raise yet other issues in the abortion debate, issues of a man's inability to procreate without a woman's consent, his right to progeny, and his desire to support a wife's choice. Husbands who support their wives demonstrate a conflicted concern that Edward Lodi explores in "Rock-A-Bye" (1992). The couple had adopted a cat from a shelter, and it had earned its keep as a "mouser." Now, it has carried a creature into the house, which the husband, fearing he is going mad, hopes he has imagined. Knowing he must find some way to dispose of the creature before his wife returns, he stops to consider how like her it is, with its "blond, taut, kinky little pubic wires," only all over its head (92). He flips it with the tip of his shoe to examine its perfect parts, tiny and pink, and to consider its erect penis, pronged "like a tuning fork . . . with a pointed venomous stinger, just like the tail end of a wasp—on each tine" (92). Feeling himself coming apart, he weeps at not having resisted enough when she wanted to have an abortion. Although he had convinced himself they were not yet ready for children, he had wanted a child. Cradling the discarded body and nuzzling its head, he holds it up for his wife to see as she opens the screen door: "Hi, Debs. Look what the cat dragged in. . . . Baby's home!" (93). A conflicted husband who felt he had no standing to object to his wife's decision, he is yet deeply invested in the life they created together and undone by its termination.

The conflicted husband role is carried to its ultimate expression in Diane Slatton's "Seventh Son of a Seventh Son" (1992). A farmer, the father of eight, struggles with several seasons of drought. He beseeches his reluctant wife to abort her most recent pregnancy as she introduces him to their son's ultrasound image. He squints "at the tornado funnel of an ultrasound picture there that threatened to suck him into the pit where his own father had been devoured." When he had wanted a vasectomy, she, a Catholic opposed to any form of contraception, had objected. Now she was ill and refused to consider ending the pregnancy. The husband finds himself saddled with an obstetrician, close to tears himself, who can only offer that he is not permitted to discuss terminations. In his desperation, the husband dreams "of reaching into her uterus—hand smoothly swimming the path his sperm had traveled" (201) to grasp the unformed body and snap its fragile bones. He gasps out to the swelling in her body to die, that he does not love it. Torn by his need for his wife, his responsibility for the children he feeds by stealing meat from his second job at a slaughterhouse, and his desire to destroy his own seed, his eyes glancingly meet his hunting gun, a reminder of his own father's messy suicide. Continuing his dream, he slides back into the uterus, becoming tangled in the noose of the umbilical cord; his seventh and unborn son tugs the dream noose "snakelike from its father's throat" (206) as he blasts back from his wife's body into sleep.

Torn between love for his family, his respect for his wife's wishes, and their dire straits, the husband's conflict is expressed in a heart attack that rips through his body as the premature baby pushes to be delivered. From the floor, on his knees, he breathes life into the blue body, directs his eldest son to cut the cord and name the boy. He provides for its incubation and hot towels for its mother as his own life's breath ebbs away, traded for that of the new life he has brought into the world. Exacting the price of his own life, his life insurance will cover them all. He promises them all college, even the newest addition. All the while, his own father's death shadows him, recalling his words to his father, "Where are you going, Pop?" "Can I go with you?" His oldest son picks up the gauntlet his father has thrown down, "That's what all the bullshit you've been talking comes down to. I gave the boy his name so now it's up to me to hold on tight and try to raise him as good as . . ." (208).

Like Slatton's farmer-husband, men who refuse or are unable to assert their own choice seem to bear the burden of picking up the pieces and making the best of it. Left with their own regrets, they are often isolated and alone. Lawrence Dorr in "Two Hundred Yards past Wordsworth's House" (1987) expresses the male perspective as one in which "the inadequacy of all males, bystanders at births . . . made it impossible for them to demand that their child's life, hardly begun, not be terminated" (73). In Dorr's story, the choice is even less the man's to make, for the pregnancy at issue is the result of his extramarital affair. The sense of loss comes from both the termination of his son and from the knowledge that his own father would have preferred to have terminated him. In his eyes, both his father, who thought he had a choice to make, and his mother, who had to tell her son about that choice, were iniquitous "in a world that cried out for love" (74). In his own failed romanticism, he feels reduced to "a scapegoat banished to the desert" (74), wishing they were all washed clean.

The male partner whose status is unlegitimated by marriage has the least standing to object to a woman's choice for an abortion. At the same time, his own insecure status may increase his desire to have a say or his vulnerability at being denied one. Stephen Dixon's "Newt Likes the House Neat" (1979) presents a couple in an unmarried relationship in which, having parented two children already, the woman wants to abort her pregnancy. The male partner insists that she bring the pregnancy to term. His motivation is to have his own child, for if it is someone else's, he admits, "I'd ask you to abort it and then conceive just with me. . . . Or I'd tell you if you wanted to have it, this other fellow's baby . . . then have it just with him" (107). For her, the issue is one of being psychologically prepared, of wanting to plan for a child, and of wanting to be financially independent, none of which overlap with his concerns. He asks her one final time to allow him to be a father. They could support each other, he would pick up more than his half, if needed, and they could marry. Having resisted, he must now accede. At the abortion clinic, the distinction between them and the three other patients is clear: one is on the phone, complaining to some man that he should be with her; a second, a mere child, depends upon her mother; a third, with her husband, is very matter of fact. She, by contrast, is attended in a loving and caring way; he watches over her as she recovers. It is his needs that will not get met, his interests that will take a back seat. For her, the abortion had become a test that he must pass: "if there ever was a reason I'd want to have a baby with him someday, it was the way he handled the whole situation and especially [the abortion]" (115).

Warren Adler's "An Unexpected Visit" (1995) presents an unmarried couple of mixed religion, the man Jewish and the woman Catholic, whose relationship is conditioned more by their mutual desire not to have children than by religious difference. From the man's point of view, abortion had seemed right in the abstract, "attractive actually, because it foreclosed on the complication of unwanted progeny. It's an option, a choice . . . a sensible approach to a biological problem" (266). Her decision, however, had been made before he began to think with his genes; the issue for her was that she was the one carrying the child. Picturing his child as a young boy, he considers his own father and their walks in the park and the zoo. His visit to the old man, a widower in a retirement "dumping ground for aged Jewish parents of a certain working-class social strata" (261), finds his father living with a woman, which makes it harder to introduce the subject. Moreover, he was unsure why he had come. Did he want advice? Did he want to be validated? How important can children be, he thought, and how much did his own father think of him? A neglectful son, he is surprised to find that, like everyone at the retirement home, his father brags about him, saying "In this place, sometimes I wonder if anybody thinks about anything else. . . .You'd think we produced a race of genuises" (271). His failure to call or visit his father, with whom he shared his past and the tradition of his ancestors, seems strange. He contrasts it with the long talks, the pouring out of words he shared with his partner, Janice, "who carried his seed, the seed of his ancestors" (272). That his father worries about him, just because he is his child, makes it harder to share his worries with him. Can he really introduce him to the idea that Janice will kill his grandchild before he even knows there is a possibility of grandchildren? The visit, nevertheless, makes clear why he was troubled at the idea of the abortion. His father, after all, had said it: his father worried simply because he was his son. His mind had cleared in the presence of a way of thinking that transcended generations. He wouldn't let anyone do away with his child. The three of them, he was thinking, when Janice broke the news that the problem was gone. She took care of it while he was gone, leaving him to try and drown what was inside of him. Made doubly impotent—by the loss of his issue as well as by the coopting of his decision— he will have no child; he will not, unlike his ancestors, have made fruitful his seed.

Race and Abortion

Race constitutes a significant variable addressed in short stories on abortion, allowing us to consider gender not only in relation to both class and race attributes but in a variety of richly overdetermined constructions. Alice Walker's "The Abortion" (1980)[2] is perhaps the best-known story on race and abortion. It considers the effect of race on the relation of husband and wife, a woman's sense of her own need for growth, and the significance of abortion inside a marriage as well as inside a community. The abortion in Walker's story takes place inside a black family, in which a middle-class couple already has a young daughter. The wife, Imani, has already experienced one abortion that was as much a response to societal expectations as it was to protect her status as a college student. She is now considering a second one. This time, she intends to choose for her own sake as a way of claiming ownership of herself. The connectedness she experiences within the marriage and through the pregnancy is balanced against her need to find her own voice. She has in many ways betrayed herself in her false expectations of her marriage and her life. Her husband, Clarence, needs her nurturing to pursue his own interests in black community politics even as he neglects her needs. Much of his life is defined by the patriarchy of black male life, somewhat like a priesthood that cloistered itself off from her and kept her on the outside.

For Imani, who is just coming into herself as a woman, society's definition of woman as wife and mother is vaguely disquieting. She finds herself, as a result, caught between discovering her own agency and the already existing structure of community expectations. Men are not so tied to their bodies, so that they do not experience them day to day as a limiting constraint or as central to how they participate in a culture, nor do they experience anything analogous to abortion, something that reaches inside and rips out a part that is integral to oneself. In spite of Clarence's role as a good family man, male culture takes place largely in a public sphere and does not successfully access the private world in which abortion takes place. Nor does the logical world Clarence inhabits provide ready access to experiencing his body as intimately as a pregnant woman experiences hers. But then neither does Imani understand "impotence" in the same way Clarence must as he tries to reach out to her in response to her desire for an abortion. His relation to power and his need to understand himself can only occur in terms of a male potency that relates differently, if in this case mutely, to the possibility of an abortion.

Because Clarence is in a position where he is expected to know how to fit in a woman's world and yet has not been able to figure himself in those terms, his performance is called into question. Does Imani really want him to tell her she should not have the abortion? He cannot know and therefore has no basis for reacting in one way or another. Clarence may simply feel he does not have the right to make the choice for her or may merely want to show his support for her choice. Imani, by contrast, may have put him in a position of control only to turn on him when he does not want what she secretly wants him to want (that is, not to abort her pregnancy). Moreover, Imani cannot know whether she is aborting the pregnancy because she thinks he wants it or as a means of asserting herself and thereby renarrating the asymmetry of their relationship.

In a summary way, Walker's story asks us to re-imagine marriage, asking if it can survive once a woman finds her voice. It questions whether children get in the way of a man's need to be nurtured by his wife or his need to dominate his wife or whether, on the other hand, children are not the very proof of reproductivity that a man dominates a woman to ensure. Imani may very well have essentialized Clarence in her relations with him rather than seeing in him a physically present real person. She may herself be going through a negative metamorphosis, finding her self in a decision that does not nurture her family. In this sense, she imitates the worst excesses of the atomistic self-serving male. Reading her abortion as self-serving on both their parts, Clarence's "delivery" of Imani to this very private event attended by his political crony the Mayor exemplifies his political ambitions and his public side.

The communal aspect to Walker's story requires notice as well as the opportunistic individualistic aspect. A memorial church service for Holly Monroe, a young girl "who had been shot down on her way home from her high-school graduation ceremony five years ago" (71), follows the abortion. For Imani, this is a time when she is really too weak to consider attending. She recognizes that "the white lawgivers attempted to get around assassination—which Imani considered extreme abortion—by saying the victim provoked it . . . but were antiabortionist to a man. Imani thought of this as she resolutely showered and washed her hair" (71). Holly Monroe and Imani become identified as women who have both been victimized by a death imposed on them. Indeed, Walker's story is filled with dead female bodies, if one considers that all the girls in Holly's class look like her, that Imani herself risks her life to attend the ceremony, and that black women's bodies have been used historically in ways that have left them at risk of being dead to life. Imani has finally to decide that she will love life, which she can only do by loving herself. To do so, she must shed those constraining definitions of herself that her fetus, internally, and her husband, externally, represent. In a choice between herself and this child, she chooses herself. As for her husband, she had already left the marriage and could tell the exact moment it happened. It had to have been the service at the church, the one they had discussed so many times, when she had separated from him as if he was nothing but a stranger. He had never felt it. In the presence of the dead girl's memory and her own uterus burning, Clarence and the Mayor had never come inside the church, "were still deep in conversation," though she had hissed at them "Your voices are carrying"; what she really meant was "How dare you not come inside?" (75). Imani's choice may have signaled the end of her marriage, but it expressed as well her refusal any longer to do as the first abortion doctor had recommended, "be sure to walk as if nothing is wrong" (68). Something was wrong, something men failed to acknowledge, but she wouldn't. There was, after all, a community of women in pain, and someone would have to recognize that.

The contexts that determine race-d experiences of abortion include not only the contemporary sociology of family and community cultures but historical contexts from African tribal culture, slavery, Jim Crow, and the civil rights struggle to black power; they range from cultural constructions of the black body and body politics to the archetypal roles of the black mammy, Jezebel, the welfare queen, and the bad mother (Lubiano 1992). These contexts sometimes mix indiscriminately to inform contemporary prose fiction that treats race and abortion. Toni Cade Bambara's "A Girl's Story" (1984),[3] for example, parallels two worlds within the black community: the un-self-conscious home that a brother, Horace, and sister, Rae Ann, share with their grandmother, M'Dear, and the consciousness-raising Center where black history and politics are taught by Dada Bibi through story, film, and dance. The former, which establishes constraints, constitutes a space determining which negative models are to be avoided and particular behaviors are not to be engaged in. Rae Ann, finding herself bleeding uncontrollably from what appears to the reader to be a botched abortion, has avoided talking about what it will take to be a woman: "she figures she might have to hear one of them one-way talks like M'Dear do about not letting boys feel on your tits" (155). The excessive flow of her menses means she has to face her grandmother's hot and strangled-looking face: "Watcha been going? . . . Let that filthy man go up inside you with a clothes hanger. You going to be your mama all over again" (160). Why, she asked, hadn't the girl come to her; what, she wants to know, is the name of this boy? Repeating her mother's history would extend the shame brought by sexual freedom into the next generation of Rae Ann's family. The Center, by contrast, offers a refuge that embraces without judging and that installs pride rather than shame. It provides an opening through which Rae Ann can go in or out without reprisal. Dada Bibi never fussed, never asked where she had been and why she was not stopping in; Dada Bibi did not accuse her of having no pride or not wanting to know about her heritage. And the models presented were not about failure but about proud images of a bright past, a great civilization of African queens. The norm at the Center and in its stories was one of serving people, of Africans fighting whites to make certain that hospitals and schools got built for the children. In one film, the line "To die for the people" (163) may have suggested bombing police stations and riots in the projects, but no one pretended that dying was a smart thing to do. The talk went back to schooling as a way to use your life to help blacks free blacks. Rae Ann's symbolic abortion becomes the means for her to bridge the two worlds, to bring positive images home and to turn around her bloodying experience: She was not certain she was dying, but she felt righteous feeling the pain that dying would bring. Getting through this time meant she would have time to do something worthwhile, not to die for the people but to live, however confusing that might sound and however inadequate it made her feel. If nothing else, Rae Ann had begun to experience her own power: "M'Dear fraid to come in the room and get her slippers, fraid to come near me" (165). And she had begun to consider the possibility of the power of others: "Either Dada Bibi had a powerful health to combat germs, she thought . . . or the woman was crazy" (165), even if she secretly wished "everything would be like before" (165).

Barbara Summers' "Trialogue" (1992) adds a generational perspective to the world of African-American abortion. Presented in three female voices, it represents three generations of one family in the projects. Concepcion, the granddaughter, admits in the opening section to being a pothead, which she considers "'cool' compared to the rest of the folks I know. I didn't have no baby at seventeen. That was my mother. I'm not sniffin and snortin and goin up in flames. That's my father. . . . I'm not dyin of no dread disease neither. That's Nanny's brother, Uncle Booty" (55). Living with her mother, Concepcion's cheap abortion at a nurse's house leaves her hemorrhaging profusely. Referring to the event as a bad case of backtalk, the girl refuses to tell her mother: "She said I could have told her. And then what? Have her tell me to suffer and bednot cry? Shoot, I could, I was doing that myself and not givin her the satisfaction of lookin down on me" (59). After two days in the hospital, and not feeling good about herself, Concepcion is taken in by her grandmother without a word.

The second section finds the grandmother, Virginia, congratulating herself that her "own granddaughter gonna graduate at the top of her class next June. To hell with these little spoiled bitches" (60) at the elite college cafeteria where she works. Virginia resents that the white girls think themselves better than her, that they feel they are on the right side of the counter while she is behind it. Unhappy that her granddaughter smokes pot and gives "Too much backtalk in the name of being up front" (62), Virginia finds relief in the abortion of a baby none of them would have had time for. She could not have kept up with it, nor could her daughter or her granddaughter. Whatever else and at whatever cost, the grandmother has made certain her granddaughter was as good as those rich girls she works for: "Somebody has got to hold to the center. And whether you want the job or not, Sister Virginia, the Creator has tapped you for it" (60).

Victoria, the mother, provides the voice for the third section, in which she asserts her own right to act as the center. She wants her daughter back in her house, and she wants the generations aligned in their temporal order; Virginia was Victoria's mother, and Victoria was Concepcion's. Still, a realignment will not make any of them more like any of the others, nor do they want or need to be. Their un-likeness does not mean they cannot respect each other, love each other, and find a way to believe in themselves. Like her own mother, Victoria finds her hope in the fact that her child, of all of them, did the right thing; she stood up for herself, took charge of her life. Her daughter's abortion, like Victoria's dream of a career as an actress, is a sign of the third-generational woman's freedom to achieve, a dream that, once impossible or illegal, is now accessible.

In "Luciella Louise Turner," from Gloria Naylor's *The Women of Brewster Place* (1983),[4] abortion takes a turn unrelated to a woman's need for independence or a career. Rather, abortion is tied to a desire for family and the need to hold it together, both in terms of a husband's self-image and the economic pressures of life in an impacted community. Carving the "unsupportable" out of their lives becomes identified with emptying the wife, Ciel, of the child she and her husband, Eugene, cannot afford to want. Emptying becomes the metaphor that then most completely describes the fate of the family, as the absented unborn becomes a precursor to the loss of the couple's one-year-old child. The husband, only recently returned from a self-imposed exile that covered the period of the child's young life, is once again emptied from the family on the occasion of her death. Ciel herself, relieved of all she had ever loved, is reduced to an image of a dessicated container, a wasted body that is gradually forced to give up what God had refused to take, her life. Ciel's dilemma had always been one of failing to fill herself; she is split into two women: one aborted her child to keep her husband and loses both; the other would have resisted but did not. A split self, Ciel lives through her husband's job loss and her abortion as if her life belonged to someone else, someone to whom she would willingly give it. But if one of Ciel's personas jammed everything on one side of her brain to give it away, the other felt it was up to her to do what God would not.

Friendship and community are all that stand in the way of Ciel's collapse in the person of her neighbor Mattie. Mattie refuses Ciel's exiting gesture and forces food into her, pressing life into her to exorcise the evil within and to refill her with that of which she had been emptied, mothering care. Rhythmically rocking, Mattie creates a pulse that transports Ciel "back into the womb, to the nadir of her hurt" (103). Mattie rocks her past Aegean seas so clear she could see the pink froth of "the fresh blood of sacrificial babies torn from their mother's arms." She rocked her "past Dachau, where soul-gutted Jewish mothers swept their children's entrails off laboratory floors. She flew past the spilled brains of Senegalese infants whose mothers had dashed them on the wooden sides of slave ships. And she rocked on" (103).

Eugene's reentrance is blocked; he can only position himself on the edge of Ciel's world, his seat in the funeral limousine taken by Mattie. Below the windows on Brewster Place, we find him at the dead end of the street conversing with the men who gather around the garbage cans, unable to mount the stoop and enter at number 316 as he had once done. Ciel had aborted more than her unborn; she had aborted Eugene, ejecting him from her life as surely as she had given up on her own life. But Mattie's rocking puts Ciel's split selves together and places her as an individual in the context of the collective; she rocks Ciel back through communal history into personal history and forward to a healing future. The journey sites abortion as a place of hurt historically and culturally; it is revealed as a ritual practice, a political horror, and an act of resistance whose hurt ends in being cast out of the body. Pain works its way through the body like a deliverance that births a new Ciel and puts delivery itself into perspective.

Resistance to abortion becomes the issue in Kate Green's "Abortion Journal" (1980), a story that deals with the potential offspring of mixed race alliances. Here, a mixed race baby, with skin a color between black, Indian, and Irish, would, its mother believes, be embraced by its father, Willie. Having already raised his sister and his nephew, taking care of his own, he would have her keep the baby. She is more practical; they are not living together, are not ready to be parents, have not planned for this pregnancy. Her reservations are soon exacerbated by those of her family: "Estalee: 'But you ain't going to marry him. He don't make enough money for you.' My mother: 'What could you possibly have in common?' Jim says blow it all, have the baby, wander nameless on the planet" (50).

Close to the time of an abortion clinic appointment, when she finally reveals to Willie that she is pregnant, Willie surprises her; the time is not right for them, he offers; she would always blame him. Supporting her decision, he feels her sadness when she admits the abortion has cured her of her fantasies, brought her to realize how impossible it is for them to love, given the great differences between them, the chasm between their expectations. Yet, in her farewell to the fetus, she speaks as a mother of "my dark child who will know nothing of earth but my heartbeat. . . . There is something of heaven in that dark curling" (52).

Willie asks to come to the abortion clinic, but she tells him not to bother, already reclaiming a sense of her separateness and her singularity. Her body was being returned to her, she will claim it again. How, she asks him, does he feel; having been left out, he owns to feeling both angry and lost. In the aftermath of the abortion, they are no more than a sexual brother and sister; they end by watching all the families of color along the lake, "the Black and mixed babies. Willie says, 'We're all mulatto','" a belated recognition that what had seemed impossible was so only for them. Indeed, as she remarks, "You were a little more possible. But in this age, where the choice was given me, I chose no" (58). The new body she gains in exchange for the choice she has made speaks only to a gendered freedom that has, after all, excluded race as a possibility.

Abortion in Gayl Jones' Corregidora (1986)[5] acts more like a looming horizon than Green's debated solution; in one sense it acts as the great undesired in the paradoxical legacy of slavery. In the procreation legend set down by her Great Gram, the slave of the Portuguese breeder and whoremaster Old Corregidora, breeding provides the evidence ex-slaves leave behind to testify to the history erased at abolition. Officials burned all the slave papers to erase what had happened, as if it never had. But the women are determined to bear witness and make it live again, testifies the second-generation offspring of Great Gram's womb. Great Gram herself proselytizes generativity as an indigenous birthing of evidence. She will leave evidence, as they must, she instructs them. And so must their children, so that when the time comes, they will have the evidence to show. What four generations of women must contract among themselves is to desire procreation. They will make generations as a way of keeping themselves visible. The first and second generations, Great Gram and Gram, breed by means of Corregidora himself; the third, mother, is drawn as if by a magnet to give herself to one man to ensure she will make her generation; but the fourth, Ursa, finds her pregnancy aborted through the drunken abuse of her first husband, Mutt, and her procreativity appropriated by hospital physicians who remove her womb.

Refusal or deprivation of procreativity is not a choice but an act of violence at the same time that procreation pursued by victims "could also be a slave-breeder's way of thinking" (22). It is not merely evidence that is preserved but Corregidora's legacy, so Ursa's long hair becomes his "evil in me" (42) and her songs the voice of the devil. Ursa's resistance is mixed. Preoccupied with having all that they had but without the generations; she cannot make her generation. Ursa is nevertheless intent on finding a voice separate from that of the other women in her line: "They squeezed Corregidora into me, and I sing back in return. I would rather have sung [my mother's] memory if I'd had to sing any. What about my own? . . . Look at me, I am not Corregidora's daughter" (103). The devils on her back, as her second husband tells her, are not hers but theirs. Ursa sings them out of herself, unable to give birth to her devils in any other way. Her body has been reduced in her eyes to "a piece of shit" (165) knocked down some stairs to abort her child, to a "Piece a ass for sale" (159) that Mutt tries to auction off at the club where she sings. She is still a woman because she can fuck and "Long as a woman got a hole, she can fuck" (100), as both her husbands remind her. But for Ursa, her womb is silent, and in the space between her thighs nothing ever bleeds.

Unlike the other women in the family, for Ursa Corregidora will never be enough. She must either find something to replace her aborted pregnancy or accept her abortion as the end of perpetuating Corregidora's legacy. Ursa has been mind-fucked by the Portuguese slavemaster in her memory of the testimony of the generations. In dream, she both births him and is raped by him; he has seen her inside ("'It looks ugly in there,' he concludes; 'no worse than what you did,'" she retorts [77]), and she has been made to touch her past. It is clear that generation for her is her music and that she shall not pollute it. But the music that will make her generation cannot exist without that which touches her life and their lives, that reaches into the "suppressed hysteria" and "genital fantasies" (59) that are Corregidora's legacy. Ursa got her songs from the testimonies of those who came before in her line and to whom she will provide witness in her way. If her body cannot make a fetus to give evidence, then when it comes time to witness she will grind coffee grounds into her eyes to make a fetus. If she cannot birth in reality, then she can witness in dream, where, as with Leda and the swan, "I felt the humming and beating of wings. And I felt a stiff penis inside me. . . . Who are you? Who have I born? His hair was like white wings, and we were united at birth. 'Who are you?' 'You don't even know your own father?'" (76–77). Just as old Corregidora both rapes her and is a product of that rape, so is the product itself made up equally of him and her.

Still, Ursa's ways of giving life—in her song, in memory, in dream—are an abortion of her life narrative. They implicate the evil of her origins; they hold her hostage to others' devils. Contending that your roots come from wherever you take them, her mother stands corrected by her lesbian friend, Cat. Roots are what you cannot pull up; all you can do is cut off from them, but they are still there. Ursa's response, reflecting her own aborted connection to maintaining the line of generations, is that, having cut off, you cannot stitch yourself back.

Perhaps the only abortion Ursa is able to address successfully is the aborted relationship with men that has plagued the preceding three generations. Here, she finds the secret of reconnecting, but it, too, comes from the history of slave relationships, this time echoing the secret of what Great Gram had done to Corregidora. A sexual solution that arises from the act of fellatio to produce combined pleasure and great pain, Ursa's act is no worse that what had been done to Great Gram by Corregidora or to Ursa by Mutt. Indeed, Ursa's liberating revelation is itself so rooted in the past that it conflates one couple with the other and Ursa with Great Gram in a single indistinguishable voice.

Slavery aborts the possibility of blacks asserting themselves unproblematically as a race—given the holocaust of the "Sixty million or more" to whom Toni Morrison dedicates *Beloved* (1987).[6] So, too, do aborting and infanticidal acts against the children of slavery by slaves themselves embrace the thinking of slavers, in this case through a self-inflicted holocaust. It happens in much the same paradoxical way that *Corregidora* presents breeding among blacks as a legacy of slavemasters. Once again, control over procreation is at the center of the fate of a race as a means of either testifying by providing evidence of the evils of slavery or aborting the slave trade by denying the material means of its survival.

More is aborted in *Beloved* than merely the fate of a race, however. The theft of children from a mother—whether ripped untimely from the womb in forced abortions to preserve the labor force for the fields or stolen as youths to fill the coffles of slave traders—aborts individual maternal histories. Slave mothers are cut short in their ability to mother, to define their own motherhood, even to "speak" their motherhood. The preemptive self-abortion, provoked miscarriage, or infanticide thereby becomes a statement of self-defense, denial of the master's seed, or refusal to accept the role of designated breeder. Such "speech" expresses the complexity of slave experience as well as the "badness" of choosing to mother under such conditions, requiring a deeper understanding that allows the "bad" to be heard and easy judgment to be superseded by a more complex sense of subjectivity.

Where motherhood finds its voice in this context, it is as likely to kill its child to save it from a hellish future as it is to birth it into an enslavement that serves the devil. In *Beloved*, Sethe's mother, Sethe herself, and the ex-slave Ella are all suggested as such voices with which to speak. This is a speech preferred to that of biting off the tip of one's tongue as Sethe does when she is pregnant and beaten over a pit that protects her swollen belly and the master's next-generation slave. The beating and outrages that tell her "story" are written on her back in the form of a chokeberry tree, in Schoolteacher's notebook, and in the newpaper she cannot read, each a space in which Sethe loses her story to others who control its writing. Her site of control is her womb and what comes out of it; what she cannot write she inscribes through the choices she makes over her own procreativity: to deliver Denver in the hope of an end to slavery; to dispatch Beloved in despair at its return.

Unlike the case of Margaret Garner, the slave whose story inspires *Beloved*, the murdered child in Morrison's work is not the spawn of a white master nor the offspring of a rape. The moral ambiguity of Sethe's choice separates her from her own mother's destruction of all her white children conceived by rape. Sethe will not be an easy case; rather, she offers the broadest possible test by which to consider all the facets of such an act. The murder may have been the right thing to do but Sethe had no right to do it, as Morrison suggests; or it may have been the only thing to do at the same time that it was the wrong thing to do. Sethe's dilemma leaves her damned equally whether she uses the only means at her disposal to resist or whether she goes back to hell like a lamb. Indeed, the very same dangerous love that leads her out of slavery to get to her children in freedom is the love that leads her to murder. Like the world of the Middle Passage in which Beloved drowns before she returns to her mother as a resident succubus, Sethe's dilemma is one of being neither truly alive nor truly dead. Until her "madness" convinces the slave catchers otherwise, Sethe is in captivity between freedom and slavery, in transition between death and birth. The child born into slavery is the child who is killed; the child born into freedom is the child who escapes her fate. The murderous system that gave Beloved to the world is the same system that is responsible for her death, while Sethe strikes out to resist that system by killing that to which it compelled her to give birth. Like a phantom limb, Beloved becomes that which is lost not because it cannot be found but because no one is looking for it (Rushdy 1992). She is like the aborted fetus, dis-connected, dis-membered, and therefore dis-re-membered. She is, like slavery and like abortion, left behind, both forgotten and not forgotten because forever recol-lected as a haunting that is unforgiving.

Denver, by contrast, is the child too closely aligned with its mother; boundaries have not set her off so that, indivisible from her mother, she is an un-individuated child, a pre-born. If Beloved exists in an infantile state because the past has not been incorporated, understood, and addressed, Denver exists in an un-born state because the future has not been recognized and embraced. Beloved may have fed from her mother's body in a reverse pregnancy in which the child swells as the mother shrinks. And Ella must respond to the community sentiment that claims "You can't just up and kill your children" by affirming, "No, and the children can't just up and kill the mama" (256). But Denver takes no such sustenance from Sethe, even as the child of a birthing that is privileged by multiple iterations throughout the novel. It is up to her grandmother, Baby Suggs, to provide for Denver's true re-birth in a dream in which she claims that Denver has no defense against paying the price of slavery. She can only know it and go out into the yard, joining her story—and by implication Sethe's—to that of the community, like the bits and pieces of Baby Sugg's quilt. They must be linked together in a synergy of stories to attach to a larger communal wholeness that binds all the bits together. In this way, the "natal alienation" (Scruggs 1992) of the Margaret Garner story is recuperated, and the mother buried beneath the child she murdered is revived to face her unrecognized need to be mothered by the community. A slave may be denied rights to her child because she is the property of the slavemaster who raped her, but this is an act that offends the natural law of property rights and the black community's relations of kinship. The story must be made whole again if those people are to survive.

Rooted like *Corregidora* and *Beloved* in slave history, Maryse Conde's *I, Tituba, Black Witch of Salem* (1992)[7] is situated in colonial America and the Caribbean and incorporates African memories and practices. Conde creates in Tituba a figure of re-sistance born of the rape of a slave by a sailor during the Middle Passage. As she as-serts, she was born out of aggression, out of hatred and contempt. When her mother is hanged in Barbados for striking a white man and her assigned slave father com-mits suicide in despair by swallowing his tongue, Tituba is taken in by a sorceress and takes on a fearful aspect in her community. She becomes the subject of story as the offspring of a woman who was hanged and as one who lives outcast at the edge of society. A free woman married to a slave by a new master, she is transported her-self as a slave to Salem where, discovering she is pregnant, she uses her herbal lore to be rid of her undesired ripeness. The difficulty, as she finds, will be in surviving the murder of her own child, in spite of the clarity of her feelings on the rightness of her course of action and its prevalence as a shared value among slaves. Tituba has seen the unhappiness of slave motherhood and constructs her act as no more than expulsing an innocent who can never influence its fate, having been cast into a world of abjection. She acts in a context in which slaves killed their babies by puncturing their egg-like heads with a thorn, by abandonment, or by poisoning the severed umbilical cord. The women in Tituba's world concocted recipes to sterilize the womb to render it a tomb for further procreation. Tituba is nevertheless haunted by the image of the child she will never have, presaging her fate never to bear a child to term; indeed, she is destined to die on the gallows where all about her are strange trees "bristling with strange fruit" (172), an unborn child in her womb.

Her fertile life framed by an abortion of choice and an abortion brutally imposed, Tituba, like her mother, signifies the condition of slavery. But she also signifies the condition of women, for, like Tituba, Hester Prynne dies in *I, Tituba* with her unborn in her womb. Consigned to an older husband whose seed she has repeatedly aborted with the numerous formulas she self-administered when she was pregnant, Hester ends her torture as a damned woman; she hangs herself in her jail cell accused of an adultery the evidence of which dies with her. For both their un-borns, Tituba repeats a lament in which a moonstone drops into the water and her fingers cannot reach it; a hunter engages to recover it but drowns in the attempt. Referring to the lost children as "children we spared, but whom, strangely enough, I pity" (113), Tituba's preoccupation with how and by whom a woman's womb can be used is extended to her own simulated rebirth. Freed from captivity in a witch's jail cell, she is delivered to the relative freedom of a new master who will pay her prison costs and employ her services: "I screamed, and this scream, the terrified cry of a newborn baby, heralded my return to this world. I had to learn how to speak again. . . . I had to learn how to speak again. . . . I had to learn how to look them in the eyes again" (122). And yet such rebirth is no more than a new bondage; it is only a gift if one chooses it, and if that choice frees one from exploitation and humiliation.

Tituba's vision was to be born again "in the steely army of conquerors" (120). It is this vision she pursues in her ultimate return to her native land, through a pregnancy that she believes will hang on in its mother's womb until the world has changed. Carrying the child of the leader of escaped slaves who established camps in the hills and the jungles, Tituba realizes the maroons have reached an accommodation with the planters to denounce slave revolts. She consults with the spirits of her mother, the sorceress Mama Yaya, and her adoptive father who advise her the time is not ripe, that their misfortune has no end, and that history must see blood before it is done. In a dream, her slave husband, the maroon leader, and her first slavemaster in Salem appear to her wearing black hoods, in their hands a pointed stick. As they lift her skirts, she screams, racked by terrible pain. Tituba's options have been foreclosed in dream, memory, and in reality, as she accepts that a new generation must replace her murdered child. Even as she does so, and as her second pregnancy stirs in her womb, she slits open a rabbbit and splatters her face with blood; two balls of rotting flesh gush forth in an image of aborted birth that signals the failure of the revolt and Tituba's own end in the gallows, her fetus within her.

Tituba's final experience with birth, in the afterlife, rewards her at last with a choice of her own. Like her desire to choose for herself the womb from which she would be born, she chooses her own descendant. The chosen child is the progeny of a mother who has lost three children at birth and who dies in birthing her; the fetus refuses to follow into death and fights "furiously to enter the universe" (176): "A child I didn't give birth to but whom I choose!" Tituba cries, "What motherhood could be nobler!" (177).

Conde's Tituba has, in the larger reading of her story, herself been treated as an aborted presence, a party to history whose voice in the Puritan witch trials record was effectively erased. *I, Tituba* becomes in this sense a "creation," the myth of Tituba. She is birthed in an act that raped and humiliated her people, an act that occurred neither in the Old World of her tribal origins nor in the New World of her race's obliteration, but in the liminal zone of the Middle Passage, a place of transition between freedom and slavery. Her identification as a witch links her with the invisible world of spirits, a space outside the control of her masters and the source of a power of resistance that Tituba exercises in both Barbados and Salem. Tituba's mediating presence between the physical and spirit realms and her back and forth passage between the world of slavery and that of the maroon camp, between the plantation system and the forest outside, places her in an interstitial position whereby she escapes the logic of her masters and evades their control. But Tituba is not self-created; she does not author her own death—as Hester does—just as she does not author her own birth. Rather, she operates within the frame of a resistance that is itself tainted by both the blood of her murdered children and the blood of a revolt aborted in its birth. At the hanging of Goody Glover and at Hester's suicide, Tituba expresses muted women enraged at giving birth. To reclaim control, she asserts her liminality. She becomes in her rage her own aborted child, refusing to be born and constructing her own death: "I *screamed* down the door of my mother's womb. . . . I shall remain crouched in your waters, deaf, dumb, and blind, clinging like kelp to your womb. I shall cling so tightly you'll never expell me . . . without ever having known the curse of day" (111).

Conclusion

From Patty Lou Floyd's "Voice in the Whirlwind" to Gish Jen's "Birthmates," abortion has proved to be an issue in fiction about which families and communities feel deeply and in which they are intimately involved, as influence agents, as providers of the means and access to abortion, and as supports for those who undergo them. Such influence and support necessarily entail dependency but sponsor as well growth and the ability to come to terms with who one is or wants to be. The debilitating effects of both the choice itself and the pressure it puts on family and community relationships inevitably result in fiction that expresses shared anguish, recriminations, and resistance and that tests generational expectations and traditions. At the same time, the moment of choice allows connections to be made or reestablished, losses to be relieved or reversed. The unforgiving closeness of parent and child contains the risk of elided identities, as in Bobbie Ann Mason's "Marita," or of imposing preferred choices, as in Andre Dubus' "Miranda over the Valley." Such risks are matched by the suffocating protectiveness of a father whose daughter never gets to truly grow up in Ellen Gilchrist's "1957, a Romance" or the resistance of a daughter whose only growth is a secretive act of rebellion, as in Sara Paretsky's "The Man Who Loved Life."

Within the relationships that most stand out, the relationship between responsible partners stands at the center. This relationship gives rise to the need to understand the male perspective on abortion, both because men are intimate parties to the abortion experience and because their perspective informs public policy and dialogue on the issue. Privately, fiction offers us insights into a world in which men have become peripheralized emotionally while still expected to function as economic centers of social, interpersonal, and family units. The social and biological pressure on men to justify themselves procreatively as well as male dependence upon a female partner to do so, leaves men with little control over the abortion event. They may remain stoic and supportive while anguishing silently, like the husband in Edward Lodi's "Rock-A-Bye," or implore to no effect, like the farmer-husband in Diane Slatton's "Seventh Son of a Seventh Son" and the significant other in Stephen Dixon's "Newt Likes the House Neat." Even so, men provide a range of reactions from the retrograde soldier pal who finds his friend a cheap abortionist in John Miller's "Bethune, South Carolina" to the icily pragmatic parent who assumes the role of overseer of his daughter's undesired abortion in Greg Johnson's "Little Death."

The experience of abortion tends to split partnerships where there are race differences, as in the Asian/white relationship in Gish Jen's "Birthmates" and the black/white relationship in Kate Green's "Abortion Journal." It tests them in often-unforgiving ways where there is a religious difference, like the Jewish/Catholic difference in Warren Adler's "An Unexpected Visit." Where family lineage, heritage, or the broken links of an persecuted people become an issue, as they do in abortions that recall the history of slavery or the Holocaust, the anxiety that attends them implicates others well beyond the immediate partnership. Grandparent survivors of a Polish pogrom figure in Joseph Epstein's "Low Anxiety" in a way that raises not principled objections to individual life-taking but the weight of a much greater horror inflicted on a people as a whole. Generativity itself becomes an issue in Gayl Jones' *Corregidora*, acting as a looming horizon for four generations of black females who cannot escape the use value to which female ancestor-slaves' bodies were put. Holding fast to the positive notion of reproducing as a way of testifying to the outrage, the four-generation tradition ends with a drunken assault that **raises** the twin questions of losing one's voice and racial suicide.

Generations figure in other, more personal ways in a variety of black family settings, from the nuclear family in Alice Walker's "The Abortion" and a grandmother's caretaking in Toni Cade Bambara's "A Girl's Story" to the generational conflicts of women-only householders in Barbara Summers' "Trialogue." Abortions become the occasion of reexamining family units, personal identities, and generational perspectives, and of considering the parallel worlds, political and personal, that coexist without converging in black communities. Race-ing itself raises questions of the female-headed family in which the husband is absent, calling up images of the emasculation of black males and the breaking up of black families under slavery. In Toni Morrison's *Beloved* and Maryse Conde's *I, Tituba, Black Witch of Salem,* such images express the strong sense of a singular female aborting to resist perpetuating the slavery of a race. Gloria Naylor's "Luciella Louise Turner" presents abortion as a signifier of emptiness and exile within and from the black family. In a differently race-d experience, that of the Asian American family in Marshall Klimasewiski's "Jun-Hee," abortion becomes an image of broken links between the present and the past and between East and West that elicit an other-worldly reconciliation to reclaim the dead and restore connectivity.

Abortion, in sum, takes on in prose fiction the very aspect Zoe Sofia, Donna Haraway, and others suggest it would, that of an image at the small end of the cosmic funnel that serves as a metaphor for large-scale effects in the human universe. Abortion is as much the negation of generativity as it is an opening to a world of order and control. In an image that owes much to chaos theory, it stands at the cusp of the moment when change returns to stability, when growth and inventiveness are morphed into stasis, when the universe moves from complexity to simplicity, from expansion to contraction. Abortion is both a pivot and a balance; it maintains a planet that has luxuriated by pruning back its lush outcroppings.

In its many fictions, abortion implicates a community of roles, none in isolation, all in a nexus of experienced connections that depend, if not upon the whole in all its parts, upon each other in a variety of combinations that come together and dissolve in a continuous back and forth of building and un-building relationships. As we discovered with the poetry of abortion, abortion prose fiction provides such a range and variety of types and occasions, of motives, conditions, and outcomes that its insights move its readers toward less unyielding positions, to a middle ground of deeper sympathy for and openness to other experiences **and** positions.

Abortion literature thus offers the most complex expression of human life at its most fundamental point and is therefore a fit subject for scrutiny for those who wish to understand both the aspirations and the limitations inherent in the human picture of abortion.

Notes

1. On motherhood, reproduction, and literature, see Adams (1994), Ashe (1988, 1992), Cosslett (1994), Daly and Reddy (1991), Herrera et al. (1997), Meaney (1993), Dance (1979), and Wilt (1991).
2. On Walker, see Butler-Evans (1989), Gates and Appiah (1993), Willis (1985), and Walker (1983).
3. On Bambara, see Butler-Evans (1989).
4. On Naylor, see Fraser (1989), Montgomery (1994), and Palumbo (1985).
5. On Jones, see Bell (1979), Dixon (1984), Harris (1980), Simon (1997), and Ward (1984).
6. On Morrison, see Bennett (1991), Brooker (1996), Butler-Evans (1989), Corti (1992), Davies (1991), Harris (1991), Heller (1998), Henderson (1991), Keenan (1993), Krumholz (1992), Ashe (1992), Rushdy (1992), Scruggs (1992), Tobin (1993), Fitzgerald (1993), and Otten (1993).
7. On Conde, see Baluntansky (1992), Dukats (1998), Mudimbe-Boyi (1993), Becel (1995), Pfaff (1996), Smith (1995), Snitgen (1989), and Shelton (1993).

CONCLUSION

Splitting the Baby

And now, O Lord my God, thou hast made thy servant king . . . and I am but a little child: I know not how to go out or come in. . . .

Give therefore thy servant an understanding heart to judge thy people, that I may discern between good and bad: for who is able to judge this thy so great a people?

. . . .

Then came there two women that were harlots, unto the king, and stood before him.

And the one woman said, O my lord, I and this other woman dwell in one house; and I was delivered of a child with her in the house.

And it came to pass the third day after I was delivered, that this woman was delivered also: and we were together; there was no stranger with us in the house.

And this woman's child died in the night; because she overlaid it.

And she arose at midnight, and took my son from beside me, while thine handmaid slept, and laid it in her bosom, and laid her dead child in my bosom.

And when I rose in the morning to give my child suck, behold, it was dead: but when I had considered it in the morning, behold, it was not my son, which I did bear.

And the other woman said, Nay; but the living is my son, and the dead is thy son. And this said, No; but the dead is thy son, and the living is my son. Thus they spake before the king.

Then said the king. The one saith, This is my son that liveth, and thy son is the dead: and the other saith, Nay; but thy son is the dead, and my son is the living.

And the king said, Bring me a sword. And they brought a sword before the king.

And the king said, Divide the living child in two, and give half to the one, and half to the other.

Then spake the woman whose the living child was unto the king, for her bowels yearned upon her son, and she said, O my lord, give her the living child, and in no wise slay it. But the other said, Let it be neither mine nor thine but divide it.

Then the king answered and said, Give her the living child, and in no wise slay it: she is the mother thereof.

And all Israel heard of the judgment which the king had judged; and they feared the king: for they saw that the wisdom of God was in him, to do judgment. 1 Kings 3

In legal narratives of the last quarter of the century, the Court's legitimacy in abortion law has become an issue. Its endangered status raises questions about its ability to resist political influence as well as the likely effect of seeking public acceptance and public consensus. The Court's own changeability becomes an issue as well as its fairness in trying to resolve an issue whose divisiveness impacts national unity. Recomposing the bench across a quarter of a century of abortion opinions, realignments through coalitioning, additions, and replacements of the justices have occurred from the *Roe v. Wade* court—which included Justices Burger, Stewart, Powell, Marshall, Douglas, and Brennan—to the *Planned Parenthood v. Casey* court—which included Justices Stevens, Souter, Scalia, Thomas, O'Connor, and Kennedy—with only Justices White, Rehnquist, and Blackmun serving on both courts; subsequent changes find Justices White and Blackmun replaced by Justices Ginsburg and Breyer.

Its authority is at risk; its justice is suspect, and its law is likely to be civilly, and not so civilly, disobeyed. The judge, like the doctor, has after all been sworn to heal; a wounded polity asks, on the one hand, that the law do no harm, and, on the other, that it kill in order to cure in actions that are dissonant with a caring or just legal identity. An oppositional dialogue has, as a result, redefined abortion as a legal, medical, social, and moral issue, legitimizing two alternative Solomonic narratives: a collision of courses and an escape from judgment. Both narratives imply a condition in which narratives either collapse or rupture in confusion or irresolution. The failure of a coherent proposition, of the authority of a single text, allows cataclysm to thrive.

Justice Scalia's strategy in *Planned Parenthood v. Casey* (1992) (dissent in part, concurrence in part) was to cut through the entangled claims of the two abortion camps and to rescue reason from confusion in what was figured as a Solomonic solution.[1] In his subsequent *Madsen v. Women's Health Center* (1994) dissent, Scalia labels as "Solomonic wisdom" the Court's insistence only in abortion cases on allowing in part and disallowing in part rather than reversing. Referring to the Court, in this regard, as "an ad hoc nullification machine" (785), Scalia would prefer it applied uncontroversial legal doctrines evenhandedly. In cartoon commentary on the Solomon analogy (Jim Borgman 1992b; Ed Fischer 1992b), the Court is presented with the same kind of stark choice that Scalia offers—split the baby, either by overturning or definitively upholding *Roe v. Wade*. The alternative, of course, is to refuse to choose.

The story of King Solomon and the contested child is a parable that refracts choice in socially authorized terms to circumscribe the mother's ability to choose— the ancient equivalent of the 1992 *Casey* decision in which one chooses under conditions not of one's choosing. In effect, the balance struck is neither that of the state or the mother choosing nor of one choosing in the voice of the other, but of a not-so-delicate dance of choice in which one partner choreographs the possible steps and the other improvises within those constraints. Interestingly, the good of the child is never explicitly raised as a standard of judgment or as a point of reference. Neither is the mother considered in her aspect as a child cut off by her "mother" (the state) should she assert her own right independent of state authorization. Infantilized by her disconnection from decisional autonomy over her own conduct, she is "allowed"; asserting her autonomy, she is "aborted," cut off and cast into the wasteland of disenfranchised mothers. Indeed, by failing to indicate initially who is the real mother, 1 Kings 3 suggests that the point is about neither the mother nor the child but, rather, about patriarchy inventing the patriarchal mother (Hansen 1997, 22–25). Having proved "complicitous with a system that devalues motherhood and oppresses women, the patriarchal mother wins the case and gets to keep the child" (24). Little concern is expressed that the test itself has the effect of destroying good motherhood in either woman by erasing the authority of one and drawing the other into infanticide. The Samaritanism called for in the complicitous mother is such that she must not, on the one hand, love the child so much that she cannot give it up, nor must she fight for her child. On the other hand, she must not consider resisting the larger harm of a patriarchal terrorism that will both victimize her and undermine her maternal subjectivity. A modern reading of the tale of Solomon would pit one woman against another while the alpha male divides and conquers to maintain control over a woman's independent sexual conduct within the borders of male law (23–24). It would subordinate the interests of the individual to those of the community rather than balance them.

The double bind in Solomon is that a mother affirmed by patriarchy must give up being a mother in any other sense, that is, she must give up the motherhood of a decisionally autonomous individual who would resist the tyranny of the community or male judge-made law. The Solomonic court will thus fail to reinforce the autonomy or authority of the mother and will leave her decisionally disabled so long as she insists on an independent right to make her own choice. By contrast, the mother who yields her authority to outside intervention is rewarded for yielding, which leaves her decisionally disabled as well (Althouse 1992). It thus becomes clear that Solomon is not about creating autonomy for its subjects but dependence, not about empowering mothers (who would always be unpredictable) but about creating a superordinate Mother of mothers—the state, and its stand-ins the judge and the patriarchal mother—who would be determinate and unambiguous.

The first move by each mother is for a judgment on her behalf and disenfranchisement of the other mother, an unhealthy decision for the welfare of the nation as a whole, given the need for social comity. The second move is the abdication by one mother of her rights in order to preserve the child's life. This act is akin to abortion rights ceding its claim to choice under the threat of violence by the antiabortion movement and the law's inability to protect abortion rights. This alternative accedes to vigilantism as a force of self-made law and undermines confidence in the willingness and competence of the legal establishment to protect its citizens and en-sure public safety. The last move is that suggested by the second mother who pro-poses a fifty-fifty split that tears the child apart. Such a stalemate in contemporary abortion law would throw abortion back to the states, yielding a patchwork of laws that gives some women rights denied to others based on the luck of their geography. By taking the decision away from women and resolving it without giving them a voice, Solomon confirms what abortion law still presumes—that women are not au-tonomous agents and that at best they share their right with other interested agents with whom they must collaborate or to whose decision they must accede. The preg-nant woman who aborts—and who is thereby constructed as dissonant with her so-cial role as mother—has embraced what is construed as a selfish personal act that disconnects her from the network of family and community. Her choice for her own life is a form of social suicide; her assertion of a right over that which has been part of her body is a sign of a disconnect from that which is outside her body.

If we were to consider the Solomon tale through the eyes of the judge rather than the mother, we are no closer to comfort. Solomon, or the Supreme Court, is in the unenviable position of deciding under fire. The King's condition is one of having to unify his people from a position of weakness as a ruler who has yet to establish his credibility and who is concerned to make a show of strength that will make determi-nate that which is ambiguous. Under threat of delegitimization, neither the Court nor the King is in a position to lead a split people to wholeness. Solomon relies not upon reason but upon a gift of God, good instincts, and folk wisdom; the Court relies upon shifting standards that flip from strict scrutiny to undue burden, allowing the "out-lawed" provisions of *Thornburgh v. American College of Obstetricians and Gynecologists* (1986) to be brought back into the law in *Casey*. In the case of the King, the reality of the sword ensures resolution rather than reason; in the case of the Court it is the mere appearance of certainty that rescues law from ambiguity, while reason remains the handmaid of doubt. The head that wears the crown is thus not secure in either the Supreme Court's or King Solomon's reign. Going out and coming in is as big a problem for the Supremes as it is for the King.

The tale of Solomon proves a useful metaphor for the abortion wars for a num-ber of reasons. The threat of violence to resolve a dilemma, the usurpation of a woman's autonomy and her self-representation, and the use of the child as a pawn without rights in the context of the judgment, all suggest themselves as compara-tive themes. Equally important to the analogy, however, are more arcane themes such as the validity of novel, creative, or ad hoc modes of resolving disputes, the assault on reason as a standard of judgment, the appropriation of legislative func-tions by judicial law-making, the challenge to the law's authority and objectivity posed by controversial legal issues, and the threat to legitimacy posed by jurispru-dential hesitancy and the public's lack of consensus on the wisdom of the law and its holdings.

As an abortion analogy, the Solomon tale in 1 Kings 3 reflects the argument that a woman's right over the fetus ensures its enslavement to her will (or her lack of one). The likelihood of giving over one's child to a false parent's fraud or to state tyranny—allowing the violence that severs the child, the mother-child bond, or both—models a parent's refusal to fight for offspring and the willingness to allow terrorism to dictate one's choice (Ashe 1991). The woman's limited choice of life or death over her child victimizes not only the child but the woman; the woman must both give up her right or connection to her child and experience a loss that does her a grievous injury. The severable child is, in the abortion analogy, threatened with bisection or with being cut off from its mother. The accommodating mother is put in the position (like the seduced serving girl of early American history) of internalizing social pressures by "aborting" her relationship with what must, for her, become the undesired child. The mother who would prefer the child be split in two has learned to resolve her relationship through the seductive brutality of selective violence. The lesson of threatened violence thus becomes a reference point for both mothers, expressing the differentiated results of forced separation either by child murder or by forced adoption, both of which abort the connectedness of mother and child. Indeed, both women, as a further expression of the violence of abortion, have been erased as mothers. If we distinguish choice from defaulting, the already-erased woman of Solomon is not, by definition, capable of a moment of choice. Rather, Solomon provides an image of the abortion experience as a double bind, a no-win dilemma. Like a woman coerced into an abortion (again, a prototypical portrait of early American seduced and abandoned womanhood), the yielding mother can also be compared to a rape victim who fails to resist. In effect, she repeats Solomon's legal rape of her will by failing to call his bluff; she not only renders herself unfit both as a woman and a mother, but she confirms Solomon's initial doubt of her claim as a mother.

If there is an element of choice in 1 Kings 3, it lies in the choice of both mothers to rely on the King's instincts for resolving the dilemma. This high-risk dependence relies upon an arbitrary act that reinforces personalistic law and is without precedent in law or morality. Rooted in the experience of a newly-installed ruler who "know[s] not how to go out or come in," such law is human (Baron 1999) and responsive to the personal but hardly subscribes to the rule of law (Allegretti 1992). If the Solomonic choice is considered in the light of resolution by the intervention of an external agency, it is still a losing proposition. Here, the presumed "objective" agency of an intermediate party has neither the intimate knowledge of direct interest to speak for it nor true neutrality. Because its legitimacy as a decisive authority is in question, it dares not entangle itself further in that which is irresoluble. Rather, its most prudent "choice" in the face of such complexity is the reductive slicing of the Gordian knot. In spite of the considerable importance to the King's authority, the dilemma in which the judge himself is placed is, interestingly, never made the focus of the contest between the two mothers. The struggle the King faces is between determinate rule—that which is nevertheless violent, arbitrary, and potentially guilty of "uncontrolled social engineering" (Baron, 16)—and the possibility of the loss of wisdom that attends a law based not on insight but on due process and the rule of law (25). Balanced, they constrain "judges from imposing their own values in the guise of law" (16).

The kind of mediating role the Supreme Court is capable of performing itself necessarily contains, in one argument, an element of abortive violence (Minow 1992). Splitting the difference in an abortion decision is not so much a balancing act or a compromise as a way to close off conversation by embracing false respect for the rule of law (White 1990). Indeed, forced commensurability of incommensurate positions on abortion might suggest itself as a way to avoid the kind of collision (between maternal and fetal interests) that Justice O'Connor was concerned about in her dissent in *City of Akron v. Akron Center for Reproductive Health* (1983), but it fails to account for legitimate parallel and non-convergent interests. The Supreme Court may, in fact, be caught in the unenviable position of arbitrary royalty making either of two improbable choices: making a spectacular cut that splits the difference and thereby satisfying no one or refusing a necessary cut and thereby perpetuating the split in democratic wholeness.

As we move from the world of Solomon to consider the prospect for mediating the abortion wars in our own times, it becomes clear that escaping judgment and slicing the Gordian knot are no longer reasonable options. We have only to look to Bertolt Brecht's modern-day version of the Solomon story in *The Caucasian Chalk Circle* to see that an improvisatory approach may well be a better fit for an unsettled world.[2] Brecht's version considers the character of the judge who renders a "splitting" decision (Gray 1962). Azdak, a rascal judge, makes his decision in favor of a good peasant woman who has struggled to save the life of a deserted child under the impossible conditions of war. The nurturing mother is variously described as having been given the child of a privileged family by a servant of the household, having kidnapped the child, and having herself attempted to desert the child. While the complexity of her struggle at times appears to render her unfit for her role as a mother, it equally qualifies her by having tested her commitment.

In Azdak, the twin elements of the power of class revenge and the victory of common sense and folk wisdom are celebrated. His wisdom is situational, arising as if by default rather than by intention. Used to cutting his sails to society's winds and keeping an eye out for any opportunity to do himself some good, Azdak delights in keeping his justice unpredictable. This Solomon keeps his subjects off balance and at his mercy, a peculiarly self-aggrandizing form of judicial "discretion." But if he privileges a law that is responsive to its times, that vindicates popular logic, and that reclaims vulgar humanism for the detritus of society, he does no more than reflect his times. These attributes speak persuasively to a kind of abortion law that adjusts the law by endowing economically and socially impacted groups with rights. They speak to a certain inventiveness, an instinctive approach to the law that weaves variations on precedents where possible and breaks new legal ground where necessary, attributes, like it or not, of present-day Supreme Court abortion jurisprudence. A modern-day *Caucasian Chalk Circle* would likely have encouraged an expression of "rascality" on the bench to create new legal doctrines that keep the law relevant even as it would have endorsed the variety of sexual roles women adopt in society and would have returned self-representation and agency to the subjects of abortion law.

In Mark Twain's version of the Solomon tale in *Huckleberry Finn*, we find an approach based on the direct and personal experience of parenting. Twain resists the pull of entrenched or hegemonic discourses and offers the hope of incorporating the views of outsiders.[3] The slave Jim locates the problem squarely as the threat to the child of chopping it in two, even as a game. Solomon's failure to fact-find is transformed in Jim's commentary into the arrogance of one who relies on inspiration to avoid perspiration. Twain thus displaces the emphasis from the "wisdom" of Solomon to the implied message that "life is cheap." Using the life of the child to illustrate how good a judge he is, Solomon has only undermined the sanctity of life, inherent in the child itself, to prefer the child's instrumental value as a legal lesson on point. But the "point" is lost on Jim, who finds no reason to create two halves to preserve a whole. What, after all, he asks, is the use of winning half a child.

Having seen his own family severed on the auction block in much the same way that Solomon proposes creating half a child (Lewis 1972), Jim understands Solomon not only in terms of his personal family but in terms of his racial family. The judgment of legal authority under slavery meant that the slaveowner endowed his many black children with little value; he was, indeed, in Jim's terms, "gwyne to be waseful o'chillen." The superior wisdom in Twain is that of the slave, the legally marginalized figure, outcast like the prostitute mothers. Having regained his voice, Jim offers an understanding superior to that of transcendent justice if only because it is rooted in human feelings and the perspective of one who has been the object of an illicit law.

Twain's Solomon not only puts the focus squarely on the absurdity of making a party whole for its loss by splitting a whole (democratic society) into half, but he ensures that two "disappeared" voices get re-appeared. He voices, first, the anguish of a father deprived of his progeny, reprising the history of the voicelessness of the slave. Second, he gives credence to the voice of the child, exposing the instrumental value given to child life and the property value ascribed to slave families as personal chattels. In his instinctive understanding of the deep structure of the scene, Jim implicitly reminds us of the foundational rights of equality and freedom granted to black slaves in the Fourteenth Amendment. These rights, extended to women in abortion law and asserted by proponents of fetal rights equally, create the very collision course with which this work has concerned itself.

One possibility to be considered is that outsider critiques will transform social discourse. The variety of what Jean Francois Lyotard calls "petit recits" (Myrsiades 1998, 201–205)[4]—representing the voices of the largest possible number of stakeholders—has the potential to enrich abortion discourse by giving us a range and depth of experience like that which we encountered in our readings of cartoons, poetry, and short fiction. We would neither be reduced to the rhetoric of oppositionality nor be constrained by the discontinuity of our history and traditions regarding the abortion issue. Indeed, the social split—the abortion fault line—that runs through the nation may already have experienced some of the worst tremors over abortion. A line drawn in the ideological sand that has given definition to our values, it has, as well, given value to our definitions. Parties on either side of the divide discover common concerns in lived life so that, like human tectonic plates, they find their ideological land floes shifting as they move from experience to experience. It is not so much that a house divided shall not stand as that a house divided shall not long remain divided. We find our rhetoric moving to the center, reaching out to shared concerns and mutual values. In the visual worlds of advertisements and cartoons, imagery opens up different ways of seeing and knowing to try on other ideas or invent new ones. The literatures of poetry and prose fiction offer us worlds of experience that give body to alternative ways of being and feeling. Nothing stays the same if the conversation is on-going; if the discussion, however explosive its dialectic, continues, it will evolve. In what direction, we may not be able to say, but change is likely to occur with a necessity that reflects different patterns of life and new sets of pressures, all of which require adaptation if we are to survive as a society. Life, to remain life, must and will be reproductive, even as, as history teaches us, it will also be abortive. That the dichotomy that arises from this conflicting agenda will reduce itself to a confrontation goes without saying. But, as the abortion film *Rain Without Thunder* (directed by Gary Bennett in 1992) reminds us in its closing quote from Frederick Douglass, "If there is no struggle, there is no progress. Those who profess to favor freedom and yet avoid confrontation are people who want crops without plowing up the ground. They want rain without thunder and lightning. They want the ocean without the roar of its waters."

Notes

1. For Scalia, the creation of doubt by the *Casey* plurality opinion and its fudging of the issues (regarding as peripheral to *Roe v. Wade* what he considers its core) are central concerns. Upholding a false precedent and a perverse arrogance in pretending to stand firm against public disapproval led the court, in Scalia's view, to rely on an invented principle of law (undue burden) and an ad hoc form of justice. (See Brisbin 1997.)

2 With Azdak, the people get the kind of justice they deserve, for he is very much the image

of a man who reflects the society of which he is a part. His justice expresses the ad hoc nature of an unsettled world in which people are pushed on impulse from pillar to post. The
operational principles of Azdak's justice include detachment from arbitrary rules and an
improvisatory originality that bespeaks flexibility. He is nothing if not responsive to facts
on the ground and has a penchant for representing the poor when possible.

Michael Freeman (1999) considers Azdak to be Brecht's "Mounted Messenger." He
rides in almost as a deus ex machina to rescue a convoluted situation with a decisive
cutting of the Gordian knot. In Freeman's reading of the play, property is best left to that
party which will most productively use it, as we find when the valley is conceded to a collective that can best manage it (199). The blood-tie argument made by the biological
mother is no more than a claim based on a right to property (203) rather than a best use
claim, the latter arguing for the adoptive mother. Morality and social utility thus trump
property rights, but without acknowledging that human property (the child) has itself any
rights. This is not a principled legal argument but judgment based solely on the facts of a
case absent guidance by rights-based theory, the legitimacy of court-made law, or the effect
of court-made law as precedent. Moreover, Azdak's justice fails to account for the rights of
those who have been socially marginalized, a consideration posed by Freeman through
such alternative hypotheses as the possibility that the adoptive mother could have been a
lesbian or the biological mother a Jewish victim of Nazi persecution (208).

Expanding the orbit of the law to represent the poor and dispossessed, as Azdak does—
on however irregular a basis—would create an inconsistent or "broken-up" law, even as it
leaves justice open to being "bribed" by popular opinion (Sterne 1994, 140–152). It is just
as likely that the judge is both a redeemer and a rascal, one who redeems an unresponsive
law even as he wrecks it (Lind 1999). Just as Brecht allows in Azdak an expression of ad
hoc, popularly responsive law, he also warns against the dangers of the humanity of such
law. Not only does the law depend upon the threat of violence as well as require deceit on
the part of the good mother, but it produces the unwelcome effect of delivering a child
more likely, as a result of Azdak's judgment, to be eaten alive in the world of violence into
which he has been born.

3. A revision of Solomon authored by Mark Twain in "Was Solomon Wise"—a stand-alone
piece that nonetheless serves as Chapter 14 of *Huckleberry Finn* (Quirk 1986)—stakes a
wholly different claim on the judgment of the King. This version considers a child-rights
approach to the tale. Huck Finn's slave friend Jim offers a homespun, down-to-earth critique of Solomon's solution in which he refers to the King's judgment as "de dad-fetchedes
ways I ever see" and compares the splitting of a child to the splitting of a dollar bill: "what's
de use er da half a bill." Solomon's solution, according to Jim, is the work of someone who
doesn't know enough to come in out of the rain, someone who failed to "go round to the
neighbors" to discover to whom the disputed child belongs.

Asking basic human questions, Jim concludes that the child, the judge, and the dispu-
tants all lose in the tale of Solomon. The point is "down furder—it's down deeper," in the
way Solomon himself was raised. In Jim's view, Solomon must be a man who, having had a
lot of children, did not know their value: "He as soon chop a chile in two as a cat. Day's
plenty mo.' A chile er two, mo'er less, warn't no consekens to Sollerman." A creature of
ancient culture, Solomon indeed acts within the context of laws that tolerate infanticide,
that allow a patriarch the right to dispose of his offspring as he judges fit, and that permit
men a harem of disposable wives and children. "[H]aving so much of everything, including
wives and children, . . . slaughtering one would matter little" (Chadwick-Joshua 1998, 51).

As a slave, Jim sees Solomon as nothing so much as "the figure of the slaveholder, the white Southerner who regards the Negro as chattel" (Mensh and Mensh 2000, 50). Even as Jim argues for family, he is a man forbidden his own family, which has been as violently ripped away from him as Solomon proposes to rip apart the child under dispute.

Jim's wisdom does not, in any case, extend beyond race or the rights of children to the rights of women. The mothers are fairly left to their own devices, making Solomon "the victim of quarrelsome women, not women the victims of a tyrannical, licentious man" (Mensh and Mensh 2000, 50). But the point of introducing Solomon's harem was never Twain's way of raising the issue of the victimization of the mothers. Rather, Jim's statement ("I reck'n de wives quarrels considerable; en dat 'crease de racket. . . .why: would a wise man want to live in de mids' er sich a blim-blammin' all de time?") becomes a critique of the harem master/slaveowner's indulgence in the sexual favors of his female slaves and his freedom to do as he wishes with the women whose bodies are his legal property.

Jim's "wisdom" operates outside the common reading of what is a community text when he critiques Solomon. Culturally excluded, he is, at the same time, free from being constrained or defined, as Huck is, by the Solomon story (West 1988, 138). This exclusion both liberates him and makes his questioning of Solomon's social code irrelevant, so that, as Robin West holds, "the critique that emerges from this process will be muted, and the transformation of the community will be minor" (140). That is to say, the story from Jim's point of view has been subverted by Jim's lack of status to tell the tale.

4. In an effort to avoid recourse to the terrorism of one language game over another or to a single metanarrative, Lyotard (1988a, 1988b, 1985, 1984) searches for an "indeterminate law" that is always in the future, yet to be determined, and continually under discussion. He resists the notion of a social consensus (sensus communis), concerned that the only consensus we should be worried about is that which would encourage heterogeneity or "dissensus" (1988b, 44). Indeed, consensus suggests to him a "community of hostages" (38).

Works Cited

Primary Sources

Cases

Bailey v. Alabama, 219 U.S. (1911)
Beal v. Doe, 432 U.S. 438 (1977)
Bellotti v. Baird, 428 U.S. 132 (1979)
Bray v. Alexandria Women's Health Clinic, 506 U.S. 263 (1993)
City of Akron v. Akron Center for Reproductive Health, 462 U.S. 416 (1983)
Colautti v. Franklin, 439 U.S. 379 (1979)
Doe v. Bolton, 410 U.S. 179 (1973)
Griffin v. Breckenridge, 403 U.S. 88 (1971)
Griswold v. Connecticut, 381 U.S. 479 (1965)
Harris v. McRae, 448 U.S. 297 (1980)
Hodgson v. Minnesota, 497 U.S. 417 (1990)
Madsen v. Women's Health Center, Inc., 512 U.S. 753 (1994)
Maher v. Roe, 432 U.S. 464 (1977)
NOW v. Scheidler, 510 U.S. 249 (1994)
Planned Parenthood v. ACLA, 41 F. Supp. 2d 1130 (D. Or. 1999); 2001 U.S. App. LEXIS
    4974
Planned Parenthood of Central Missouri v. Danforth, 428 U.S. 476 (1976)
Planned Parenthood of Southeast Pennsylvania v. Casey, 505 U.S. 833 (1992)
Poelker v. Doe, 432 U.S. 519 (1977)
Roe v. Wade, 410 U.S. 113 (1973)
Rust v. Sullivan, 500 U.S. 173 (1991)
Singleton v. Wulff, 428 U.S. 106 (1976)
Stenberg v. Carhart, 530 U.S. 914 (2000)
Thornburgh v. American College of Obstetricians and Gynecologists, 476 U.S. 747 (1986)
U.S. v. Amistad, 40 U.S. (1841)
U. S. v. Hill, 893 F. Supp. 1044 (N.D. Fla. 1994)
Webster v. Reproductive Services, 492 U.S. 490 (1989)

Literature

Adler, Warren. "An Unexpected Visit." *Never Too Late for Love*. Florida: Homestead Publishing, 1995. 261–274.

Ai. "Abortion." *A Book of Women Poets from Antiquity to Now*. Aliki Barnstone and Willis Barnstone, eds. New York: Schocken Books, 1980. 562.

Ai. "The Country Midwife: A Day." *The Garden Thrives: Twentieth-Century African-American Poetry*. Clarence Major, ed. New York: HarperPerennial, 1996. 294.

Anonymous. "Epitaph on a Child Killed by Procured Abortion." *The New Oxford Book of Eighteenth Century Verse*. Roger Lonsdale, ed. Oxford: Oxford UP, 1984. 335.

Atkins, Russell. "Lakefront, Cleveland." *The Garden Thrives: Twentieth-Century African-American Poetry*. Clarence Major, ed. New York: HarperPerennial, 1996. 83–84.

Atkinson, Michael. "Same Troubles with Beauty You've Always Had." *The Best American Poetry 1993*. Louise Gluck, ed. New York: Macmillan, 1993. 28–29.

Atwood, Margaret. "Christmas Carols." *Selected Poems II: Poems Selected and New 1976–1986*. Boston: Houghton Mifflin, 1987. 70–71.

Bambara, Toni Cade. "A Girl's Story." *The Sea Birds Are Still Alive*. London: The Women's Press, 1984. 152–165.

Beernick, K. D. "Anonymous: Spontaneous Abortion." *Ward Rounds*. Wallingford, PA: Washington Square East, 1970. 14–15.

Berlin, Lucia. "Tiger Bites." *Homesick: New and Selected Stories*. Santa Rosa, CA: Black Sparrow Press, 1990. 91–107.

Brooks, Gwendolyn. "The Mother." *A Street in Bronzeville* in *The World of Gwendolyn Brooks*. New York: Harper and Row, 1971. 5–6.

Carroll, Kenneth. "The Truth About Karen." *In Search of Color Everywhere: A Collection of African-American Poetry*. E. Ethelbert Miller, ed. New York: Stewart, Tabori, and Chang, 1994. 172.

Clifton, Lucille. "The Lost Baby Poem." *Good Woman: Poems and a Memoir, 1969–1980*. Brockport, NY: Boa, 1987.

Conde, Maryse. *I, Tituba, Black Witch of Salem*. New York: Ballantine Books, 1992.

Davies, W.H. "The Inquest." *The New Oxford Book of English Verse 1250–1950*. Helen Gardner, ed. Oxford: Oxford UP, 1972. 836–837.

DiPrima, Diane. "Brass Furnace Going Out: Song, After an Abortion." *The Portable Beat Reader*. Ann Charters, ed. New York: Viking Penguin, 1992. 363–369.

Dixon, Stephen. "Newt Likes the House Neat." *Quite Contrary: The Mary and Newt Story*. New York: Harper and Row, 1979. 100–116.

Dorr, Lawrence. "Two Hundred Yards past Wordsworth's House." *A Slight Momentary Affliction*. Baton Rouge, LA: Louisiana State UP, 1987. 67–74.

Dubus, Andre. "Miranda over the Valley." *Selected Stories*. Boston: David R. Godine, 1988. 1–19.

Epstein, Joseph. "Low Anxiety." *The Golden Boys*. New York: W.W. Norton, 1991. 35–54.

Floyd, Patty Lou. "The Voice in the Whirlwind." *The Silver De Soto*. Tulsa, OK: Council Oak Books, 1987. 167–194.

Gibson, Margaret. "Country Woman Elegy." *Long Walks in the Afternoon*. Baton Rouge, LA: Louisiana State UP, 1982. 105-106.

Gibson, Margaret. "Unborn Child Elegy." *Long Walks in the Afternoon*. Baton Rouge, LA: Louisiana State UP, 1982.

Gilchrist, Ellen. "1957, a Romance." *In the Land of Dreamy Dreams: Short Fiction by Ellen Gilchrist*. New York: Little, Brown, 1981. 81-95.

Gluck, Louise. "The Egg." *Firstborn*. New York: The New American Library, 1968. 4-5.

Gluck, Louise. "Firstborn." *Firstborn*. New York: The New American Library, 1968. 34.

Gluck, Louise. "The Wound." *Firstborn*. New York: The New American Library, 1968. 11.

Gray, Nowick. "New Moon." *Abortion Stories: Fiction on Fire*. Rick Lawler, ed. Sacramento, CA: MinRef Press, 1992. 173-185.

Green, Kate. "Abortion Journal." *Believing Everything: An Anthology of New Writing*. Mary Logue and Lawrence Smith, eds. Minneapolis, MN: Holy Cow Press, 1980. 49-58.

Hewett, Dorothy. "This Version of Love." *The Bloodaxe Book of Modern Australian Poetry*. John Tranter and Philip Mead, eds. Bloodaxe Books, 1991. 121-122.

Jen, Gish. "Birthmates." *The Best American Short Stories 1995*. Jane Smiley and Katrina Kenison, eds. New York: Houghton Mifflin, 1995. 110-125.

Johnson, Greg. "Little Death." *I Am Dangerous*. Baltimore, MD: Johns Hopkins UP, 1996. 104-116.

Jones, Gayle. *Corregidora*. Boston: Beacon Press, 1986.

Jonson, Ben. "To Fine Lady Would-Bee." *The Complete Poetry of Ben Jonson*. William B. Hunter, Jr., ed. New York: New York UP, 1963. 26.

Jonson, Ben. "On My First Sonne." *The Complete Poetry of Ben Jonson*. William B. Hunter, Jr., ed. New York: New York UP, 1963. 20.

Jonson, Ben. "On My First Daughter." *The Complete Poetry of Ben Jonson*. William B. Hunter, Jr., ed. New York: New York UP, 1963. 11-12.

Klimasewiski, Marshall N. "Jun-Hee." *The New Yorker* 66 (January 14, 1991): 26-36.

Lochhead, Liz. "An Abortion." *The New British Poetry 1968-88*. Gillian Allnutt, Fred D'Aguiar, Ken Edwards, and Eric Mottram, eds. London: Paladin Grafton Books, 1988. 110-111.

Lodi, Edward. "Rock-A-Bye." *Abortion Stories: Fiction on Fire*. Rick Lawler, ed. Sacramento, CA: MinRef Press, 1992. 91-93.

Lowell, Robert. "Fetus." *Day by Day*. New York: Farrar, Straus and Giroux, 1975. 34-35.

Mason, Bobbie Ann. "Marita." *Love Life*. New York: Harper & Row, 1989. 54-67.

Miller, John A. "Bethune, South Carolina." *Jackson Street and Other Soldier Stories*. Berkeley, CA: Orloff Press, 1995. 57-67.

Moeller, Eileen. "ten years ago." *Cries of the Spirit; A Celebration of Women's Spirituality*. Marilyn Sewell, ed. Boston: Beacon Press, 1991. 104.

Morrison, Toni. *Beloved*. New York: Alfred A. Knopf, 1987.

Naylor, Gloria. *The Women of Brewster Place: A Novel in Seven Stories*. New York: Penguin, 1983.

O'Hara, Frank. "An Abortion." *The Collected Poems of Frank O'Hara*. Donald Allen, ed. New York: Alfred A. Knopf, 1972.

Paretsky, Sara. "The Man Who Loved Life." *The Country of Herself*. Karen Lee Osborne, ed. Chicago: Third Side Press, 1993. 158–169.

Peacock, Molly. "Chriseaster." *A Formal Feeling Comes: Poems in Form by Contemporary Women*. Annie French, ed. New York: Story Line Press, 1994. 182–183.

Piercy, Marge. "The Provocation of the Dream." *Circles on the Water: Selected Poems of Marge Piercy*. New York: Alfred A. Knopf, 1982. 167–169.

Piercy, Marge. "The Sabbath of Mutual Respect." *Circles on the Water: Selected Poems of Marge Piercy*. New York: Alfred A. Knopf, 1982. 270–272.

Piercy, Marge. "Right to Life." *Circles on the Water: Selected Poems of Marge Piercy*. New York: Alfred A. Knopf, 1982. 263–265.

Rich, Adrienne. "To a Poet." *The Dream of Common Language*. New York: W.W. Norton, 1978.

Ritchie, Elisavietta. "Natalie." *Life on the Line: Selections on Words and Healing*. Sue Brannan Walker and Rosaly Demaios Roffman, eds. Mobile, AL: Negative Capability Press, 1992. 44.

Sexton, Anne. "The Abortion." *The Complete Poems*. Boston: Houghton Mifflin, 1981. 192.

Sexton, Anne. "Unknown Girl in the Maternity Ward." *The Complete Poems*. Boston: Houghton Mifflin, 1981. 24–25.

Shiffrin, Nancy. "For My Neverborn." *Editor's Choice III: Fiction, Poetry and Art from the U.S. Small Press (1984–1990)*. Marty Sklar, ed. New York: The Spirit That Moves Us Press, 1991. 254

Slatton, T. Diane. "Seventh Son of a Seventh Son." *Abortion Stories: Fiction on Fire*. Rick Lawler, ed. Sacramento, CA: MinRef Press, 1992. 199–208.

Snodgrass, W.D. "The Mother." *Selected Poems, 1957–1987*. New York: Soho Press, 1987.

Summers, Barbara. "Trialogue." *Nouvelle Soul*. New York: Amistad Press, 1992. 55–64.

Walker, Alice. "The Abortion." *You Can't Keep a Good Woman Down*. Orlando, FL: Harcourt Brace Jovanovich, 1980.

Walker, Alice. "Ballad of the Brown Girl." *Her Blue Body Everything We Know: Earthly Poems 1965–1990*. New York: Harcourt Brace Jovanovich, 1991. 135–136.

Williams, William Carlos. "A Cold Front." *The Collected Poems of William Carlos Williams: Volume II 1939–1962*. Christopher MacGowan, ed. New York: New Directions, 1988. 92–93.

Cartoons

Addis, Don. "Any Fruits, Exotic Pets or Pregnant Teens?" *St. Petersburg Times. Reproductive Freedom News* (RFN) (November 1998).

Asay, Chuck. "Guess Which Guest Speaker the Supreme Court Banned at the Graduation Ceremony?" *Colorado Springs Gazette Telegraph*. Christine Anne Marley. *Political Cartoons: A Playful Analysis of the Supreme Court: 1991–1992*. Diss. University of Oklahoma, 1994. Ann Arbor: UMI, 1992a. 216.

Asay, Chuck. "Having Rendered Yet Another Landmark Decision, the U.S. Supreme Court Exits the Courtroom." *Colorado Springs Gazette Telegraph*. Marley. 1992b. 189.

Asay, Chuck. "'We Found in This Document'. . . 'The Right of Women to Take the Lives of Their Unborn Children'. . . 'But Only in Moderation.'" *Colorado Springs Gazette Telegraph.* Marley. 1992c. 296.

Asay, Chuck. "Which Constitutionally Protected Expression Should Taxpayers Help Pay For?" *Colorado Springs Gazette Telegraph.* Marley. 1992d. 311.

Auth, Tony. "Choice—What a Beautiful Life." *Philadelphia Inquirer.* Universal Press Syndicate. RFN 6.9 (May 23 1997).

Auth, Tony. "Equal Justice Under the Law." *Philadelphia Inquirer.* Universal Press Syndicate. *Editorials on File* (EF) (1981): 761.

Auth, Tony. "Harry Blackmun, 1908–1999." *Philadelphia Inquirer.* Universal Press Syndicate. RFN 8.4 (April 1999).

Auth, Tony. "Hatchet. . . ." *Philadelphia Inquirer.* Universal Press Syndicate. RFN 3.14 (July 22, 1994a).

Auth, Tony. "I Have the Right to Choose Who Forfeits the Right to Life." *Philadelphia Inquirer.* Universal Press Syndicate. RFN 7.2 (March 1, 1998).

Auth, Tony. "In the Name of the Father, and of the Son." *Philadelphia Inquirer.* Universal Press Syndicate. EF (1984): 1379.

Auth, Tony. "Number Three May Not Look Like the Other Racketeers. . . ." *Philadelphia Inquirer.* Universal Press Syndicate. RFN 3.2 (January 28, 1994b).

Auth, Tony. "Quit Complaining. You Still Have a Right to Abortion." *Philadelphia Inquirer.* Universal Press Syndicate. RFN 5.4 (February 23, 1996).

Beattie, Bruce. "We've Added a Few More Restrictions." Copley News Service. Marley. 1992. 258.

Beck, Chip. "Waiting for the Big One." Associated Features, Inc. Marley. 1992. 179.

Borgman, Jim. "On, My Furies! On to *Planned Parenthood v. Casey!*" *Cincinnatti Enquirer/King Features Syndicate.* Marley. 1992a. 154.

Borgman, Jim. "Well, I'll Be Danged! He Pulled It Off!!" *Cincinnatti Enquirer/King Features Syndicate.* Marley. 1992b. 191.

Britt, Chris. "And Don't Get Any Ideas About Throwing It Out." *The News Tribune.* RFN 3.9 (May 13, 1994).

Britt, Chris. "The Only Black Group in America." *The News Tribune.* Marley. 1992a. 160.

Britt, Chris. "So We Overturn *Roe v. Wade.* . . ." *The News Tribune.* Marley. 1992b. 156.

Conrad, Paul. [A balance of hangers.] *Los Angeles Times* Syndicate. EF (1989a): 761.

Conrad, Paul. "*Bush v. Roe.*" *Los Angeles Times* Syndicate. EF (1992a): 90.

Conrad, Paul. "Only in America." *Los Angeles Times* Syndicate. Marley. 1992b. 308.

Conrad, Paul. "The *Roe v. Wade* Abortionists." *Los Angeles Times* Syndicate. Marley. 1992c. 150.

Conrad, Paul. "What a Reversal of *Roe v. Wade* Would. . . ." *Los Angeles Times* Syndicate. EF (1989b): 380.

Conrad, Paul. "What If?" *Los Angeles Times* Syndicate. Marley. 1992d. 133.

Danziger. "Judge Thomas Is Fascinated, Intrigued, and Engrossed. . . ." *The Christian Science Monitor/Los Angeles Times* Syndicate. Marley. 1992a. 292.

Danziger. "'With Partial Support'; 'We've Made a Partial Change'. . . ." *The Christian Science Monitor/Los Angeles Times* Syndicate. Marley. 1992b. 85.

Day, Bill. "I Gotta Admit, Lem." *Detroit Free Press*. Marley. 1992. 164.

Duffy, Brian. "Pro Choice/Supreme Court/Pro Life." *Des Moines Register*. Marley. 1992. 186.

Englehart, Bob. "Mom, Dad . . . There Are Several Bills Before the Legislature. . . ." *The Hartford Courant*. RFN 4.8 (April 21, 1995).

Fischer, Ed. "*Roe vs. Wade*." Extra Newspaper Features. Marley. 1992a. 256.

Fischer, Ed. "Solomon's Court." Extra Newspaper Features. Marley. 1992b. 194.

Gorrell, Bob. "Me? Pregnant? Well, Maybe Just a Little!" Copley News Service. Marley. 1992. 129.

Handelsman, Walt. "Operation Rescue/Choice/ 'Rescue me!'" *The Times Picayune*. EF (1992): 487.

Haynies, Chuck. "Compromise Abortion Law." *Los Angeles Times* Syndicate. EF (1977a): 1580.

Haynies, Chuck. "In Order to Appreciate Our Opinion on This Matter." EF (1980): 761.

Haynies, Chuck. "Supreme Court Ruling: The (Poor) Woman Always Pays." *Los Angeles Times* Syndicate. EF (1977b): 835.

Herblock. "Directional Road Signs." *Washington Post*. EF (1995): 42.

Herblock. "It's Very Simple—If You Could Afford Children. . . ." *Washington Post*. EF (1977): 833.

Hitch, David. "Campaign '92/Abortion Decision." Worcester *Telegram and Gazette*. Marley. 1992. 273.

Hollander, Nicole. "A Bill Was Narrowly Defeated Today. . . ." RFN 4.5 (March 10, 1995).

Hollander, Nicole. "The Sylvia School of Writing." RFN 5.17 (October 25, 1996).

Jorgensen, Bob. "The Court/Hate Crimes." Extra Newspaper Features. Marley. 1992a. 166.

Kelley, Steve. "Don't Believe Everything You Read." Copley News Service. EF (1993): 287.

Luckovich, Mike. "Pro-Life/'Burn Baby Burn!'" *Atlanta Constitution*. Marley. 1992. 104.

Luckovich, Mike. "Whoever Has These Numbers Gets the $295 Million Powerball Jackpot." *Atlanta Constitution*. *Newsweek* (December 28, 1998): 105.

Margulies, Jimmy. "Abortion Provider Targeted by Pro-Life Extremists." Hackensack *The Record*. RFN (December 1998a).

Margulies, Jimmy. "And This Is My Lamaze Coach." Hackensack *The Record*. EF (1989): 765.

Margulies, Jimmy. "I Said I Promise I Won't Tell Your Parents." Hackensack *The Record*. EF (1990): 721.

Margulies, Jimmy. "I'm Not Really a Doctor . . . but I Play One on TV." Hackensack *The Record*. RFN 4.1 (January 13, 1995).

Margulies, Jimmy. "It's Developing Nicely." Hackensack *The Record*. Marley. 1992. 147.

Margulies, Jimmy. "The Torch Is Passed." Hackensack *The Record*. RFN 7.4 (May 2, 1998b).

Ohman, Jack. "Blackmun Returns." *The Oregonian*. Marley. 1992a. 197.

Ohman, Jack. "Past Supreme Court Burning Decision." *The Oregonian*. Marley. 1992b. 305.

Oliphant. "Abortion Aid." *Los Angeles Times* Syndicate. EF (1977): 1577.

Peters, Mike. "Nightmares of Chief Justice Rehnquist." *Dayton Daily News*/United Features Syndicate, Inc. Marley. 1992. 145.

Peters, Mike. "What! You Want a Birth Control Device?" *Dayton Daily News*/United Features Syndicate, Inc. RFN 4.12 (June 16, 1995a).

Peters, Mike. "You've Been Found Guilty of Being Poor, Female, and Raped." *Dayton Daily News*/United Features Syndicate, Inc. RFN (July 28, 1995b).

Pett, Joel. "Clarence 'Never Discussed *Roe*' Thomas." *Lexington-Herald-Leader*/University Press Syndicate. RFN 4.4 (February 24, 1995).

Pett, Joel. "You Have Rights." *Lexington-Herald-Leader*/University Press Syndicate. RFN 6.14 (August 8, 1997).

Priggee, Milt. "It's Worse Than White Sheets." *The Spokesman Review*/*Spokane Chronicle*. Marley. 1992a. 162.

Priggee, Milt. "Yup! The Supreme Court Said Burning Crosses Is Constitutional." *The Spokesman Review*/*Spokane Chronicle*. Marley. 1992b. 322.

Rogers, Rob. "I Survived the Reagan Court." *The Pittsburgh Press*/United Features Syndicate, Inc. Marley. 1992. 89.

Rogers, Rob. "25 Years Ago Women Seeking Abortions Had to Live with the Fear. . . ." *The Pittsburgh Press*/United Features Syndicate, Inc. 1998.

Sack, Steve. "Supreme Court Abortion Rights Richter Scale." *State Tribune*. Marley. 1992. 82.

Schorr. "Life Begins at Conception . . . And Ends at Assassination." *New York Daily News*. *Newsweek* (December 28, 1998): 104.

Schorr. "Court Approved Abortion Clinic." *New York Daily News*. Marley. 1992. 253.

Shelton, M. "The Supreme Court Upholds Abortion." *Orange Country Register*. EF (1986): 663.

Smith, Mike. "Supreme Court Ruling." North American Syndicate. Marley. 1992. 80.

Stayskal, Wayne. "Death Row/Death *Roe*." *The Tampa Tribune*. Marley. 1992. 102.

Stephanos, Dale. "Start Praying." *Haverhill Gazette*. Marley. 1992. 116.

Summers, Dana. "Choice/'Please Don't Kill Our Baby.'" *The Orlando Sentinel*. Marley. 1992. 131.

Szed. "Abortion Kills." *The Boston Globe*. RFN 3.19 (November 4, 1994).

Templeton. "Supreme Court/'OK, Let's Vote on the Abortion Issue.'" Associated Features, Inc. Marley. 1992. 202.

Toles, Tom. "Dear Lord Above, Please Strike Justice William Brennan Dead." *The Buffalo News*/Universal Press Syndicate. 1986. Dallas A. Blanchard and Terry J. Prewitt. *Religious Violence and Abortion: The Gideon Project*. Gainesville, FL: UP of Florida, 1993. 258.

Trever, John. "Guess Which Form of Expression the Supreme Court Considers Harmful?" *The Albuquerque Journal*. Marley. 1992a. 214.

Trever, John. "Hey, They Can't Block Free Access." *The Albuquerque Journal*. Marley. 1992b. 87.

Trever, John. "I'm Proud to Stand with You in the Long March to Protect Life!" *The Albuquerque Journal*. EF (1985): 89.

Wasserman. "Nurse—Should I Have an Abortion?" *The Boston Globe*/*Los Angeles Times* Syndicate. RFN 4.21 (November 24, 1995).

Wasserman. "*Roe v. Wade.*" *The Boston Globe/Los Angeles Times* Syndicate. Marley. 1992. 313.

Wilkinson, Signe. "Butch's Abortions: No Parental Consent Required." Cartoonist and Writers Syndicate. RFN 5.2 (January 26, 1996).

Wilkinson, Signe. "Natural Family Planning." Cartoonist and Writers Syndicate. RFN 4.7 (April 7, 1995).

Wright, Don. "The Court Can Hardly Wait for Mrs. O'Connor to Get Here." *The Palm Beach Post.* EF (1981): 767.

Wright, Don. "'Enter Here'; 'Abortion Performed Here.'" *The Palm Beach Post.* Marley. 1992a. 252.

Wright, Don. "If, on the Other Hand, This Unwanted, Deprived, Uncared for Precious Little Life. . . ." *The Palm Beach Post.* Marley. 1992b. 106.

Wright, Don. "Medican't." *The Palm Beach Post.* RFN 4.18 (October 13, 1995).

Wright, Don. "Operation Rescue's Position on the RICO Ruling." *The Palm Beach Post.* EF (1994).

Wright, Don. "Supreme Court: *Roe v. Wade.*" *The Palm Beach Post.* EF (1989): 373.

Websites

armyofgod.com
cais.com
choiceusa.org
christiangallery.com/atrocity
crip.org
ippf.org
meonline.com
mint.net/life4me/nws-sp99.htm
naral.org
nrlc.org
planned parenthood.com
prochoice connection.com
prochoice.org
protectchoice.org
wcla.org
wifo.unimanheim.org

Secondary Sources

Adamek, Raymond J. "On the Salience of Arguments." *When Life and Choice Collide: Essays on Rhetoric and Abortion.* David Mall, ed. Libertyville, IL: Kairos Books, 1994. 65–89.

Adams, Alice E. *Reproducing the Womb: Images of Childbirth in Science, Feminist Theory, and Literature.* Ithaca, NY: Cornell UP, 1994.

Alexander, Mark C. "Religiously Motivated Murder: The Rabin Assassination and Abortion Clinic Killings." *Arizona Law Review* 39 (1997): 1161–1208.

Allegretti, Joseph. "Rights, Roles, Relationships: The Wisdom of Solomon and the Ethics of Lawyers." *Cardozo Law Review* 25.4 (1992): 1119-1139.

Althouse, Ann. "Beyond King Solomon's Harlots: Women in Evidence." *Southern California Law Review* 65 (1992): 1265-1278.

Alvesson, Mats. "The Play of Metaphors." *Postmodernism and Organizations*. John Hassard and Martin Parker, eds. London: Sage, 1993. 114-131.

Annas, George J. "The Supreme Court, Liberty, and Abortion." *The New England Journal of Medicine* 327.9 (August 27, 1992): 651-654.

Appleton, Susan Frelich. "Doctors, Patients and the Constitution: A Theoretical Analysis of the Physician's Role in 'Private' Reproductive Decisions." *Washington University Law Quarterly* 63.2 (1985): 183-236.

The Army of God Manual. 3/31/00. http://armyof god/AOGhistory.html.

Ashe, Marie. "Abortion of Narrative: A Reading of the Judgment of Solomon." *Yale Journal of Law and Feminism* 4 (1991): 81-92.

Ashe, Marie. "Law-Language of Maternity: Discourse Holding Nature in Contempt." *New England Law Review*, 22 (1988): 521-559.

Ashe, Marie. "Theoretics of Practice: The Integration of Progressive Thought and Action: The 'Bad Mother' in Law and Literature: A Problem of Representation." *Hastings Law Journal* 43 (1992): 1017-1036.

Balsamo, Anne. *Technologies of the Gendered Body: Reading Cyborg Women*. Durham, NC: Duke UP, 1996.

Balutansky, Kathleen M. "Creating Her Own Image: Female Genesis in *Memoire d'une amnesique* and *Moi, Tituba sorciere*." *L'Heritage de Caliban*. Maryse Conde, ed. Guadeloupe: Jasor, 1992. 29-47.

Baron, Jane B. "Storytelling and Legal Legitimacy." *Un-disciplining Literature: Literature, Law, and Culture*. Kostas Myrsiades and Linda Myrsiades, eds. New York: Peter Lang, 1999. 13-27.

Barnes, Paula C. "Meditations on Her/Story: Maryse Conde's *I, Tituba, Black Witch of Salem and the Slave Narrative Tradition*." *Arms Akimbo: Africana Women in Contemporary Literature*. Janice Lee Liddell and Yakini Belinda Kemp, eds. Gainesville, FL: UP of Florida, 1999. 193-204.

Barstow, Anne Llewellyn. *Witchcraze: A New History of the European Witch Hunts*. New York: HarperCollins, 1994.

Becel, Pascale. "*Moi, Tituba Sorciere . . . Noire de Salem* as a Tale of Petite Marronne." *Callaloo* 18.3 (1995): 608-615.

Bell, Roseann P. "Gayl Jones Takes a Look at *Corregidora*: An Interview." *Sturdy Black Bridges: Visions of Black Women in Literature*. Roseann P. Bell, Bettye J. Parker, and Beverly Guy-Sheftall, eds. Garden City, NY: Anchor, 1979. 282-287.

Bennett, Paul. "The Mother's Part: Incest and Maternal Deprivation in Woolf and Morrison." *Narrating Mothers: Theorizing Maternal Subjectivities*. Brenda O. Daly and Maureen T. Reddy, eds. Knoxville, TN: U of Tennessee P, 1991. 125-138.

Benshoof, Janet. "*Planned Parenthood V. Casey*: The Impact of the New Undue Burden Standard on Reproductive Health Care." *JAMA* 269.17 (May 5, 1993): 2249-2257.

Berenstein, Rhona. "Mommie Dearest: *Aliens, Rosemary's Baby* and Mothering." *Journal of Popular Culture* 24.2 (Fall 1990): 55-74.

Bhabha, Homi K. "A Good Judge of Character: Men, Metaphors, and the Common Culture." *Race-ing Justice, En-gendering Power: Essays on Anita Hill, Clarence Thomas, and the Construction of Social Reality.* Toni Morrison, ed. New York: Pantheon, 1992. 232–250.

Blanchard, Dallas A. *The Anti-Abortion Movement and the Rise of the Religious Right: From Polite to Fiery Protest.* New York: Twayne Publishers, 1994.

Blanchard, Dallas A., and Terry J. Prewitt. *Religious Violence and Abortion: The Gideon Project.* Gainesville, FL: UP of Florida, 1993.

Booth, Stephen. *Precious Nonsense: The Gettysburg Address, Ben Jonson's Epitaphs on His Children, and Twelfth Night.* Berkeley, CA: U of California P, 1998.

Bopp, James Jr., and Curtis R. Cook. "Partial-Birth Abortion: The Final Frontier of Abortion Jurisprudence." *Issues in Law and Medicine* 14.1 (1998): 3–57.

Bray, Michael. *Time to Kill: A Study Concerning the Use of Force and Abortion.* Portland, OR: Advocates for Life Publications, 1994.

Brisbin, Richard A., Jr. *Justice Antonin Scalia and the Conservative Revival.* Baltimore, MD: Johns Hopkins UP, 1997.

Brodie, Janet Farrell. *Contraception and Abortion in Nineteenth Century America.* Ithaca, NY: Cornell UP, 1994.

Brooker, M. Keith. "Approaches to *Beloved*, by Toni Morrison." *A Practical Introduction to Literary Theory and Criticism.* White Plains, NY: Longman, 1996. 285–315.

Brownstein, Alan. "How Rights Are Infringed: The Role of Undue Burden Analysis in Constitutional Doctrine." *Hastings Law Journal* 45 (1994): 867–950.

Buelow, William E. "To Be and Not To Be: Inconsistencies in the Law Regarding the Legal Status of the Unborn Fetus." *Temple Law Review* 71 (1998): 963–994.

Bundtzen, Lynda. "Monstrous Mothers: Medusa, Grendel, and Now Alien." *Film Quarterly* 40 (1987): 11–17.

Butler, J. Douglas, and David F. Walbert, eds. *Abortion, Medicine and the Law.* New York: Facts on File, 1985.

Butler-Evans, Elliott. *Race, Gender, and Desire: Narrative Strategies in the Fiction of Toni Cade Bambara, Toni Morrison, and Alice Walker.* Philadelphia: Temple UP, 1989.

Callahan, Joan C., and James W. Knight. "Women, Fetuses, Medicine, and the Law." *Feminist Perspectives in Medical Ethics.* Helen Bequaert Holmes and Laura M. Purdy, eds. Bloomington, IN: Indiana UP, 1992. 224–239.

Cassidy, Keith. "Abortion and the Rhetoric of Legitimacy." *When Life and Choice Collide: Essays on Rhetoric and Abortion.* David Mall, ed. Libertyville, IL: Kairos Books, 1994. 9–31.

Chadwick-Joshua, Jocelyn. *The Jim Dilemma: Reading Race in Huckleberry Finn.* Jackson, MS: UP of Mississippi, 1998.

Chambers, Ross. *Room for Maneuver: Reading the Oppositional Narrative.* Chicago: U of Chicago P, 1991.

Clifton, Lucille. "A Simple Language." *Black Women Writers (1950–1980): A Critical Evaluation.* Mari Evans, ed. Garden City, NY: Anchor Books, 1984. 137–138.

Cobbs, John L. "*Alien* as an Abortion Parable." *Literature and Film Quarterly* 18.3 (1990): 198–201.

Cohen, Daniel A. *Pillars of Salt, Monuments of Grace: New England Crime Literature and the Origins of American Popular Culture, 1674–1860*. New York: Oxford UP, 1993.

Colker, Ruth. "Feminist Litigation: An Oxymoron? A Study of the Briefs Filed in *William L. Webster v. Reproductive Health Services*." *Harvard Women's Law Journal* 13 (1990): 137–188.

Colker, Ruth. *Pregnant Men: Practice, Theory, and the Law*. Bloomington, IN: Indiana UP, 1994.

Condit, Celeste Michelle (Railsback). "The Contemporary American Abortion Controversy: Stages in the Argument." *Quarterly Journal of Speech* 70 (1984): 410–424.

Condit, Celeste Michelle. *Decoding Abortion Rhetoric: Communicating Social Change*. Urbana, IL: U of Illinois P, 1990.

Cornell, Drucilla. "The Doubly-Prized World: Myth, Allegory, and the Feminine." *Cornell Law Review*, 75 (1990): 644–699.

Corti, Lillian. "*Medea* and *Beloved*: Self-Definition and Abortive Nurturing in Literary Treatments of the Infanticidal Mother." *Disorderly Eaters: Texts in Self-Empowerment*. University Park, PA: Pennsylvania State UP, 1992.

Cosslett, Tess. *Women Writing Childbirth: Modern Discourses of Motherhood*. Manchester: Manchester UP, 1994.

Crewe, Jonathan. "Baby Killers." *differences* 7.3 (1995): 1–23.

Daly, Brenda O., and Maureen T. Reddy. *Narrating Mothers: Theorizing Maternal Subjectivities*. Knoxville, TN: U of Tennessee P, 1991.

Daly, Erin. "Reconsidering Abortion Law: Liberty, Equality, and the New Rhetoric of *Planned Parenthood v. Casey*." *The American University Law Review* 45 (1995): 77–150.

Dance, Daryl C. "Black Eve or Madonna?: A Study of the Antithetical Views of Mother in Black American Literature." *Sturdy Black Bridges: Visions of Black Women in Literature*. Roseann P. Bell, Bettye J. Parker, and Beverly Guy-Sheftall, eds. Garden City, NY: Anchor, 1979. 123–133.

Daniels, Cynthia R. *At Women's Expense: State Power and the Politics of Fetal Rights*. Cambridge: Harvard UP, 1993.

Dash, Irene. "The Literature of Birth and Abortion." *Regionalism and the Female Imagination* 3.1 (1977): 8–13.

Davies, Carole Boyce. "Mother Right/Write Revisited: *Beloved* and *Dessa Rose* and the Construction of Motherhood in Black Women's Fiction." *Narrating Mothers: Theorizing Maternal Subjectivities*. Brenda O. Daly and Maureen T. Reddy, eds. Knoxville, TN: U of Tennessee P, 1991. 44–57.

Davis, Angela Y. *Women, Race, and Class*. New York: Random House, 1981.

Davis, Peggy Cooper. "Neglected Stories and the Lawfulness of *Roe v. Wade*." *Harvard Civil Rights-Civil Liberties Law Review* 28 (1993): 299–394.

Davis, Peggy Cooper. *Neglected Stories: The Constitution and Family Values*. New York: Hill and Wang, 1997.

Dayton, Cornelia Hughes. "Taking the Trade: Abortion and Gender Relations in an Eighteenth-Century New England Village." *The William and Mary Quarterly* 48.1 (January 1991): 19–49.

Dayton, Cornelia Hughes. *Women Before the Bar: Gender, Law, and Society in Connecticut, 1639-1789*. Chapel Hill, NC: U of North Carolina P, 1995.

Dellapenna, Joseph W. "Brief of the American Academy of Medical Ethics." *Planned Parenthood of Southeastern Pennsylvania v. Robert P. Casey*. Nos. 91-744 and 91-902. April 6, 1992. 420-463.

DeMarco, Donald. "Grace and the Word." *When Life and Choice Collide: Essays on Rhetoric and Abortion*. David Mall, ed. Libertyville, IL: Kairos Books, 1994. 205-228.

Demos, John Putnam. *Entertaining Satan: Witchcraft and the Culture of Early New England*. New York: Oxford UP, 1982.

Dessner, Lawrence Jay. "Anne Sexton's 'The Abortion' and Confessional Poetry." *Anne Sexton Telling the Tale*. Steven E. Colburn, ed. Ann Arbor, MI: U of Michigan P, 1988.

Devereux, George. *A Study of Abortion in Primitive Societies*. New York: International Universities P, 1955.

Diamond, Sara. *Roads to Dominion: Right-Wing Movements and Political Power in the United States*. New York: The Guilford Press, 1995.

Dillon, Michele. "Argumentative Complexity of Abortion Discourse." *Public Opinion Quarterly* 57.3 (1993): 305-323.

Dimock, Wai Chee. *Residues of Justice: Literature, Law, and Philosophy*. Berkeley, CA: U of California P, 1996.

Dixon, Melvin. "Singing a Deep Song: Language as Evidence in the Novels of Gayle Jones." *Black Women Writers (1950-1980): A Critical Evaluation*. Mari Evans, ed. Garden City, NY: Anchor Books, 1984. 236-248.

Dolliver, Mark. "Choosing Not to Use the Unpopular Word." *Adweek* 48.19 (11 May 1998): 21-25.

Dresden-Coenders, Lene. "Witches as Devils' Concubines." *Saints and She-Devils: Images of Women in the 15th and 16th Centuries*. London: Rubicon Press, 1987. 59-82.

Dukats, Mara L. "The Hybrid Terrain of Literary Imagination: Maryse Conde's Black Witch of Salem, Nathaniel Hawthorne's Hester Prynne, and Aime Cesaire's Heroic Poetic Voice." *Race-ing Representation Voice, History, and Sexuality*. Kostas Myrsiades and Linda Myrsiades, eds. New York: Rowman and Littlefield, 1998. 119-140.

Dworkin, Ronald. *Life's Dominion: An Argument About Abortion, Euthanasia, and Individual Freedom*. New York: Knopf, 1993.

"Editorial: *Courier Journal*." *Editorials on File*, June 23, 1977, 833.

Ehrenreich, Barbara, and Deirdre English. *For Her Own Good: 150 Years of Experts' Advice to Women*. New York: Anchor Books, 1978.

Ehrenreich, Nancy. "The Colonization of the Womb." *Duke Law Journal* 43 (1993): 492-587.

Eisenberg, Rebecca. "Beyond *Bray*: Obtaining Federal Jurisdiction to Stop Anti-Abortion Violence." *Yale Journal of Law and Feminism* 6 (1994): 155-227.

Estrich, Susan, and Kathleen M. Sullivan. "*Webster v. Reproductive-Health Services*; Abortion Politics: Writing for an Audience of One." *University of Pennsylvania Law Review* 138 (1989): 119-155.

Evans, Mari, ed. *Black Women Writers (1950-1980): A Critical Evaluation*. Garden City, NY: Anchor Books, 1984.

Falwell, Jerry. *If I Should Die Before I Wake. . . .* Nashville, TN: T. Nelson, 1986.

Fineman, Martha Albertson, and Isabel Karpin, eds. *Mothers in Law: Feminist Theory and the Legal Regulation of Motherhood.* New York: Columbia UP, 1995.

Finkelman, Paul, ed. *Slavery and the Law.* Madison, WI: Madison House, 1997.

Fisher, Walter R. *Human Communication as Narration: Toward a Philosophy of Reason, Value, and Action.* Columbia, SC: U of South Carolina P, 1987.

Fitzgerald, Jennifer. "Selfhood and Community: Psychoanalysis and Discourse in *Beloved.*" *Modern Fiction Studies* 39.3–4 (Fall/Winter 1993): 669–687.

Foot, Philippa. "Killing and Letting Die." *Abortion: Moral and Legal Perspectives.* Jay L. Garfield and Patricia Hennessey, eds. Amherst, MA: U of Massachusetts P, 1984. 177–185.

Fox-Genovese, Elizabeth. *Within the Plantation Household: Black and White Women of the Old South.* Chapel Hill, NC: U of North Carolina P, 1988.

Franklin, Sarah. "Fetal Fascinations: New Dimensions to the Medical-Scientific Construction of Fetal Personhood." *Off-Centre: Feminism and Cultural Studies.* Sarah Franklin, Celia Lury, and Jackie Stacey, eds. New York: HarperCollins Academic, 1991. 190–205.

Franklin, Sarah, Celia Lury, and Jackie Stacey, eds. *Off-Centre: Feminism and Cultural Studies.* New York: HarperCollins Academic, 1991.

Franklin, Sarah, and Helen Rangone, eds. *Reproducing Reproduction: Kinship, Power, and Technological Innovation.* Philadelphia: U of Pennsylvania P, 1998.

Fraser, Celeste. "Stealing B(l)ack Voices: The Myth of Matriarchy and *The Women of Brewster Place.*" *Critical Matrix* 5 (Fall-Winter 1989): 65–88.

Freedman, Estelle. "Historical Interpretation and Legal Advocacy: Rethinking the *Webster* Amicus Brief." *The Public Historian* 12.3 (Summer 1990): 27–32.

Freeman, Michael. "Truth and Justice in Bertolt Brecht." *Cardozo Studies in Law and Literature* 11.2 (1999): 197–214.

Friedman, Leon, ed. *The Supreme Court Confronts Abortion: The Briefs, Argument, and Decision in Planned Parenthood v. Casey.* New York: Farrar, 1993.

Garfield, Jay, and Patricia Hennessey, eds. *Abortion: Moral and Legal Perspectives.* Amherst, MA: U of Massachusetts P, 1984.

Gates, Henry Louis, Jr., ed. *Reading Black, Reading Feminist: A Critical Anthology.* New York: Meridian, 1990.

Gates, Henry Louis, Jr., and K. A. Appiah, eds. *Alice Walker: Critical Perspectives Past and Present.* New York: Amistad, 1993.

Gayle, Addison, Jr. "Gwendolyn Brooks: Poet of the Whirlwind." *Black Women Writers (1950–1980): A Critical Evaluation.* Mari Evans, ed. Garden City, NY: Anchor Books, 1984. 79–87.

Genovese, Eugene D. *Roll Jordan, Roll: The World the Slaves Made.* New York: Vintage, 1976.

Getman, Karen A. "Sexual Control in the Slaveholding South: The Implementation and Maintenance of a Racial Caste System." *Harvard Women's Law Journal* 7 (1984): 115–152.

Gey, Steven G. "The *Nuremberg Files* and the First Amendment Value of Threats." *Texas Law Review* 78.3 (2000): 541–598.

Gillespie, Gary. "Abortion and Symbolic Action: Fetal Victimage in Pro-Choice and Pro-Life Politics." *When Life and Choice Collide: Essays on Rhetoric and Abortion*. David Mall, ed. Libertyville, IL: Kairos Books, 1994. 229–253.

Ginsburg, Faye D. "The Case of Mistaken Identity: Problems in Representing Women on the Right." *When They Read What We Write: The Politics of Ethnography*. Caroline B. Brettell, ed. Westport, CT: Bergin and Garvey, 1993. 163–176.

Ginsburg, Faye D. *Contested Lives: The Abortion Debate in an American Community*. Berkeley, CA: U of California P, 1989.

Ginsburg, Faye D. "The 'Word-Made' Flesh: The Disembodiment of Gender in the Abortion Debate." *Uncertain Terms: Negotiating Gender in American Culture*. Faye Ginsburg and Anna Lowenhaupt Tsing, eds. Boston: Beacon Press, 1990. 59–75.

Ginsburg, Faye D., and Anna Lowenhaupt Tsing, eds. *Uncertain Terms: Negotiating Gender in American Culture*. Boston: Beacon Press, 1990.

Givner, Jessie. "Reproducing Reproductive Discourse: Optical Technologies in *The Silent Scream* and *Eclipse of Reason*." *Journal of Popular Culture* 28.3 (Winter 1994): 229–244.

Gray, Peter. "On Brecht's *The Caucasian Chalk Circle*." *Brecht: A Collection of Critical Essays*. Peter Demetz, ed. Englewood Cliffs, NJ: Prentice-Hall, 1962. 151–156.

Gross, Ariela. "Pandora's Box: Slave Character on Trial in the Antebellum Deep South." *Slavery and the Law*. Paul Finkelman, ed. Madison, WI: Madison House, 1997. 291–328.

Guitton, Stephanie, and Peter Irons, eds. *May It Please the Court: Arguments on Abortion*. New York: The New Press, 1995.

Gutman, Herbert G. *The Black Family in Slavery and Freedom, 1750–1925*. New York: Pantheon Books, 1976.

Guy-Sheftall, Beverly. "The Women of Bronzeville." *Sturdy Black Bridges: Visions of Black Women in Literature*. Roseann P. Bell, Bettye J. Parker, and Beverly Guy-Sheftall, eds. Garden City, NY: Anchor, 1979. 157–169.

Hakin, Marilyn G. "Mother v. Fetus: New Adversaries in the Struggle to Define the Rights of Unborn Children." *Journal of Juvenile Law* 18 (1997): 99–111.

Halberstam, Judith, and Ira Livingston, eds. *Posthuman Bodies*. Bloomington, IN: Indiana UP, 1995.

Hall, Kermit L. *The Magic Mirror: Law in American History*. New York: Oxford UP, 1989.

Hansen, Elaine Tuttle. *Mother Without Child: Contemporary Fiction and the Crisis of Motherhood*. Berkeley, CA: U of California P, 1997.

Haraway, Donna J. "The Promise of Monsters: A Regenerative Politics for Inappropriate/d Others." *Cultural Studies*. Lawrence Grossberg, Cary Nelson, and Paula Treichler, eds. New York: Routledge, 1992. 295–337.

Haraway, Donna J. *Modest Witness @ Second Millennium. FemaleMan Meets OncoMouse: Feminism and Technoscience*. New York: Routledge, 1997.

Haraway, Donna J. *Simians, Cyborgs, and Women: The Reinvention of Nature*. New York: Routledge, 1991.

Harding, Susan. If I Should Die Before I Wake: Jerry Falwell's Pro-Life Gospel." *Uncertain Terms: Negotiating Gender in American Culture*. Faye Ginsburg and Anna Lowenhaupt Tsing, eds. Boston: Beacon Press, 1990. 76–97.

Harley, David. "Historians as Demonologists: The Myth of the Midwife-Witch." *Social History of Medicine* 3.1 (1990): 1–26.

Harris, Angela P. "Race and Essentialism in Feminist Legal Theory." *Stanford Law Review* 42 (1990): 581–615.

Harris, Janice. "Gayl Jones' *Corregidora*." *Frontiers* 5.3 (Fall 1980): 1–5.

Harris, Trudier. *Fiction and Folklore: The Novels of Toni Morrison*. Knoxville, TN: U of Tennessee P, 1991.

Hartouni, Valerie. "*Brave New World* in the Discourses of Reproductive and Genetic Technologies." *The Nature of Things: Language, Politics, and the Environment*. Jane Bennett and William Chaloupka, eds. Minneapolis, MN: U of Minnesota P, 1993. 85–110.

Hartouni, Valerie. *Cultural Conceptions: On Reproductive Technologies and the Remaking of Life*. Minneapolis, MN: U of Minnesota P, 1997.

Hartouni, Valerie. "Fetal Exposures: Abortion Politics and Optics of Allusion." *The Visible Woman: Imaging Technologies, Gender, and Science*. Paula A. Treichler, Lisa Cartwright, and Constance Penley, eds. New York: New York UP, 1998. 198–216.

Hartouni, Valerie. "Reproductive Technologies and the Negotiation of Public Meanings: The Case of Baby M." *Provoking Agents: Gender and Agency in Theory and Practice*. Judith Kegan Gardiner, ed. Urbana, IL: U of Illinois P, 1995. 115–132.

Heller, Dana. "Reconstructing Kin: Family, History, and Narrative in Toni Morrison's *Beloved*." *Race-ing Representation: Voice, History, and Sexuality*. Kostas Myrsiades and Linda Myrsiades, eds. New York: Rowman and Littlefield, 1998. 213–230.

Henderson, Mae G. "Toni Morrison's *Beloved*: Re-Membering the Body as Historical Text." *Comparative American Identities: Race, Sex, and Nationality in the Modern Text*. Hortense J. Spillers, ed. New York: Routledge, 1991. 62–86.

Herrera, Andrea O'Reilly, Elizabeth Mahn Nollen, and Sheila Reitzel Foor, eds. *Family Matters in the British and American Novel*. Bowling Green, OH: Bowling Green State U Popular P, 1997.

Higginbotham, A. Leon, Jr. *In the Matter of Color: Race and the American Legal Process: The Colonial Period*. New York: Oxford UP, 1978.

Hill, Paul. *Should We Defend Born and Unborn Children with Force?* Pensacola, FL: Paul Hill, 1993.

Hoffer, Peter C., and N.E.H. Hull. *Murdering Mothers: Infanticide in England and New England, 1558–1803*. New York: New York UP, 1981.

Holbrook, H. L. *Parturition Without Pain: A Code of Directions for Escaping from the Primal Curse*. New York: Wood and Holbrook, 1882.

Holcombe, William H. *The Sexes Here and Hereafter*. Philadelphia: J.B. Lippincott and Co., 1869.

Holmes, Helen Bequaert, and Laura M. Purdy, eds. *Feminist Perspectives in Medical Ethics*. Bloomington, IN: Indiana UP, 1992.

Howard, C. Elaine. "The *Roe*'d to Confusion: *Planned Parenthood v. Casey*." *Houston Law Review* 30 (1993): 1457–1508.

Hunter, James Davison. *Before the Shooting Begins: Searching for Democracy in America's Culture Wars*. New York: Free Press, 1994.

Hurley, Kelly. "Reading Like an Alien: Posthuman Identity in Ridley Scott's *Alien* and David Cronenberg's *Rabid*." *Posthuman Bodies*. Judith Halberstam and Ira Livingston, eds. Bloomington, IN: Indiana UP, 1995. 203–224.

Ikemoto, Lisa C. "The Code of Perfect Pregnancy: At the Intersection of the Ideology of Motherhood, the Practice of Defaulting to Science, and the Interventionist Mindset of Law." *Ohio State Law Journal* 53 (1992): 1205–1305.

Ireland, Patricia. "Transcript: The Rescue Racket, Organized Crime, and Mob Violence Against Women and Doctors." *Ohio Northern University Law Review* 21 (1995): 845–854.

Jameson, Fredric. *The Political Unconscious: Narrative as Socially Symbolic Act*. Ithaca, NY: Cornell UP, 1981.

Joffee, Carole. *Doctors of Conscience: The Struggle to Provide Abortion Before and After Roe v. Wade*. Boston: Beacon Press, 1995.

Johnson, Barbara. "Apostrophe, Animation, and Abortion." *Diacritics* (Spring 1986): 29–47.

Johnson, Miriam M. "Maternal Agency vs. the Brotherhood of Males." *Provoking Agents: Gender and Agency in Theory and Practice*. Judith Kegan Gardiner, ed. Chicago: U of Illinois P, 1995. 152–166.

Jones, Marvin D. "Darkness Made Visible: Law, Metaphor, and the Racial Self." *Georgetown Law Journal* 82 (1993): 437–510.

Jordanova, Ludmilla J. *Sexual Visions: Images of Gender in Science and Medicine Between the Eighteenth and Twentieth Centuries*. Madison: U of Wisconsin P, 1989.

Kairys, David. "Privacy." *With Liberty and Justice for Some: A Critique of the Conservative Supreme Court*. New York: New Press, 1993. 147–166.

Kaplan, Laura. *The Story of Jane: The Legendary Underground Feminist Abortion Service*. New York: Pantheon Books, 1995.

Karlsen, Carol F. *The Devil in the Shape of a Woman: Witchcraft in Colonial New England*. New York: Vintage, 1987.

Keenan, Sally. "'Four Hundred Years of Silence': Myth, History, and Motherhood in Toni Morrison's *Beloved*." *Recasting the World: Writing After Colonialism*. Jonathan White, ed. Baltimore, MD: Johns Hopkins UP, 1993. 45–81.

Kellough, Gail. *Aborting Law: An Exploration of the Politics of Motherhood and Medicine*. Toronto: U of Toronto P, 1996.

Kennedy, Randall. *Race, Crime, and the Law*. New York: Vintage, 1997.

Keown, John. *Abortion Doctors and the Law*. Cambridge: Cambridge UP, 1988.

Knickerbocker, Brad. "Anti-Abortion Web Sites: Free Speech or 'Threats'?" *Christian Science Monitor*, January 12, 1999, 1.

Kolbert, Kathryn. "After *Webster*, Where Will Court Go on Abortion?" *The National Law Journal* (August 1989a): S4.

Kolbert, Kathryn. "On Behalf of *Planned Parenthood et al*." *The Supreme Court Confronts Abortion: The Briefs, Arguments, and Decision in Planned Parenthood v. Casey*. Leon Friedman, ed. New York: Farrar, Straus, and Giroux, 1993. 311–322.

Kolbert, Kathryn. "*Webster v. Reproductive Services*: Reproductive Freedom Hanging by a Thread." *Women's Rights Law Reporter* 11 (1989b): 153–162.

Kolbert, Kathryn and David H. Gans. "Responding to *Planned Parenthood v. Casey*: Establishing Neutrality Principles in State Constitutional Law." *Temple Law Review* 66 (1993): 1151–1171.

Koppelman, Andrew. "Forced Labor: A Thirteenth Amendment Defense of Abortion." *Northwestern University Law Review*, 84 (1990): 480–534.

Korn, Peter. *Lovejoy: A Year in the Life of an Abortion Clinic*. New York: Atlantic Monthly Press, 1996.

Krumholz, Linda. "The Ghosts of Slavery: Historical Recovery in Toni Morrison's *Beloved*." *African American Review* 26.3 (1992): 395–408.

Lake, Randall A. "The Metaethical Framework of Anti-Abortion Rhetoric." *Signs: Journal of Women in Culture and Society* 11.3 (1986): 478–499.

Lake, Randall A. "Order and Disorder in Anti-Abortion Rhetoric: A Logological View." *Quarterly Journal of Speech* 70 (1984): 425–443.

Langer, Lawrence L. *Holocaust Testimonies: The Ruins of Memory*. New Haven, CT: Yale UP, 1991.

Langer, William L. "Infanticide: A Historical Survey." *History of Childhood Quarterly* 1.3 (Winter 1974): 355–365.

Lauro, Patricia Winters. "Advertising: An Abortion Rights Coalition Hopes Its Campaign Will Get Young Women to Discuss Their Choices." *New York Times*, December 16, 1999, C 13.

Law, Sylvia A. "Conversations Between Historians and the Constitution." *The Public Historian* 12.3 (Summer 1990): 11–17.

Leavitt, Judith W. "Why Women Suffer So: Meddlesome Midwifery and Scrupulous Cleanliness." *Brought to Bed: Childbearing in America, 1750–1950*. New York: Oxford UP, 1986.

Lenz, Kathryn E. "*NOW v. Scheidler*: RICO's Reach Now Extends to Antiabortion Protestors." *Journal of Pharmacy and Law* 4 (1994): 111–122.

Lewis, Stuart. "Twain's *Huckleberry Finn*." *The Explicator* 30.7 (March 1972): #61.

Lifton, Robert Jay. *The Nazi Doctors: Medical Killing and the Psychology of Genocide*. New York: Basic Books, 1986.

Lind, Douglas. "Azdak, the Rascal Judge." *Canadian Journal of Law and Jurisprudence* 12.2 (1999): 223–252.

Lindemann, Barbara S. "'To Ravish and Carnally Know': Rape in Eighteenth-Century Massachusetts." *Signs: Journal of Women in Culture and Society* 10.1 (1984): 63–82.

Lomicky, Carol S., and Charles S. Salestrom. "Anti-Abortion Advertising and Access to the Airwaves: A Public Interest Doctrine Dilemma." *Journal of Broadcasting and Electronic Media* 42.4 (Fall 1998): 491–507.

Lubiano, Wahneema. "Black Ladies, Welfare Queens, and State Minstrels: Ideological War by Narrative Means." *Race-ing Justice, En-gendering Power: Essays on Anita Hill, Clarence Thomas, and the Construction of Social Reality*. Toni Morrison, ed. New York: Pantheon, 1992. 323–363.

Lyotard, Jean Francois. *The Differend: Phrases in Dispute*. Trans. G. Van Den Abbeele. Minneapolis, MN: U of Minnesota P, 1988a.

Lyotard, Jean Francois. *Peregrinations: Law, Form, Event*. New York: Columbia UP, 1988b.

Lyotard, Jean Francois. *The Postmodern Condition: A Report on Knowledge*. Trans. Geoff Bennington and Brian Massumi. Minneapolis, MN: U of Minnesota P, 1984.

Lyotard, Jean Francois. *Just Gaming*. Trans. Wlad Godzich. Minneapolis, MN: U of Minnesota P, 1985.

Madhubuti, Haki. "Lucille Clifton: Warm Water, Greased Legs, and Dangerous Poetry." *Black Women Writers (1950–1980): A Critical Evaluation*. Mari Evans, ed. Garden City, NY: Anchor Books, 1984. 150–160.

Mall, David. "The Catholic Church and Abortion: Persuading Through Public Relations." *When Life and Choice Collide: Essays on Rhetoric and Abortion*. David Mall, ed. Libertyville, IL: Kairos Books, 1994. 107–156.

Mall, David M., ed. *When Life and Choice Collide: Essays on Rhetoric and Abortion*. Libertyville, IL: Kairos Books, 1994.

Maltz, Earl M. "Abortion, Precedent, and the Constitution: A Comment on *Planned Parenthood of Southeastern Pennsylvania v. Casey*." *Notre Dame Law Review* 68 (1992): 11–32.

Mann, Patricia S. "Cyborgean Motherhood and Abortion." *Provoking Agents: Gender and Agency in Theory and Practice*. Judith Kegan Gardiner, ed. Chicago: U of Illinois P, 1995. 133–151.

Manning, Peter K. "Metaphors of the Field: Varieties of Organizational Discourse." *Administrative Science Quarterly* 24 (December 1979): 660–669.

Markens, Susan, C.H. Browner, and Nancy Press. "Feeding the Fetus: On Interrogating the Notion of Maternal-Fetal Conflict." *Feminist Studies* 23.2 (Summer 1997): 351–372.

Marley, Christine Anne. *Political Cartoons: A Playful Analysis of the Supreme Court 1991–1992*. Diss. University of Oklahoma, 1994. Ann Arbor: UMI, 1994.

Mason, Carol. "Terminating Bodies: Toward a Cyborg History of Abortion." *Posthuman Bodies*. Judith Halberstam and Ira Livingston, eds. Bloomington, IN: Indiana UP, 1995. 225–243.

McClerren, B.F. "The Rhetoric of Abortion: A Weaverian Method of Analysis." *When Life and Choice Collide: Essays on Rhetoric and Abortion*. David Mall, ed. Libertyville, IL: Kairos Books, 1994. 269–283.

McClusky, Audrey T. "Tell the Good News: A View of Lucille Clifton." *Black Women Writers (1950–1980): A Critical Evaluation*. Mari Evans, ed. Garden City, NY: Anchor Books, 1984. 139–149.

McConnell, Joyce E. "Beyond Metaphor: Battered Women, Involuntary Servitude and the Thirteenth Amendment." *Yale Journal of Law and Feminism*, 4 (1992): 207–253.

McDonagh, Eileen L. *Breaking the Abortion Deadlock: From Choice to Consent*. New York: Oxford UP, 1996.

McDonald, Timothy B. "When Does a Fetus Become a Child in Need of an Advocate?: Focusing on Fetal Pain." *Children's Legal Rights Journal* 17.2 (Spring 1997): 12–19.

McGowan, Philip. "Uncovering the Female Voice in Anne Sexton." *Revista Canaria de Estudios Ingleses* 37 (1998): 125–141.

McKeegan, Michele. *Abortion Politics: Mutiny in the Ranks of the Right.* New York: The Free Press, 1992.

McKenna, George. "On Abortion: A Lincolnian Position." *The Atlantic Monthly* 276.3 (September 1995): 51-64.

Means, Cyril C. Jr. "The Law of New York Concerning Abortion and the Status of the Foetus, 1664-1968: A Case of Cessation of Constitutionality." *New York Law Forum* 14.3 (Fall 1968): 411-515.

Means, Cyril C. Jr. "The Phoenix of Abortional Freedom: Is a Penumbra or Ninth-Amendment Right About to Arise from the Nineteenth-Century Legislative Ashes of a Fourteenth-Century Common-Law Liberty?" *New York Law Forum* 17.2 (1971): 335-410.

Meaney, Geraldine. *(Un)Like Subjects: Women, Theory, Fiction.* London: Routledge, 1993.

Medhurst, Martin J., and Michael A. DeSousa. "Political Cartoons as Rhetorical Form: A Taxonomy of Graphic Discourse." *Communication Monographs* 48 (September 1981): 197-236.

Mensh, Elaine, and Harry Mensh. *Black, White and Huckleberry Finn: Re-Imagining the American Dream.* Tuscaloosa, AL: U of Alabama P, 2000.

Middlebrook, Diane Wood. *Anne Sexton: A Biography.* Boston: Houghton Mifflin, 1991.

Miklitsch, Robert. "Assembling a Landscape: The Poetry of Louise Gluck." *The Hollins Critic* 19.4 (1982): 2-13.

Minow, Martha, Michael Ryan, and Austin Sarat, eds. *Narrative, Violence, and the Law: The Essays of Robert Cover.* Ann Arbor: U of Michigan P, 1992.

Mishkin, Tracy, ed. *Literary Influence and African-American Writers: Collected Essays.* New York: Garland, 1996.

Mohr, James C. "Historically Based Legal Briefs: Observations of a Participant in the *Webster* Process." *The Public Historian* 12. 3 (Summer 1990): 19-26.

Mohr, James C. *Abortion in America: The Origins and Evolution of National Policy, 1800-1900.* New York: Oxford UP, 1978.

Montgomery, Maxine Lavon. "Rewriting the Apocalypse: The End of the World in Gloria Naylor's *The Women of Brewster Place.*" *The Literary Griot* 6.2 (Fall 1994): 46-53.

Moran, Terence. "Hanging by a Thread; When *Roe* Is Gone, What Happens to Privacy." *Legal Times,* December 30, 1991, 6.

Morgan, Gareth. "Paradigms, Metaphors, and Puzzle Solving in Organization Theory." *Administrative Science Quarterly* 25 (1980): 605-621.

Myrsiades, Linda. "A Language Game Approach to Narrative Analysis of Sexual Harassment Law in *Meritor v. Vinson.*" *College Literature* 25.1 (1998): 200-230.

Mudimbe-Boyi, Elisabeth. "Giving a Voice to Tituba: The Death of the Author." *World Literature Today* 674 (Autumn 1993): 751-756.

Neilson, Joanne. "*Madsen v. Women's Health Center, Inc.*: Protection Against Antiabortionist Terrorism." *Pace Law Review* 16 (1996): 325-357.

Newman, Karen. *Fetal Positions: Individualism, Science, Visuality.* Palo Alto, CA: Stanford UP, 1996.

Noonan, John, John T. Noonan Jr., et al., eds. *The Morality of Abortion: Legal and Historical Perspectives.* Cambridge: Harvard UP, 1970.

Oaks, Laury. "Smoke-Filled Wombs and Fragile Fetuses: The Social Politics of Fetal Representation." *Signs* 26.1 (2000): 63–107.

Olasky, Marvin W. *Abortion Rites: A Social History of Abortion in America.* Wheaton, IL: Crossway Books, 1992.

Ostriker, Alicia. "'Kin and Kin': The Poetry of Lucille Clifton." *Literary Influence and African-American Writers: Collected Essays.* Tracy Mishkin, ed. New York: Garland, 1996. 301–323.

Otten, Terry. "Horrific Love in Toni Morrison's Fiction." *Modern Fiction Studies* 39.3–4 (Fall/Winter 1993): 651–667.

Palumbo, Kathryn. "The Uses of Female Imagery in Naylor's *The Women of Brewster Place.*" *Notes on Contemporary Literature* 15.3 (May 1985): 6–7.

Pang, Amber M. "Speech, Conduct, and Regulation of Abortion Protest by Court Injunction: From *Madsen v. Women's Health Center* to *Schenck v. Pro-Choice Network.*" *Gonzaga Law Review* 34.1 (1998/99): 201–227.

Parker, Alexander M. "Stretching RICO to the Limit and Beyond." *Duke Law Journal* 45 (1996): 819–848.

Petchesky, Rosalind Pollack. *Abortion and Woman's Choice: The State, Sexuality, and Reproductive Freedom.* Boston: Northeastern UP, 1990.

Petchesky, Rosalind Pollack. "Fetal Images: The Power of Visual Culture in the Politics of Reproduction." *Feminist Studies* 13.2 (1987): 263–292.

Pfaff, Francoise. *Conversations with Maryse Conde.* Lincoln, NE: U of Nebraska P, 1996.

Posner, Richard A. *Sex and Reason.* Cambridge: Harvard UP, 1992.

Powers, Edwin. *Crime and Punishment in Early Massachusetts, 1620–1692: A Documentary History.* Boston: Beacon Press, 1966.

Press, Andrea L., and Elizabeth R. Cole. *Speaking of Abortion: Television and Authority in the Lives of Women.* Chicago: U of Chicago P, 1999.

Quirk, Thomas. "'Learning a Nigger to Argue': Quitting *Huckleberry Finn.*" *American Literary Realism* 20.1 (1986): 18–33.

Reagan, Leslie. *When Abortion Was a Crime: Women, Medicine, and the Law in the United States, 1867–1973.* Berkeley, CA: U of California P, 1997.

Reagan, Ronald. *Abortion and the Conscience of the Nation.* Nashville, TN: Thomas Nelson Publishers, 1984.

Reicher, Steve, and Nick Hopkins. "Seeking Influence Through Characterizing Self-Categories: An Analysis of Anti-Abortionist Rhetoric." *British Journal of Social Psychology* 35 (1996): 297–311.

Ricoeur, Paul. *History and Truth.* Trans. and ed. Charles A. Kebley. Evanston, IL: Northwestern UP, 1965.

Riddle, John M. *Contraception and Abortion from the Ancient World to the Renaissance.* Cambridge: Harvard UP, 1992.

Risen, James, and Judy L. Thomas. *Wrath of Angels: The American Abortion Wars.* New York: Basic Books, 1998.

Roberts, Dorothy E. "Punishing Drug Addicts Who Have Babies: Women of Color, Equality, and the Right to Privacy." *Harvard Law Review* 104 (1991): 1419–1482.

Roberts, Dorothy E. "Racism and Patriarchy in the Meaning of Motherhood." *Mothers in Law: Feminist Theory and the Legal Regulation of Motherhood.* Martha Albertson Fineman and Isabel Karpin, eds. New York: Columbia UP, 1995.

Ross, Loretta J. "African-American Women and Abortion." *Abortion Wars: A Half Century of Struggle, 1950-2000.* Rickie Solinger, ed. Berkeley: U of California P, 1998. 161-207.

Rothman, Barbara Katz. *Recreating Motherhood: Ideology and Technology in a Patriarchal Society.* New York: W.W. Norton, 1989.

Rudy, Kathy. *Beyond Pro-Life and Pro-Choice: Moral Diversity in the Abortion Debate.* Boston: Beacon Press, 1996.

Rushdy, Ashraf H. A. "Daughters Signifyin(g) History: The Example of Toni Morrison's *Beloved.*" *American Literature* 64.3 (September 1992): 567-597.

Rushing, Janice Hocker. "Evolution of 'The New Frontier' in *Alien* and *Aliens*: Patriarchal Co-optation of the Feminine Archetype." *Quarterly Journal of Speech* 75.1 (February 1989): 1-24.

"Safety Valve Closed: The Removal of Nonviolent Outlets for Dissent and the Onset of Anti-Abortion Violence." *Harvard Law Review* 113 (2000): 1210-1227.

Samuels, David. "The Making of a Fugitive." *The New York Times Magazine,* Section 6, March 21, 1999, 47.

Sandelowski, Margarete. "Separate but Unequal: Fetal Ultrasonography and the Transformation of Expectant Mother/Fatherhood." *Gender and Society* 8.2 (June 1994): 230-245.

Savage, David. "Abortion Issue Argued Before Supreme Court." *Los Angeles Times,* April 23, 1992a, A1.

Savage, David G. *Turning Right: The Making of the Rehnquist Supreme Court.* New York: John Wiley and Sons, 1992b.

Savitt, Todd L. *Medicine and Slavery: The Diseases and Health Care of Blacks in Antebellum Virginia.* Urbana, IL: U of Illinois P, 1978.

Scarr, Amy. "Coming to Terms with the Politics of Discourse: A Critique of Robin West's *Jurisprudence and Gender.*" *Wisconsin Women's Law Journal* 5 (1990): 147-159.

Schafer, Judith Kelleher. "'Details are of a Most Revolting Character': Cruelty to Slaves as Seen in Appeals to the Supreme Court of Louisiana." *Slavery and the Law.* Paul Finkelman, ed. Madison, WI: Madison House, 1997. 241-268.

Scheidler, Joseph M. *Closed: 99 Ways to Stop Abortion.* Westchester, IL: Crossway Books, 1985.

Schemanske, Mark. "Working for the Company: Patriarchal Legislation of the Maternal in *Alien.*" *Authority and Transgression in Literature and Film.* Bonnie Braendlen and Hans Braendlen, eds. Gainesville, FL: UP of Florida, 1996.127-135.

Schoen, Johanna. "Reconceiving Abortion: Medical Practice, Women's Access, and Feminist Politics Before and After *Roe v. Wade.*" *Feminist Studies* 26.2 (2000): 349-376.

Scholten, Catharine M. "'On the Importance of the Obstetrick Art': Changing Customs of Childbirth in America, 1760-1825." *The William and Mary Quarterly* 34.3 (July 1977): 426-445.

Scruggs, Charles. "The Invisible City in Toni Morrison's *Beloved.*" *Arizona Quarterly* 48.3 (Autumn 1992): 95–132.

Sernett, Milton C. "Widening the Circle: The Pro-Life Appeal to the Abolitionist Legacy." *When Life and Choice Collide: Essays on Rhetoric and Abortion.* David Mall, ed. Libertyville, IL: Kairos Books, 1994. 159–187.

Shapiro, Ian, ed. *Abortion: The Supreme Court Decisions.* Indianapolis, IN: Hackett, 1995.

Shaw, Anne E., and Alane C. Spinney. "Rhetoric, Repetition, and Violence: A Case Study of Clinic Conflict in Milwaukee." *Un-Disciplining Literature: Literature, Law, and Culture.* Kostas Myrsiades and Linda Myrsiades, eds. New York: Peter Lang, 1999. 47–71.

Shelton, Marie-Denise. "Conde: The Politics of Gender and Identity." *World Literature Today* 674 (Autumn 1993): 717–722.

Siegel, Reva B. "Reasoning from the Body: A Historical Perspective on Abortion Regulation and Questions on Equal Protection." *Stanford Law Review* 44 (1992): 261–380.

Simon, Bruce. "Traumatic Repetition: Gayl Jones's *Corregidora.*" *Race Consciousness: African-American Studies for the New Century.* Judith Jackson Fossett and Jeffrey A. Tucker, eds. New York: New York UP, 1997. 93–112.

Smith, Daniel Scott, and Michael S. Hindus. "Premarital Pregnancy in America 1640–1971: An Overview and Interpretation." *Journal of Interdisciplinary History* 5.4 (Spring 1975): 537–570.

Smith, Lynn. "An Equality Approach to Reproductive Choice: *R. v. Sullivan.*" *Yale Journal of Law and Feminism* 4 (1991): 93–132.

Smith, Michelle. "Reading in Circles: Sexuality and/as History in *I, Tituba, Black Witch of Salem. Callaloo* 18.3 (1995): 602–607.

Smith-Rosenberg, Carroll, and Charles Rosenberg. "The Female Animal: Medical and Biological Views of Woman and Her Role in Nineteenth-Century America." *Concepts of Health and Disease: Interdisciplinary Perspectives.* Arthur L. Caplan, H. Tristram Engelhardt, Jr., and James J. McCartney, eds. Reading, MA: Addison-Wesley, 1981. 281–303.

Snitgen, Jeanne. "History, Identity and the Constitution of the Female Subject: Maryse Conde's *Tituba.*" *Black Women's Writing: Crossing the Boundaries.* Carole Boyce Davies, ed. Frankfurt: Holger Ehling, 1989. 55–73.

Sofia, Zoe. "Exterminating Fetuses: Abortion, Disarmament, and the Sexo-Semiotics of Extraterrestrialism." *Diacritics,* 14 (1984): 47–59.

Solinger, Rickie, ed. *Abortion Wars: A Half Century of Struggle, 1950–2000.* Berkeley, CA: U of California P, 1998.

Solinger, Rickie. *The Abortionist: A Woman Against the Law.* New York: The Free Press, 1994.

Solomon, Martha. "Redemptive Rhetoric: The Continuity Motif in the Rhetoric of Right to Life." *Central States Speech Journal* 31 (Spring 1980): 52–62.

Squier, Susan M. "Reproducing the Posthuman Body: Ectogenetic Fetus, Surrogate Mother, Pregnant Man." *Posthuman Bodies.* Judith Halberstam and Ira Livingston, eds. Bloomington, IN: Indiana UP, 1995. 113–132.

Stabile, Carol. "Shooting the Mother: Fetal Photography and the Politics of Disappearance." *The Visible Woman: Imaging Technologies, Gender, and Science.* Paula A. Treichler, Lisa Cartwright, and Constance Penley, eds. New York: New York UP, 1998. 171–197.

Staggenborg, Susanne. *The Pro-Choice Movement: Organization and Activism in the Abortion Conflict.* New York: Oxford UP, 1991.

Stanworth, Michelle. "Reproductive Technologies and the Deconstruction of Motherhood." *Reproductive Technologies: Gender, Motherhood, and Medicine.* Michelle Stanworth, ed. Minneapolis, MN: U of Minnesota P, 1987. 10–35.

Starr, Paul. *The Social Transformation of American Medicine: The Rise of a Sovereign Profession and the Making of a Vast Industry.* New York: Basic Books, 1982.

Sterne, Richard Clarke. *Dark Mirror: The Sense of Injustice In Modern European and American Literature.* New York: Fordham UP, 1994.

Stormer, Nathan. "Prenatal Space." *Signs: Journal of Women in Culture and Society* 26.1 (2000): 109–144.

Swigert, Jane. "The Double Vision of Anne Sexton and Sylvia Plath." *The Myth of the Bad Mother: The Emotional Realities of Mothering.* New York: Doubleday, 1991. 213–237.

Tate, Claudia, ed. "Gayl Jones." *Black Women Writers at Work.* New York: Continuum, 1983. 89–99.

Taylor, Janelle S. "Image of Contradiction: Obstetrical Ultrasound in American Culture." *Reproducing Reproduction: Kinship, Power, and Technological Innovation.* Sarah Franklin and Helen Rangone, eds. Philadelphia: U of Pennsylvania P, 1998. 15–38.

Taylor, Janelle S. "The Public Fetus and the Family Car: From Abortion Politics to a Volvo Advertisement." *Public Culture* 4.2 (Spring 1992): 67–80.

Terry, Randall. *Operation Rescue.* Springfield, PA: Whitaker House, 1988.

Terry, Randall. *Accessory to Murder: The Enemies, Allies, and Accomplices to the Death of Our Culture.* Brentwood, TN: Wolgemuth and Hyatt, 1990.

Thomas, Laurence. "Abortion, Slavery, and the Law: A Study in Moral Character." *Abortion: Moral and Legal Perspectives.* Jay L. Garfield and Patricia Hennessey, eds. Amherst, MA: U of Massachusetts P, 1984. 227–237.

Thomson, Judith Jarvis. "A Defense of Abortion." *Philosophy and Public Affairs,* 1 (1971): 47–66.

Tobin, Elizabeth. "Law and Literature: Imagining the Mother's Text: Toni Morrison's *Beloved* and Contemporary Law." *Harvard Women's Law Journal* 16 (1993): 233–273.

Treichler, Paula A., Lisa Cartwright, and Constance Penley, eds. *The Visible Woman: Imaging Technologies, Gender, and Science.* New York: New York UP, 1998.

Tribe, Lawrence H. *Abortion: The Clash of Absolutes.* New York: W.W. Norton and Co., 1990.

Tsing, Anna Lowenhaupt. "Monster Stories: Women Charged with Perinatal Endangerment." *Uncertain Terms: Negotiating Gender in American Culture.* Faye Ginsburg and Anna Lowenhaupt Tsing, eds. Boston: Beacon Press, 1990. 282–299.

Tushnet, Mark V. *The American Law of Slavery, 1810–1860: Considerations of Humanity and Interest.* Princeton: Princeton UP, 1981.

Tyler, Tom R., and Gregory Mitchell. "Legitimacy and the Empowerment of Discretionary Legal Authority: The United States Supreme Court and Abortion Rights." *Duke Law Journal* 43 (1994): 703–798.

Ulrich, Laurel Thatcher. *A Midwife's Tale: The Life of Martha Ballard, Based on Her Diary, 1785–1812*. New York: Vintage Books, 1990.

Vanderford, Marsha L. "Vilification and Social Movements: A Case Study of Pro-Life and Pro-Choice Rhetoric." *Quarterly Journal of Speech* 75 (1989): 166–182.

Verhovek, Sam Howe. "Anti-Abortion Site on Web has Ignited Free Speech Debate." *New York Times*, January 13, 1999a, A1, 13.

Verhovek, Sam Howe. "Creators of Anti-Abortion Web Site Told to Pay Millions." *New York Times*, February 3, 1999b, A9.

Von Rosenvinge Sheppard, Hille. "The Federal Communication Act and the Broadcast of Aborted Fetus Advertisements." *The University of Chicago Legal Forum* (1993): 395–415.

Walker, Alice. *In Search of Our Mothers' Gardens: Womanist Prose*. New York: Harcourt Brace, 1983.

Ward, Jerry W., Jr. "Escape from Trublem: The Fiction of Gayl Jones." *Black Women Writers (1950–1980): A Critical Evaluation*. Mari Evans, ed. Garden City, NY: Anchor Books, 1984. 249–257.

Ward, Roy Bowen. "The Use of the Bible in the Abortion Debate." *Saint Louis University Public Law Review* 13.1 (1993): 391–408.

Wedam, Elfriede. "Splitting Interests or Common Cause: Styles of Moral Reasoning in Opposing Abortion." *Contemporary American Religion: An Ethnographic Reader*. Penny Edgell Becker and Nancy L. Eiesland, eds. London: Altamira, 1997. 147–168.

Weinstein, Henry. "Free Speech Ruling Boon for Abortion Foes." *Los Angeles Times*, March 29, 2001, A1.

West, Robin. "Communities, Texts, and Law: Reflections of the Law and Literature Movement." *Yale Journal of Law and the Humanities* 1 (1988): 129–156.

West, Robin L. "The Nature of the Right to an Abortion: A Commentary on Professor Brownstein's Analysis of Casey." *Hastings Law Journal* 45 (1994): 961–967.

White, Deborah Gray. *"Ain't I a Woman?": Female Slaves in the Plantation South*. New York: Norton, 1985.

White, Hayden. *The Content of the Form: Narrative Discourse and Historical Representation*. Baltimore, MD: Johns Hopkins UP, 1987.

White, James Boyd. *Justice as Translation: An Essay in Cultural and Legal Criticism*. Chicago: U of Chicago P, 1990.

White, James Boyd. "*Planned Parenthood v. Casey*: Legal Judgment as an Ethical and Cultural Art." *Acts of Hope: Creating Authority in Literature, Law, and Politics*. Chicago: U of Chicago P, 1994. 153–183.

Willis, Susan. "Alice Walker's Women." *New Orleans Review* 12.1 (Spring 1985): 33–41.

Willke, John C. "The Battleground of Semantics." *When Life and Choice Collide: Essays on Rhetoric and Abortion*. David Mall, ed. Libertyville, IL: Kairos Books, 1994. 321–331.

Wilt, Judith. *Abortion, Choice, and Contemporary Fiction: The Armageddon of the Maternal Instinct*. Chicago: U of Chicago P, 1991.

Wolf, Naomi. "Our Bodies, Our Souls." *New Statesman and Society* 8.375 (October 10, 1995): 23–28.

Woodward, Bob, and Scott Armstrong. *The Brethren: Inside the Supreme Court*. New York: Simon and Schuster, 1979.

Index

ERUPTIONS
New Thinking across the Disciplines

Erica McWilliam
General Editor

This is a series of red-hot women's writing after the "isms." It focuses on new cultural assemblages that are emerging from the de-formation, breakout, ebullience, and discomfort of postmodern feminism. The series brings together a post-foundational generation of women's writing that, while still respectful of the idea of situated knowledge, does not rely on neat disciplinary distinctions and stable political coalitions. This writing transcends some of the more awkward textual performances of a first generation of "feminism-meets-postmodernism" scholarship. It has come to terms with its own body of knowledge as shifty, inflammatory, and ungovernable.

The aim of the series is to make this cutting edge thinking more readily available to undergraduate and postgraduate students, researchers and new academics, and professional bodies and practitioners. Thus, we seek contributions from writers whose unruly scholastic projects are expressed in texts that are accessible and seductive to a wider academic readership.

Proposals and/or manuscripts are invited from the domains of: "post" humanities, human movement studies, sexualities, media studies, literary criticism, information technologies, history of ideas, performing arts, gay and lesbian studies, cultural studies, post-colonial studies, pedagogics, social psychology, and the philosophy of science. We are particularly interested in publishing research and scholarship with international appeal from Australia, New Zealand, and the United Kingdom.

For further information about the series and for the submission of manuscripts, please contact:

Erica McWilliam
Faculty of Education
Queensland University of Technology
Victoria Park Rd., Kelvin Grove Q 4059
Australia

To order other books in this series, please contact our Customer Service Department at:

(800) 770-LANG (within the U.S.)
(212) 647-7706 (outside the U.S.)
(212) 647-7707 FAX

Or browse online by series at:

www.peterlangusa.com